D E S I G N E R

Q U A R K X P R E S S

L A U R E N   S M I T H

A Subsidiary of
Henry Holt and Co., Inc.

First Edition—1994

Printed in the United States of America.

10 9 8 7 6 5 4 3 2 1

Library of Congress Cataloging-in-Publication Data
Smith, Lauren, 1952-
      Designer QuarkXPress / Lauren Smith.
          p.   cm.
      Includes index.
      ISBN 1-55828-379-X : $29.95
      1. QuarkXPress (Computer file) 2. Desktop publishing. I. Title
    Z253.532.Q37S64   1994
    686.2'2544536–dc20   94-30580
                                                                  CIP

MIS:Press books are available at special discounts for bulk purchases for sales promotions, premiums, fund-raising, or educational use. Special editions or book excerpts can also be created to specification.

For details contact: Special Sales Director
                      MIS:Press
                      a subsidiary of Henry Holt and Company, Inc.
                      115 West 18th Street
                      New York, New York 10011

Development Editor, *Debra Williams-Cauley*
Production Editor, *Anne Alesi*
Copy Editor and Technical Editor, *Jack Donner*

Contents

CHAPTER ONE

Designing with a Computer

T he computer is having a dramatic influence on the way graphic designers work. It is to design and print production what Eli Whitney's cotton gin was to textiles. It has fundamentally changed the industry. Graphic designers must learn new ways to work with a new set of tools.

While reading through this chapter, consider the following issues related to designing with a computer:

- Is designing on the computer better than designing with traditional tools?

- Will working on a computer make you a better designer?

- What things does the computer do well?

- Is there anything the computer can't do?

The traditional process of creating a publication involved a small army of people: at the very least, a writer to create text, a graphic designer to develop visual concepts and page layouts, a typographer to set type, a production artist to assemble and layout the elements, and a printer to create film and do the printing. While this traditional method is still employed today, the computer has changed the way printed materials are produced. Now, at least in theory, the same person can perform all of these functions without ever leaving his or her desk. The Macintosh has made it possible to have complete creative control over the entire process.

It's interesting to note that, in a way, the entire process has come full circle. Centuries ago most publications were produced by a single person. In fact, when he wasn't busy shaping the policies of new nations and discovering electricity, Benjamin Franklin made his living as a printer. His most famous work, *Poor Richard's Almanac*, was conceived, written, and printed by Franklin on his own press. A publication in those days was like a work of art—a complete creative expression of the publisher. The computer is a very powerful tool, and coupled with software such as QuarkXPress, it places at your disposal an impressive range of capabilities—in fact, far more than most people will ever use. It's like having a sports car that you know can go 120 miles per hour even though you've never driven it above 70. It's just nice to know that the power is there if you ever need it.

As powerful as it is, though, it's important to keep in mind that the computer is just a tool, and a tool is only as good as the skills of the craftsman using it. In the hands of a skilled designer, work produced on a computer can look just like work produced traditionally. However, just having a computer won't make you a designer any more than having a scalpel will make you a brain surgeon. Having all the best tools won't make you a designer. Knowing what to do with them will. Computer hardware and software manufacturers have created the impression through their advertising that creating sophisticated publications is easy if you use their products. This is partially true. In many ways these products do make the job easier. But as a result of this myth, many people are faced with the rather daunting task of creating documents on the computer without the benefit of any formal training in design or print production. As a result, the marketplace has been flooded with amateurish printed materials of all kinds. This isn't intended as a criticism, because many people have no choice but to learn on the fly. It does underscore my point, though—that the computer is not, and can never be, a designer. Only you can be a designer and only after you've developed a working knowledge of design and publishing fundamentals.

With all of this in mind, let's take a critical look at the computer as a design tool. First, I have to tell you…I love the Macintosh. I work with it every day and I firmly believe that it can do everything. I've used it to produce my work from concept sketches through final film. But, frankly, there are some things the Mac does very well, some things that it does well with some extra effort, and some things it doesn't do well at all. It's important to understand both its strengths and its weaknesses. Knowing how to get the most out of your Mac will enhance your productivity and save you a lot of frustration. It's also important to understand that the computer itself is only a piece of hardware, and it's the computer program or software that does most of the work. Software is constantly being improved, and soon software like QuarkXPress will give you results to rival the highest quality traditional prepress methods.

WHAT THE COMPUTER DOES BEST

The computer can do a lot of things, but what does it do best? For starters, the computer is a great time-saver. It's a tremendous efficiency tool. Now it is possible to have a page layout in a matter of minutes using QuarkXPress on a Macintosh. The same layout in rough form would have taken hours using traditional methods and not look nearly as finished. The time savings is even more dramatic when you're producing large publications electronically. The computer is the ideal production tool for books and magazines. For instance, this book was produced entirely with QuarkXPress on a Macintosh. Software like QuarkXPress allows you to predetermine layout features like page grids and typographic styles. You can make decisions about where type columns will be placed, the size and style of body text, headlines, and captions before you put anything on the first page. QuarkXPress allows you to make standardized page templates, then flow the text into place. Styles can be selected with a few keystrokes or a click of the mouse. For a publication with a lot of pages, these features can save days off the production schedule.

One of the things I like best about working with the Macintosh is that I'm not chained to a drawing table. I actually own four Macs of various sizes, all of which have enough power to run QuarkXPress and the other software that I use. I have a Macintosh IIx with a color monitor that I use in the studio for most of my work. It's connected to a scanner and a laser printer. I also have a Macintosh PowerBook 170 portable that fits in my briefcase. I take it with me wherever I go. It has communications software that lets me exchange files with my office computer through the phone lines, so even if I'm on the other side of the country I can send work back and forth. I can work on airplanes or in hotel rooms. This kind of portability has allowed me to make more efficient use of my time.

Designing on the computer requires a lot less space. Several of my colleagues have been able to confine their entire design business to one small room since they began designing electronically. When I was using conventional methods I had an entire room that was used just for storage. The room housed hundreds of large envelopes containing extra galleys of type, photographs, mechanical art boards, color swatches, page grids…well, you get the idea. Each job had a great many pieces to keep track of. Now, since most projects are created and composed on the computer, the entire job can be stored on a disk.

CREATIVE CONTROL

Working with a computer gives you, the designer, more creative control. The Macintosh allows you to explore numerous design options in a short period of time: Which typeface will look best? How big should you make the headlines? Should you put the picture here? Maybe it would look better cropped horizontally and running across the bottom of the page. This kind of experimentation is essential to the creative process, and the computer makes it quick and easy. I used to spend a lot of time doing exploratory thumbnail sketches before arriving at the final design solution—and still do. But now I frequently do it at the computer. The difference is, instead of scribbles on a drawing pad, I end up with pages that look much more finished. Clients really appreciate the finished quality of rough designs produced on the computer. It leaves less to the imagination.

It's also easy to experiment with images electronically. You can import a photograph or illustration into your layout and play with the cropping and placement on the page. You can alter the contrast, value, or color hue. You can apply color to the background or see what it will look like with a special effect applied, like a special screen pattern.

The computer makes it easy to set type, and QuarkXPress offers the broadest typographic control of any Macintosh page layout software. But even so, there are some limitations to what the computer can do typographically, and these may seem like serious shortcomings if you're used to having your type set professionally. When setting type on the computer, keep in mind that the results are dependent upon both the page layout software and the fonts that are resident in your system. Most of the problems are inherent in the fonts themselves. The *kerning* (the spacing between the letters) may be uneven and the line breaks at the end of the column may be awkward. QuarkXPress has built-in typographic functions that let you control these things, but it requires a lot of extra work. Chapter 5 will discuss this in greater detail.

Computer and software manufacturers including Quark claim that high-quality *prepress* work can be performed on the Macintosh but, frankly, this technology is still evolving and quality results aren't guaranteed. (Prepress refers to the steps in the process that precede the actual printing. It includes such things as production of halftones, color separations, and final film assembly. We'll discuss these processes further in later chapters.) While it is technically possible to take a publication from design to printing electronically, truly professional results require a lot of work and often have to be processed through high-end conventional equipment anyway. If you have ambitions to do your own film work, you might want to wait a while until all the bugs are worked out. Within a decade this is how most film will be produced, but jumping in too quickly might be frustrating.

Computers can also be temperamental. This is a big disadvantage to working electronically. The Macintosh is such a great production tool that it lures you in and gets you hooked. Believe me, working this way is addicting. The trouble is, you can get absolutely dependent on the computer and then something disastrous can happen such as your hard disk crashes and you can't access any of your files. Or you might install a great new software program and then suddenly experience software conflicts that immobilize your system. This can be extremely annoying, especially if you're facing a deadline (and in the design business you're always facing a deadline!). Without getting too technical here, let's just say that there are any number of things that can happen inside your computer that can mess up your work, and unless you have a degree in programming from M.I.T., you probably won't have a clue what the problem is. If you want to get seriously involved with the Macintosh, be prepared to learn a lot about how the system works as well as some basic problem-solving techniques. But the main thing is: it's essential to save your work as you go, and back your work up on floppy disks or some other storage media. Fortunately, Quark has made this almost automatic by including an Auto Save feature within the program. When the Auto Save box is checked in the Application Preferences dialog box, QuarkXPress will record any changes you make to your document as you work (by default every 5 minutes but you can specify another time interval if you prefer). These changes will be saved to a temporary file in your document folder. When you decide to manually save your work these changes will be permanently incorporated into your document. Similarly, checking the Auto Backup box in the Preferences dialog box will allow you to automatically save multiple revisions of the document to a designated Destination folder (up to 100 versions!).

SUMMARY

In this chapter you learned that the computer is a formidable efficiency tool for the designer, but like most tools it has its strengths and weaknesses. With this in mind, answer the following questions:

1. In what ways is the computer changing the way graphic designers work?

2. What's the difference between hardware and software?

3. What are the principle advantages to working with the computer?

4. What are some of the potential problems inherent in working with a computer?

CHAPTER TWO

Design Basics

For a graphic designer, the most exciting, and at the same time frightening, task is to stare at a blank piece of paper and wonder how you're going to create a thing of function and beauty on it. And to make matters worse, you usually have to do it on a tight deadline. If you're designing electronically, the blank sheet of paper is a computer screen. Well, no need to panic yet. First let's address some fundamental questions:

- What exactly is a graphic designer and what does he or she do?

- What is meant by *gestalt*?

- Designers have a strange vocabulary. What exactly do they mean when they talk about *line, form, color, scale, texture, space,* and *value*?

- How are symbols important to graphic communication?

- What is the designer's main responsibility?

- What is the best way to use photographs and illustrations?

- What is a *creative platform*?

- What is meant by *concept*?

WHAT'S A GRAPHIC DESIGNER?

Today printed materials have become a common part of our everyday lives. It would be difficult to imagine going through a day without encountering numerous kinds of printed materials—newspapers, magazines, product packages, books, posters, billboards, signs, garment tags, brochures, labels, greeting cards, calendars—well, you get the idea. All of these printed pieces have a message for us. How effectively that message is communicated often depends on how well it is designed. Graphic designers are specialists in print communication. Their responsibility is to create the structure of a publication by determining the placement and interrelationship of text and image. The designer's objective is to combine text and image to create a visual gestalt. *Gestalt* is a German word that loosely translated means "a configuration of elements that results in something bigger than the sum of its individual parts." In other words, the creative arrangement of text and image should communicate better than text or visuals alone. The elements should have a synergistic relationship—the eye naturally wants to create this kind of order when viewing a variety of elements and the brain is always trying to find relationships between disparate elements to create a meaningful whole. Understanding this principle is essential to good graphic communication (see Figure 2.1).

FIGURE 2.1

The brain intuitively tries to find relationships between elements in order to attach significance or meaning. A tangram is an ancient Chinese puzzle where symbols are created from abstract shapes. On the right are the elements of the tangram placed randomly. On the left the same elements are arranged in meaningful way.

The professional graphic designer is responsible for the creative and strategic impact of a publication and wears many hats. He or she needs to be proficient in fundamentals of composition, form, and color. The designer must know typography, illustration, and photography. It's important to be familiar with the various types and grades of printing papers and to understand the various printing and binding processes. And now, in the age of computers, it doesn't hurt to know something about bits and bytes and how publications are produced electronically. It's kind of like being an artist, art director, typographer, and computer and printing expert all at the same time. Discouraging? Well, as daunting as all this may sound, learning a few fundamentals in each of these areas can dramatically improve the appearance and effectiveness of your publications.

How effectively a message is communicated often depends on how well it is designed.

There isn't anything magical about design. It's really just a matter of putting those fundamental principles to work and using some common sense. Most people design things all the time without realizing it. When you arrange the furniture in your house, for instance, you consider such things as how the room should function, how the colors and textures work together, and the space relationships between the various pieces of furniture. A graphic designer makes the same kind of judgments with type and pictures on paper.

Learning a few fundamentals can dramatically improve the appearance and effectiveness of your publications.

THE BASIC ELEMENTS OF A LAYOUT

All graphic design is made up of *line, form, color, scale, texture, space,* and *value.* These are the building blocks of design. In fact, if you think about it, everything visual is made up of these elements. Look around you—you can see all of these things in the natural world. But in design you actually have creative control over them. You can decide how they can be used to your best advantage. You can arrange them to create a specific impression or elicit a particular response.

Line

Lines, when used in the context of a layout, can add interest to the page and are often used to separate and organize the elements. They can also be used to direct attention by creating a path for the reader's eye to follow. They take the form of *rules* (a typesetter's term for a line within a page of text), *boxes,* and *arrows.* They can be solid, dashed, dotted, thick, or thin. They can be used as a decorative border or to underscore text. Notice in Figure 2.2 how the designer used rules to add organization to the layout.

Design: Kit Hinrichs

FIGURE 2.2 Notice how the designer used rules to provide a sense of organization to the page.

Form

Form refers to the broad shapes used within the context of the layout. Forms can be clearly defined shapes within the page structure, such as a rectangular box to set off a section of type, or a photo cropped in the shape of a circle. Sometimes type can be set to conform to a specific shape. These shapes can often take on symbolic significance or have psychological connotations. We react differently to precise, straight-edged shapes such as squares than we do to soft, rounded shapes like circles or ellipses, or loose free-form shapes like brush strokes or ink splatters. The human mind has a hard time dealing with things to which it can't attach significance. It always tries to find meaning in abstract forms. For this reason, abstract forms can be used quite effectively as symbols. For instance, arranging four stars in a horizontal line might make you think of a military general. Abstract shapes are often used in the design of logos. Notice how the abstract shapes in Figure 2.3 imply specific meaning.

FIGURE 2.3 What meaning do you find in these abstract shapes?

Color

In much the same way that abstract shapes can have a psychological impact on the viewer, *color* can influence the mood of a printed piece. Bright warm colors such as reds, yellows, and oranges, and strong pure colors can convey a sense of action and excitement. Cool colors such as blues, violets, greens, and muted or grayed colors create feelings of peace and tranquility and appear more conservative. Before applying color to your publication, take a few moments to consider how that color will influence the overall tone.

Often inexperienced designers use too much color. When viewing the page, the reader's eye always responds to color first. Make sure that you place color where you want to add emphasis.

Generally, the eye is attracted to the largest elements first and the smallest ones last, so make sure that you design the page so that the most important elements have priority of scale.

Scale

Scale refers to the relative size relationship between graphic elements. Varying the scale of all the graphic elements on the page can add interest to the page and can create a visual path for the reader to follow. Generally, the eye is attracted to the largest elements first and the smallest ones last, so make sure that you design the page so that the most important elements have priority of scale. This is an excellent way to create a strong focal point within a layout.

By exaggerating scale you can add tremendous dramatic impact to the page. The example in Figure 2.4 is an excellent example of this principle. Notice where your eye goes first, next, and last.

Texture

The eye loves texture. Look around you and see how many examples of textures you can find within your field of view. What if everything was absolutely smooth and unvaried—can you think of anything more boring? In the same way our eyes respond favorably to texture in the world around us, texture can add interest to the printed page. In design, texture can be either tactile or visual. Tactile texture refers to texture physically applied to a surface, such as embossing or using a paper stock with a rough finish. Visual texture is really the illusion of texture created by the elements printed on the page. Figure 2.5 illustrates how texture can be created visually.

Designers are essentially communicators. Their job is to get the attention of the reader, lead him or her into the publication, and package the message so it comes through clearly.

Space

The creative use of space on the page is absolutely fundamental to the success of a design. The objective is to create a sense of balance where all elements are placed and visually weighted to their best advantage. When designing a layout most people think in terms of the space the elements will occupy. Even more important is the space between the elements. This is called *negative space*, or white space. Sometimes designers have a tendency to be economical and fill every square inch of the page. Unless this is very skillfully done it usually results in a layout that lacks excitement. Always remember that the space you leave blank is still space

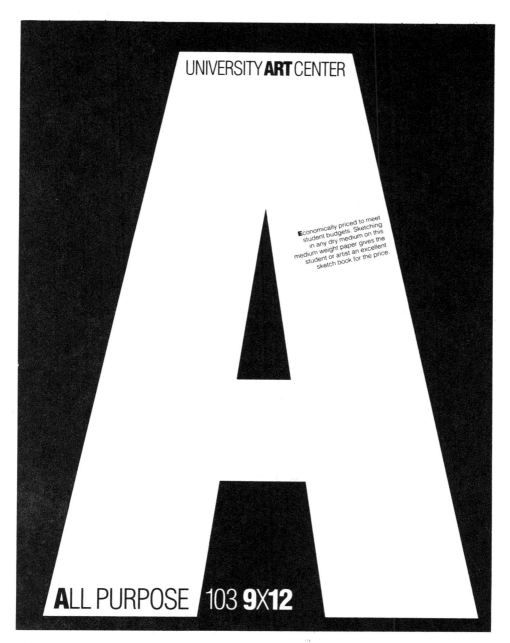

UNIVERSITY **ART** CENTER

Economically priced to meet student budgets. Sketching in any dry medium on this medium weight paper gives the student or artist an excellent sketch book for the price.

ALL PURPOSE 103 **9X12**

FIGURE 2.4 Notice how extreme difference in scale has given this design impact.

Design: Sam Smidt

FIGURE 2.5 This is a very effective example of visual texture.

that the eye is aware of, and it can actually make the other elements on the page more dynamic. Look at Figure 2.6. Can you see how the generous negative space adds interest and makes the positive elements more effective?

FIGURE 2.6 Notice the importance of the negative space in this spread from an annual report.

Value

Value refers to the relative lightness or darkness of the elements on the page. Like color, value can influence mood or add drama to the page. Values that are similar, such as multiple shades of gray, create a calm mood. Values that contrast widely, such as strong blacks and pure whites, create excitement. A word of caution: be careful applying value to type. Type is most legible when the letters are black on a white background. The more this contrast range is minimized, the less legible the type.

> *The creative use of space on the page is absolutely fundamental to the success of a design.*

IT'S NO GOOD UNLESS IT COMMUNICATES

Designers are essentially communicators. Their job is to get the attention of the reader, lead him or her into the publication, and package the message so it comes through clearly. Many beginning designers are so concerned about the way a publication looks that they lose sight of why they are creating it in the first place. There is a strong temptation to overdesign. Never make a design decision without first asking yourself if it will enhance or distract from the effectiveness of the essential communication. For example, printing an entire page of type in white on a black background may be striking to look at but nearly impossible to read, or filling the page with too many decorative elements may confuse the reader.

If the design is no more than window dressing,
it falls far short of its objective.

When you're designing a publication of any kind it's very important to consider the audience. You have to ask yourself some fundamental questions: Who's going to read this? What are their interests? What is their visual vocabulary? Every group has its own level of visual literacy. Visual literacy refers to the reader's ability to decode and absorb the visual message. There are various levels of visual literacy, and the visual vocabulary can vary greatly from audience to audience. It's important to consider such things as age, culture, education level, gender, and socioeconomic level. You would certainly design a children's book differently than a corporate annual report. This kind of sensitivity to the audience is crucial to effective communication.

The secret to good design is building just enough visual
interest into the page without going too far.

FORM FOLLOWS FUNCTION

Can you imagine deciding the answer to a mathematical equation without ever looking at the problem? Similarly, you can't design the page without first reading the text. The writing should always influence the design, not the other way around. It's important to always keep the essential message in mind when determining the design concept, which brings to mind a popular axiom from the world of design: form follows function. In addition to being a great example of alliteration, it makes a lot of sense. It simply means that the problem should dictate the solution. For example, when you stand in front of your closet in the morning trying to decide what to wear, you think about choosing an outfit that is comfortable and appropriate for the day's activities.

THE QUICK FIX

Your tenants have just moved out. In addition to the usual cleaning problems, they've left a gaping hole in the wall. Now you'll not only have to call the janitorial service and the carpet cleaners, but a contractor as well. And the new tenant wants to move in day after tomorrow! Why not call the Cleanup Crew and let us tell you about the wide range of services we have to offer. Hiring one company to handle all your maintenance and repair needs can save you both time and money. And your satisfaction is always guaranteed.

805-489-9730
805-481-4370

CLEANUP
CREW

FIGURE 2.7 High value contrasts create visual excitement in a design.

Creative Platform

Date: October 3, 1991
Client: Crosby House
Project: *Kids Are People Too!* Communications Series

Key Fact: Crosby House is a new publisher in the school curriculum market and *Kids Are People Too!* is a new type of product. We must find a way to establish an image for the company and an interest in the product.

Problem: There are a number of problems associated with this product introduction that must be solved. First, since *Kids Are People Too!* is an innovative product that breaks with traditional curriculum styles, we must overcome some initial resistance from conservative educators. We must introduce them to and encourage them to feel comfortable with this new concept of bridging affective learning and academics. It is difficult to classify this product in traditional terms. We must make the point that the *Kids Are People Too!* series is far-reaching in its effectiveness but at the same time easy to use...even fun! It is imperative that the product be perceived as non-threatening.
    In addition to these image problems there are some challenges ahead in the area of marketing. The potential audience is vast. How can we reach the widest possible audience for the least possible cost? We also need to get the attention of educators who are busy and inundated with pitches for new products from numerous sources.

Product: The *Kids Are People Too!* Communications Series is a curriculum series designed to build self-esteem in children while they learn. It accomplishes this by teaching children to become skillful communicators both on interpersonal and intrapersonal levels. The series covers an age range from Kindergarten through grade 8. The product is unique in its melding of affective learning and academics.

Audience: Teachers, school administrators, and government officials who are responsible for determining the curriculum for the public school system.

FIGURE 2.8 A simple creative platform

You wouldn't wear a tuxedo to a ball game (Sure, you might look very sharp, but you'd be totally out of place!). Similarly, when you're making design decisions, always consider the publication's function before deciding how it should look. Admittedly, often much of what a designer does is decoration. But the decoration should be appropriate to the message and the overall context of the publication.

Everything that is placed on the page should be there for a reason. If the design is no more than window dressing, it falls far short of its objective.

THE CREATIVE PLATFORM

Every publication has an objective, whether it is specifically stated or not. It's crucial that the designer understand what this objective is and develop a design strategy based on it. In some cases, especially for large projects, I find it helpful to write a creative platform. Advertising agencies use this method routinely to make sure that they are on target conceptually. The *creative platform* is usually a one-page document that specifies the following:

- What is the problem the advertising or publication must solve? Is it trying to sell a product, or to inform or persuade someone to a different point of view?

- To whom is the publication attempting to communicate? Is it targeted to the general public, or to a specific group such as bald men between 45 and 50 years old?

- What is the publication's essential message?

- What is the call to action? How should the readers respond? For example, do you want them to run right out to the store and buy a box of Corn Doodles, or do you just want to leave them with warm fuzzy feelings about the product

- What is the appropriate image or tone? You would certainly choose radically different kinds of looks for a surfboard company and a Wall Street bank.

Having the answers to questions such as these clearly in mind can make the design process much easier and will almost certainly result in a more effective publication.

KEEP IT SIMPLE

Designers are usually brimming with great ideas, and it's tempting to try to work as many of them as possible into a publication. This brings to mind yet another popular platitude from the world of design: less is more. Sometimes—well, most of the time—it's better to underdesign than overdesign. Remember going through countless problems in math class trying to reduce a fraction down to its lowest common denominator? Similarly, the secret to good design is building just enough visual interest into the page without going too far. It's also important to keep the

Maybe we don't have the hottest presses in town.

We won't do your shirts, but if you need good clean printing we can deliver. Everything from letterheads to l FOR POSITION ONLY white to full color. And we do it right–absolutely no wrinkles. For a free quotation on your next job call Steve or Doug at (415) 961-2320.

Olds Printing Services

Maybe we don't have the hottest presses in town.

We won't do your shirts, but if you need good clean printing we can deliver. Everything from letterheads to brochures. Black & white to full color. And we do it right–absolutely no wrinkles. For a free quotation on your next job call Steve or Doug at (415) 961-2320.

Olds Printing Services

FIGURE 2.9 Pictures can often communicate more than words.

basic structure of the page simple. All of us are conditioned from a very early age to assimilate information in very specific ways. For instance, we always read from left to right, generally starting in the upper-left corner of the page. We look for columns of text placed so that we can easily jump from the bottom of one to the top of the next. We tend to look at pictures first, large text next, and small text last. Deviating from any of these conventions will almost certainly confuse the reader. Keep in mind that readers are basically lazy. They will not invest time trying to read something that looks like too much work.

DON'T UNDERESTIMATE THE POWER OF GRAPHIC IMAGES

Some very effective design is done with type alone, but this requires great skill and the ability to use letterforms as graphic elements. As a rule, publications are more effective when they use some graphic devices such as photographs or illustrations to enhance and give emphasis to the written message. Everyone is familiar with the old saying "a picture is worth a thousand words." Sure, it's a cliché, but it's still true. The fact is, people would much rather look at pictures than read words. When was the last time you sat down with a magazine and read all the text before looking at the pictures? A picture can communicate much more information in a much shorter time than words can. Look at the two versions of the ad in Figure 2.9.

Whatever type of illustration you employ, it should be there for a reason. It should be included in your publication only if it makes the message clearer or the communication more effective.

Having said all that, a word of caution: Be sure that whatever you use for illustration is of good quality. In fact, it might be better to not use the illustration at all if it isn't a good one. Often graphic designers work closely with photographers or illustrators to work out the idea and ensure that the final result is of the best possible quality. This is called art direction. If you have an opportunity to create custom images for your publication, be sure to work with the most talented artists and photographers you can find. If you're not an experienced art director, these professionals can be of immeasurable benefit to you. They can often contribute a great deal to the creative process. You certainly pay more for the best, but even on a limited budget this is an area in which you shouldn't cut corners. Considering the overall cost of producing most publications, spending a little more for strong visuals will not break the budget and will pay off in effectiveness.

There are many different kinds of illustrations. Some are intended simply to inform and have an almost editorial quality. These are the kind of photographs that you see in newspapers, newsletters, and some magazines. They are concerned only with reporting the facts and accurately portraying something that is real.

Other illustrations are designed to lend a sense of reality to something imaginary. They function as catalysts to the imagination. For example, a picture of an imaginary event like Jack climbing the beanstalk can help the mind make reality out of fantasy. Such illustrations are commonly found in story books, children's books, and fiction.

Another kind of illustration is designed to elicit an emotional response. We've all been exposed to pictures that tug at our heartstrings and motivate us to respond. For example, a picture of a child in a wheelchair might motivate us to give to charity. This kind of illustration is routinely used in advertising because so many buying decisions are motivated by emotional impulse. Emotional impact can be used effectively in publications, and often the best designs utilize this kind of emotional impact (see Figure 2.10).

Pictures are essentially symbols. A *symbol* is a simple graphic device that represents a larger idea. Even a very simple symbol can communicate a great deal of information in very little space. This is why logos are so popular in the corporate world. Given enough exposure, a symbol can be an effective way to not only give the viewer a mental picture of the company but to arouse all sorts of connotations and feelings as well. For example, what do you think of when you see a swastika? No doubt you think of the Nazi Party, but it probably elicits an emotional response as well.

Our culture is rich with symbols. We see them every day and incorporate them into our visual vocabulary. They are a visual shorthand. What do you think of when you see the American flag? A heart? A dove? A stop sign? A cross? A skull and crossbones? Symbols are as much a part of our language as words themselves. For the designer they can be a very useful communication tool (see Figure 2.11).

Photo: David Powers

FIGURE 2.10 Pictures can add emotional impact to a publication.

FIGURE 2.11

Symbols are a visual shorthand. Notice how the designer used common symbols to pack more meaning into the design.

Whatever type of illustration you employ, it should be there for a reason. It should be included in your publication only if it makes the message clearer or the communication more effective. Avoid using an illustration or graphic just as filler. Here's another important rule to keep in mind: Never underestimate the intelligence of the reader. Publications that really work are well thought out, make sense, and in some way challenge the reader. Don't be afraid to use illustrations that make the reader stop and think.

COMMUNICATING IN A COMMUNICATION-SATURATED WORLD

Today there is more competition for the attention of the public than ever before. In Western cultures, people are deluged with printed material every day, all crying out for attention and trying to be noticed above the others. In the United States, the average person is subjected to hundreds, if not thousands, of advertising messages each day. Hard to believe? Maybe so, but keep in mind that most of these messages are tuned out. Think about the number of advertisements you see on television in a day. Add to that magazine and newspaper ads you might glance at, billboards, window displays, posters, advertising on buses, taxis, junk mail—the list goes on and on. Americans are exposed to twice as much advertising as Canadians, and four times as much as Europeans. This creates a great deal of demand for printed materials. This is good business if you're a graphic designer, but it also means that whatever you create has to be particularly effective and attention-grabbing in order to be noticed.

How do you create something that has enough impact to get noticed? The most obvious way is to be visually bold almost to the point of being brash. You could use bright colors and huge type and try to hit the reader right between the eyes with the design elements themselves. This works sometimes, but it obviously isn't appropriate for every situation. For example, it might be a viable approach if your client sells skateboards or is in the music industry, but what if it's a law firm or a Fortune 500 company?

Another way to get attention is to make sure that every design is driven by a *concept*. What is a concept? Well, in advertising it's often called the "Big Idea." It involves giving the message a "twist" to make it more interesting and attention-grabbing. Songwriters call it a "hook"—that part of a song that gets stuck in your mind and plays over and over until it nearly drives you crazy. Think of a concept as the same kind of thing, only visual (see Figure 2.12).

FIGURE 2.12

Can you define the concept
behind each of these designs?

SUMMARY

If you didn't know what a graphic designer was when you started this chapter, you should now have an idea of what the designer's responsibilities are, as well as the fundamentals of the designer's craft. Take a moment to answer the following questions:

1. If someone asked you what a graphic designer does, how would you respond?

2. What is meant by the term *gestalt*?

3. What is the designer's primary responsibility?

4. What are the building blocks of design?

5. What is meant by the phrase "form follows function"?

6. What are the components of a *creative platform*?

7. What is meant by the term *concept*, and why is it important?

CHAPTER THREE

Working with QuarkXPress

Designing with a computer means learning a new set of tools and becoming accustomed to a new way of working. Software like QuarkXPress is so powerful and has such a broad range of features that it is capable of doing far more than you will need it to do. But to accomplish even the most fundamental tasks requires a working knowledge of the software. This chapter will answer the following questions:

- What is meant by the term *user interface*?

- What are the tools available in QuarkXPress?

- How do you make the computer do what you want it to do?

- What are *palettes* and *dialog boxes*?

While I have other page layout software in my library that I use occasionally, I tend to use QuarkXPress almost exclusively. For many reasons, I believe it's the software of choice for most professional graphic designers. Among the leading software programs, QuarkXPress offers the most comprehensive and powerful features. Its typographic capabilities have more range than those of its closest competitor. If you want to do all the typographic refinements yourself that you're used to getting from a professional typesetter, you'll find them much easier to accomplish with QuarkXPress than you would with comparable applications. Typography is so fundamental to graphic design that it's worth choosing QuarkXPress for this reason alone. Let's look at exactly what the software will allow you to do and how to go about doing it.

QuarkXPress Fundamentals

Every software program is designed with a *user interface*. This term refers to the graphical framework you see on the screen, including the menus and all those little symbols or icons. It also refers to the way the user navigates through the program. If this navigation is easy, the interface is considered "friendly."

The Apple Macintosh system software also has a user interface. Quark has designed the XPress interface to be as friendly and intuitive as the Macintosh interface. There are pull-down menus at the top of the screen, floating tool palettes, and dialog boxes in which you can make decisions about how the program should perform.(See Figure 3.1.) These menus and palettes allow you to perform specific functions within the software. For instance, there's a text tool for entering or formatting type, a line tool for drawing lines or rules, and a picture box tool for making windows for pictures. In addition, there are scroll bars at the bottom and right side of the screen that allow you to scroll across the page or through the document from top to bottom or side to side. (See Figure 3.2.)

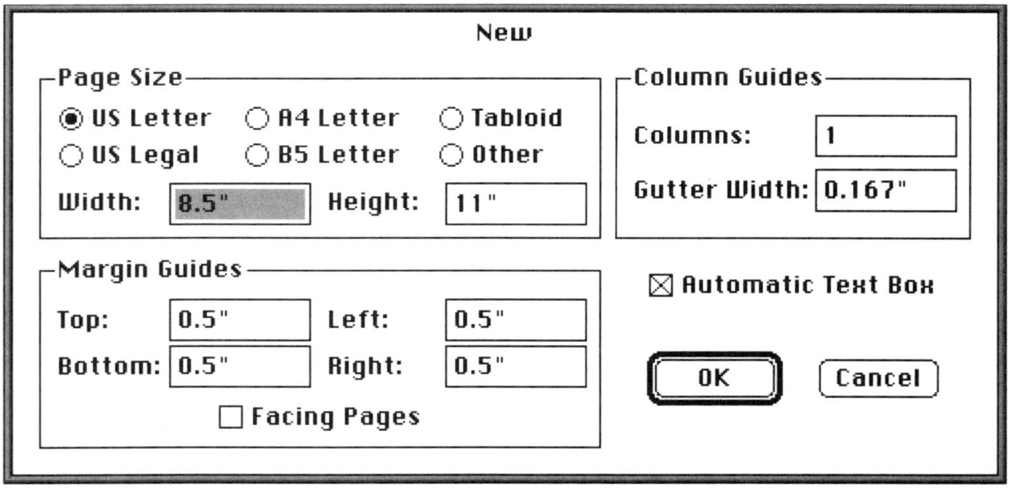

FIGURE 3.1 Use the New dialog box to set up your basic page format.

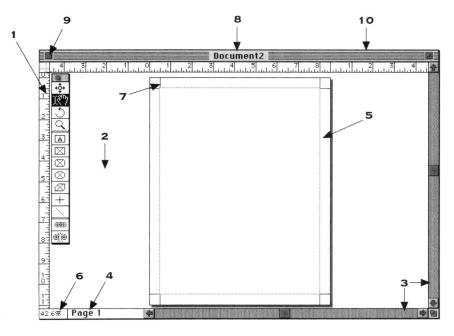

FIGURE 3.2 The QuarkXPress interface has been designed with ease of use foremost in mind.

Notice some of the important features in the QuarkXPress interface:

1. Rulers.

2. Pasteboard—imagine this is the top of your drawing table. Use it as a place to put things when you're not using them in the layout.

3. Scroll Bars—these allow you to quickly change your position within the document.

4. Page Number Indicator.

5. Automatic Text Box—this text box comes up automatically. You can determine the dimensions of the text box in the New dialog box.

6. View Percent Field—this shows you at a glance the size at which you're viewing the page. You can also use it to change the size of your view.

7. Page Guides.

8. Document Name.

9. Close Box—click on this box to put your document away.

10. Title Bar—click on this and drag to reposition the document window.

Open QuarkXPress and look at the user interface. Double-click on the QuarkXPress icon to open the program. After a few seconds you should see the QuarkXPress information window, click on this and the interface comes up with the Tool Palette on the left side. Go up to the File menu in the upper-left corner and select New Document. This will bring up the New dialog box, which contains little boxes and "radio" buttons that let you make format choices. The New dialog box is shown in Figure 3.1.

Under Page Size, click the button next to US Letter, then click OK. Clicking US Letter will automatically give you a standard 8.5" x 11" page. You also have the option of typing in the page dimensions, but US Letter saves time if you are using a standard page format. Now you should see the entire document window, with Page 1 displayed. You should also see rulers across the left side and top, and the Tool Palette on the left. If you don't see the Tool Palette, select Show Tools from the View menu.

PALETTES

Quark includes palettes in its interface, so instead of having to constantly pull down menus you can simply click on a particular tool or item to select it. Everything is out on your desktop where you can see it. (Of course, if you prefer, you can still access these same functions through pull-down menus.) I leave three palette windows open on my desktop: Tool Palette, Measurements Palette, and Document Layout Palette. (QuarkXPress also features Library Palettes, but I use them only occasionally and open them as I need them.) I should mention that I work with a 19-inch monitor, which gives me a lot of room. If you have a smaller monitor it may not be practical to leave so many palettes open. Even if you're cramped for space, try to leave the Tool Palette and the Measurement Palette open. They're the most useful and take up the least room.

THE TOOL PALETTE

The Tool Palette allows you to select a tool simply by clicking on it. If you double-click on it, the Tool Preferences dialog box will come up. This box lets you specify default settings. (Defaults are the automatic settings for each tool.) Changing

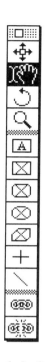

FIGURE 3.3

Using the Tool Palette makes selecting a function easy—simply click on the tool to activate it. Double-click to display the Tool Preferences dialog box. This lets you specify or change default settings.

defaults allows you to customize the way the tools function. (See Figure 3.3.) Let's take a moment to learn about each tool and what it does. We'll start at the top of the palette and work down.

Item Tool

This tool looks like little arrows in the shape of a cross. Use it to move things around on the page. You can also use it to group or ungroup items and to cut, copy, or paste elements such as lines, text boxes, and picture boxes.

Content Tool

The Content Tool is the one with the little hand in it. This is probably the most versatile of all the tools. When this tool is selected you can type text into a text box, import text or pictures from another document, edit, cut, paste, copy, and modify the contents of text and picture boxes. You can use the little hand to actually "push" a picture around inside a picture box if you want to change the way the picture is framed.

Rotation Tool

This tool lets you rotate elements on the page; for example, to put a text box on a diagonal or rotate a picture box 90 degrees.

Zoom Tool

This handy tool looks like a little magnifying glass. It lets you magnify the page to get a closer look at your work. If you select this tool and click on the area of the page you want to zoom in on, it will enlarge that section in increments of 25% (or any other increment specified in the Tool Preferences dialog box).

Text Box Tool

This is another tool you'll use a lot. It lets you create text boxes. Once text boxes are created, you can either type text into them or import text into them from another document.

Rectangular Picture Box Tool

Before you can put pictures into your document, you must create a picture box. By selecting this tool and dragging the cursor across the page, you can make a picture box of any size. Rectangular picture boxes always have square corners.

Rounded-corner Picture Box Tool

This tool lets you create a picture box with rounded corners. It works just like the Rectangular Picture Box Tool.

Oval Picture Box Tool

This tool lets you create oval-shaped picture boxes.

Polygon Picture Box Tool

If you want to get crazy and make a picture with an irregular shape, this is the tool to use. It works differently than the other picture box tools. With this tool you have to click on each corner point individually and then click on the origin point to complete the shape.

Orthogonal Line Tool

Orthogonal? Well, that just means lines that go straight up and down or straight side to side, and that's what this tool makes.

Line Tool

This is the tool used to draw lines. You can draw straight lines at any angle and in any direction by clicking and dragging the mouse.

Linking Tool

In QuarkXPress you can "flow" text from column to column or text box to text box throughout a document, but first you have to "link" the boxes together in the order in which you want the text to flow. This tool lets you connect the boxes.

Unlinking Tool

What if you link your text boxes in the wrong order? No problem. This tool lets you unlink them.

THE MEASUREMENTS PALETTE

The Measurements Palette is a handy little device that acts like a control panel. It gives you easy access to the most frequently used controls. The contents of the palette change according to which tool is selected and what kind of box or element is activated. (See Figures 3.4 through 3.7.) For instance, if you've selected the Content Tool and a text box is active, you will see a palette that lets you easily change the location of the text box, change leading or line spacing of text, alter tracking or letterspacing between type characters, choose the alignment of the type, and select or change font or typeface as well as change style and size of type.

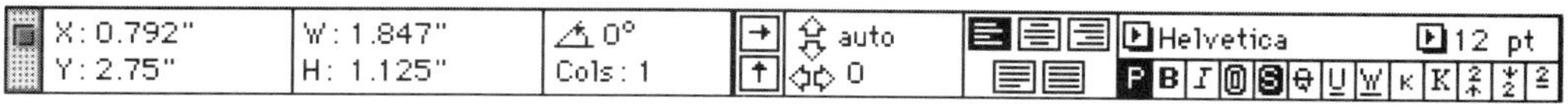

| X: 0.792" | W: 1.847" | ⊿ 0° | → ⇕ auto | Helvetica | 12 pt |
| Y: 2.75" | H: 1.125" | Cols: 1 | ↑ ⬦⬦ 0 | P B I O S Φ U W K K | |

FIGURE 3.4 The Measurements Palette looks like this when a text box is active.

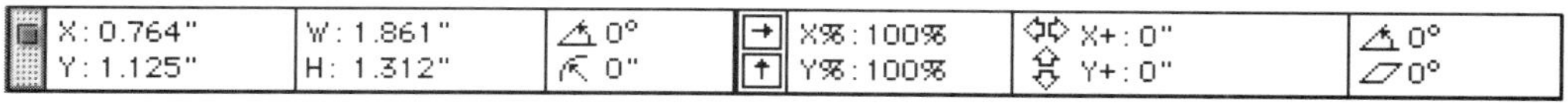

| X: 0.764" | W: 1.861" | ⊿ 0° | → X%: 100% | ⬦⬦ X+: 0" | ⊿ 0° |
| Y: 1.125" | H: 1.312" | ⟋ 0" | ↑ Y%: 100% | ⇕ Y+: 0" | ⟋ 0° |

FIGURE 3.5 The Measurements Palette looks like this when a picture box is active.

35

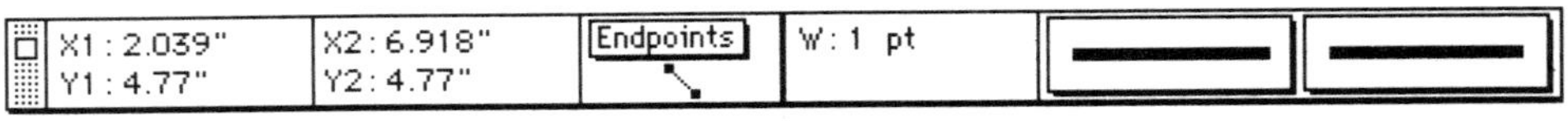

□ X1 : 2.039" Y1 : 4.77"	X2 : 6.918" Y2 : 4.77"	Endpoints	W : 1 pt	

FIGURE 3.6 The Measurements Palette looks like this when a line is selected.

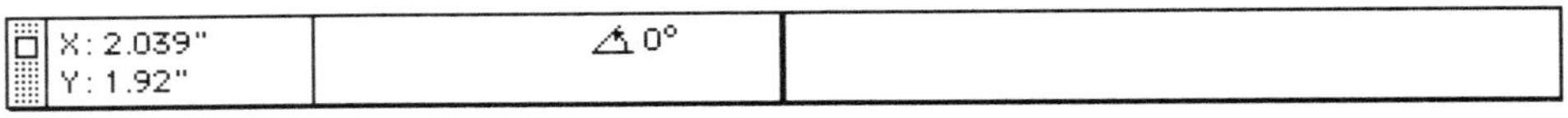

□ X : 2.039" Y : 1.92"	△ 0°	

FIGURE 3.7 When a group is active, the Measurements Palette can be used to adjust the position and angle of the grouped elements.

THE DOCUMENT LAYOUT PALETTE

This palette is very useful when you create a document with a lot of pages. It lets you create master pages, which are like templates. For instance, if you decide that your entire publication should have half-inch margins and three columns, you can set up a master page that will automatically put these things in place every time you add a new page. The Document Layout Palette also makes it easy to add, delete, or rearrange pages in your document, and it helps you find your way around your document easily. (See Figure 3.8.) If you're working on page 8, for example, and decide you need to change something on page 246, instead of tediously scrolling through your entire document a page at a time, you can jump there by simply double clicking on page 246 in the document layout. This palette also makes it simple to arrange your document in spreads.

LIBRARY PALETTES

QuarkXPress has a Librarian feature that lets you store items in libraries. You can create as many libraries as you want, and each can contain up to 2,000 entries. These libraries are useful for storing frequently used items such as logos, mastheads, or any other standard elements that you may want to use over and over again. Libraries can contain anything that can be created or imported into QuarkXPress. Once a library is set up you can access it through the Library Palette, which displays a thumbnail representation of each object contained within it. (See Figure 3.9.) You simply drag the objects back and forth between the palette window and your layout.

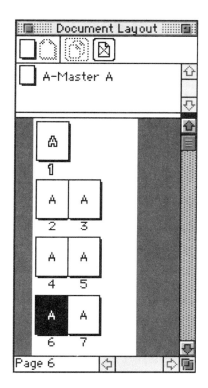

FIGURE 3.8

The Document Layout Palette makes it easy to add, delete, or rearrange pages within the document. It also lets you set up or make changes to templates called master pages.

MENUS AND DIALOG BOXES

If you've ever worked with the Macintosh you're already familiar with menus, but let's take a moment to look at the menus in the QuarkXPress interface. At the top of the screen you will see the general menu categories: File, Edit, Style, Item, Page, View, and Utilities. If you place the cursor on one of these labels and hold the mouse button down, you'll see the corresponding menu appear. The active entries are black and the inactive entries are dimmed. To select an entry, simply drag the cursor down until it is highlighted. To activate the entry, lift your finger off the mouse button.

Some menu entries have submenus, which pop up when the main entry is highlighted. With your finger still on the mouse button, drag your cursor to the right onto the submenu and highlight the desired entry. Notice that some menu entries

FIGURE 3.9

Using the Library Palette is an easy way to store and retrieve frequently used items.

are followed by a keyboard command equivalent. You can bypass the pull-down menus by using the keyboard shortcuts. Also notice that some menu entries are followed by an ellipses, or three dots. When these entries are selected, they display a dialog box. (See Figure 3.10.)

A dialog box contains fields and controls that can be used to make specifications. (See Figure 3.11 through 3.14.) The dialog box contains pop-up menus, editable pop-up menus, buttons, check boxes, and fields. In addition to general dialog boxes that allow you to specify values, there are dialog boxes that allow you to navigate to and open files, save files. These are alert dialog boxes that warn you if there is a problem. (See Figure 3.15.)

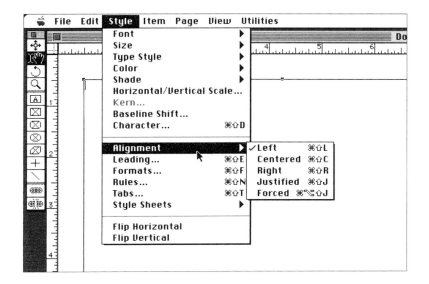

FIGURE 3.10

This is a typical pull-down menu. The black entries are active; dimmed entries are inactive. To the right of the entry is its keyboard equivalent. Items followed by ellipses will display a dialog box. An arrow-head to the right of the entry indicates a submenu.

FIGURE 3.11

The Text Box Specification box lets you enter values into fields. It displays the current values, which you can alter by simply typing over them. Some values are changed by using pop-up menus.

Picture Box Specifications

Origin Across:	0.972"	**Scale Across:**	100%
Origin Down:	9.722"	**Scale Down:**	100%
Width:	0.375"	**Offset Across:**	0"
Height:	0.236"	**Offset Down:**	0"
Box Angle:	0°	**Picture Angle:**	0°
Box Skew:	0°	**Picture Skew:**	0°
Corner Radius:	0"		

☐ Suppress Picture Printout

☐ Suppress Printout

Background

Color: *None*

Shade: ▷ 100%

[OK]   [Cancel]

FIGURE 3.12

This is what you'll see when you call up the Picture Box Specification box.

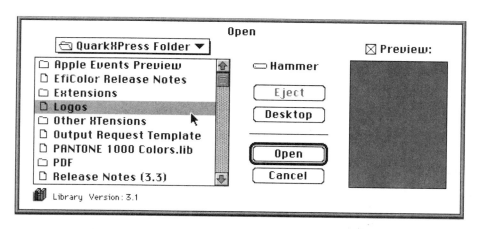

FIGURE 3.13 This dialog box makes it easy to navigate through and open files within your system.

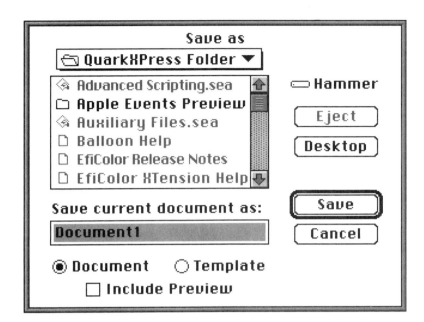

FIGURE 3.14

Dialog boxes are also used to save documents.

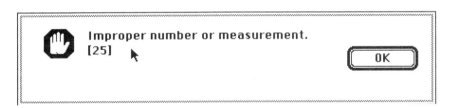

FIGURE 3.15 Sometimes a box like this one will pop onto your screen to alert you that an error has occurred.

As you can see, making changes in palettes and dialog boxes is much more convenient than using pull-down menus, but there's an even easier way. Almost every menu item has a keyboard command that performs the same function. For example, you can save your work by pulling down the File menu and clicking Save. Or you can do the same thing by holding down the Command key (the one with the apple on it) and tapping S (for Save). As you become more comfortable working with QuarkXPress, you will find it much easier to use keystrokes for the most common commands. For more keyboard shortcuts see Appendix D.

SUMMARY

QuarkXPress is the most comprehensive and powerful page layout software available today. In order to get the most from it, however, a thorough understanding of its fundamentals is essential. In this chapter we learned about the software interface and the controls that are available to the user. Consider the following questions based on the contents of this chapter:

1. What is meant by the term *interface*?

2. What is a *dialog box*?

3. What's the difference between a *menu* and a *palette*?

4. What is the principle advantage of using palettes?

5. Review the tool palette and the individual tools. What does each one do?

CHAPTER FOUR

Organizing the Page

A bove all else, the designer's job is to create pages that will be read. Communication is the essence of what we do. It's our responsibility to enhance the reader's ability to assimilate information and to encourage interaction between the publication and the reader. I'll even go one step further— our task is to manipulate the reader, to control the way he or she absorbs information. Sounds kind of Machiavellian, doesn't it? Well, there's nothing sinister about it. What we're trying to do is make the reader's job easier. This chapter will explore ways to make information more accessible to the reader as well as the actual mechanics of laying out the printed page. It will address these questions:

- What is the secret to designing a page that's attractive as well as informative?

- How do you use QuarkXPress to set up your page layout?

- What are *grids*, and why should you care about them?

- How can you use white space effectively?

- What's a *focal point*?

- How can you use lines or rules in your layout to organize information?

The Secret to Organizing Information

Well, it's not exactly a secret. A lot of people know about it, but it's surprising how few people really use it. The secret is simply this: It's not enough to just squeeze information within the borders of the page; you must also create a visual path for the reader to follow. You want the reader's eye to land on point A, then go to point B, then go to point C, and so on.

In order to do this, you need to understand how the mind works when it's confronted with something interesting to look at. The eye immediately tries to lock on to something, and it generally goes for the biggest, boldest, simplest, and most colorful object first. (See Figure 4.1.) But the eye is promiscuous—it will almost immediately get bored with the first object and will be distracted by something else. This process continues until either everything on the page is taken in or the mind decides it couldn't care less and moves on to the next page. This tendency may seem like common sense, but it's surprising how many publications are designed with little thought for it. If the page is designed so that everything has a similar visual "weight," the eye has to work much harder. It immediately tries to go everywhere at once and then resorts to scanning the page methodically to get information. Remember that readers are lazy, and unless they already have an interest in what you have to say they probably aren't going to invest much time in reading it.

What we're talking about is visual articulation. You've probably met people who seem to have a silver tongue. When they speak, their words are well ordered and thoughtful. You hang on their every word, waiting in breathless anticipation for the next syllable to roll off their tongues. Then there are the people who have trouble

It's not enough to simply squeeze information within the borders of the page; you must also create a visual path for the reader to follow.

putting two coherent thoughts together. After listening to a few minutes of "Well, uh, the thing is, uh…", you start looking for ways to escape. Similarly, there are designs that are absolutely eloquent in their execution. They are interesting to look at and they get their message across simply and gracefully. All too often, however, the opposite is true and you have to work to find the message because it is expressed so poorly visually.

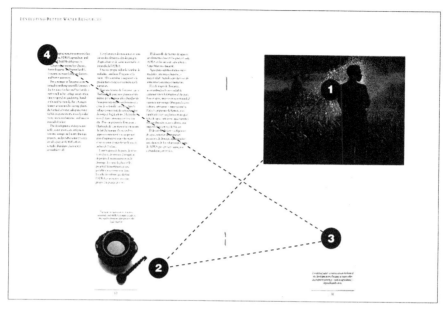

Design: Lauren Smith

FIGURE 4.1 Follow the visual path in this simple layout.

The visual path is made up of focal points. Think of a focal point as a target for the eye. Whenever the eye is confronted with something to look at, it immediately looks for a place to land. The places it chooses to land are focal points. The visual path is constructed by creating a primary focal point on the page, followed by a secondary focal point, then a third, etc. Think of it like one of those connect-the-dots puzzles, except here the eye is connecting graphic elements on the page while at the same time absorbing information. This descending order of focal points is called a *visual hierarchy*.

It's possible for a designer to create a visual path that attracts the reader's eye to all the wrong places or in the wrong order. The design may look beautiful, but ultimately it will be ineffective.

Sometimes the designer leads the reader down a visual path, but it's the wrong path. A common pitfall for even experienced designers is to design without regard for the publication's essential message. A cartoon illustrates this point: A designer is hunched over his drawing table working on a layout, and a clock is ticking above his head. His supervisor comes over, points to his layout, and says, "What did you think of that article?" The designer snarls back, "I don't have time to read it, I only have time to make it fit!"

It's easy to get so caught up in meeting a deadline or making a beautiful layout that you lose sight of the fact that the design is only a vehicle to facilitate the communication of the written word. It's possible for a designer to create a visual path that attracts the reader's eye to all the wrong places or in the wrong order. The design may look beautiful, but ultimately it will be ineffective.

Let's examine some of the devices designers use to attract the eye of the reader and create a visual path. Visual elements are usually the most effective. People seem to lock in on pictures first (especially pictures of people). Any kind of picture, whether it's a photograph, a symbol, an illustration, or even an abstract illustration, holds more interest than type. (See Figure 4.2.)

Spot color is often effective, if it's not overdone. It's best to use color sparingly and place it where you want to attract the most attention. Using it for headlines makes sense, using it for page numbers doesn't. But what if your publication is black and white? You can achieve similar effects using scale and value. In the same way that color attracts attention, the largest, boldest objects on the page get noticed first. Look at Figure 4.3. Where does your eye go first?

SETTING UP THE PAGE IN QUARKXPRESS

Before you set up a page, there are a few decisions to make. First, do you want to measure your page in inches, centimeters, or picas? (Picas are a printer's measurement. A pica contains 12 points and there are approximately 6 picas to an inch). Do you want to use autokerning? If so, in what point sizes? Do you want QuarkXPress to hyphenate automatically? Do you want QuarkXPress to automatically add pages when you come to the end of your document? Do you want your page guides in front of or in back of the page?…

Actually, you don't need to make all of these decisions every time you open a document, but you can if you want to. And there are numerous other things you can control. Most of these controls can be found under Preferences, in the Edit menu. Fortunately, QuarkXPress has built-in automatic default values based on what people most commonly use. You can override the defaults at any time, but if you

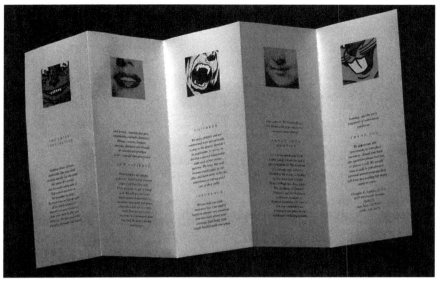

Design: Lauren Smith

FIGURE 4.2 Which element in this layout attracts your eye first? The eye is usually attracted to pictures before text. A dramatic picture enhances the effect even further.

Are you hitting the mark with your development system applications?

FIGURE 4.3 The eye is attracted to the biggest and boldest elements first.

choose not to change anything, the measurements will automatically assume Quark's default values—the guides will be behind the page for instance. You'll want to take some time to become familiar with the defaults, but for now, let's leave the standard defaults in place.

Read this chapter sitting in front of your computer. It describes the steps involved in setting up a page template, and you will find it helpful to actually perform these steps as you read.

First, open up QuarkXPress and select New Document from the File menu. When the New dialog box comes up, select US Letter. Your first decision is to decide how wide to make the margins. Make the top and side margins .5" and the bottom margin .75". You can select these values by typing them in the value boxes in the Margin Guides section. If there are values already displayed, drag the cursor across them to select them, then type over them.

You're probably wondering why I chose to make the bottom margin wider than the others. There's a strange thing that happens when you look at the page—the center of the page is not where your eye thinks it is. The eye sees the horizontal center at a point that is slightly higher than the actual center line. This point is called the *visual center*. If you were to measure the exact center of the page and mark it with a horizontal line, it would probably look too low. To compensate for this phenomenon, we beef up the bottom margin to force the type on the page up a bit. Moving it up slightly makes it "feel" centered. If you've ever had a picture framed with a mat between the picture and the frame, you may have noticed that the framer cut the mat wider at the bottom to compensate for this illusion.

Next you need to decide how many columns you want on your master page. For now, select three columns with .25" in between them. Type these values (in numerals) in the Column Guides section of the New dialog box, then click OK. You should see the page on your screen, with the columns and margins indicated with guide lines. Finally, click in the box that's labeled Facing Pages and the one marked Automatic Text Box. This will tell the computer to flow text automatically through your document and display the pages in spreads. It's important to set up your document in spreads, because when readers look at a publication they tend to see both pages as one unit. Since this is how readers see it, this is how you should design it. Facing pages should work together as one. (See Figure 4.4.)

USING GRIDS

When you set up the margins and columns, you were actually setting up a simple page grid. Grids are made up of modules that provide an understructure to the page. They give it a sense of proportion and ensure that type, illustrations, and other graphic elements are placed in a manner that is consistent from page to page. Grids can take many forms and vary widely in complexity. In the grid you just set up, you specified the margins and set up three modules that define vertical divisions within the page. More complex grids usually take into account horizontal divisions as well, and may look like a patchwork of boxes. (See Figure 4.5.)

FIGURE 4.4 Even though they consist of two pages side by side, spreads should be considered a single unit.

All publications have an underlying structure, whether it's defined or not. Many designers have an intuitive sense of proportion that makes setting up a formal grid an unnecessary step. Even experienced designers, however, use formal grids when they're working on publications with many pages, such as books, magazines, and newspapers. Formal grids are also important for periodical publications. If you're producing a magazine, for instance, you want to make sure that it's consistent not only from page to page, but also from issue to issue.

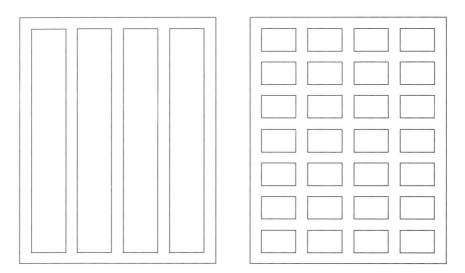

FIGURE 4.5 Grid modules are useful for imposing consistency and order on the page.

Now comes the tricky part. Once you've set up your grid, you need to put the elements into the layout so skillfully that the reader will be absolutely unaware of the grid. The grid should be invisible. The reader should be aware of an overall sense of organization and consistency, but not the specific structure.

Grids have been used for centuries. The earliest architects used grid systems. The artists of the Renaissance used grids to scale their small sketches up to the size of frescoes. But the idea of using formal grids as an understructure for publications was developed by the Bauhaus school of design in the 1950s and 1960s. Many of the designers spawned by this movement used grids religiously. As a result, this period in graphic design was typified by publications that were tightly structured to the point of being static. (See Figure 4.6.) It's interesting that modern design—that is, design trends over the last decade—has been almost anti-structure in its approach. Post-modern design, for instance, is characterized by almost random placement of elements on the page. This style of design is great fun to look at, but sometimes you really have to dig to understand what it's trying to say. I believe the most effective design falls somewhere in between these two extremes. It should have an apparent structure, but the designer should feel free to use the grid creatively. After all, isn't the essence of creativity a willingness to bend the rules?

 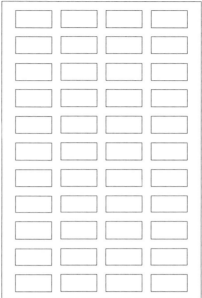

FIGURE 4.6 On the left is the publication and on the right the grid upon which it was based.

MASTER PAGES

Let's go back to the computer. Do you still have the page in front of you? It should show horizontal and vertical lines defining the margins and columns. If you don't see the entire page on your screen, select Fit in Window from the View menu. Then pull down the View menu again, and select Show Document Layout. This will put the Document Layout palette on your desktop. It should have a vertical line down the center and one little page with a dog-eared corner. One of the greatest features of QuarkXPress is that it lets you set up styles or formats that will automatically be applied to every page in your document. The margin and column values you specified in the New dialog box are now standard items that will appear on every page. You can create even more detailed formats and apply them to your document pages as well. These formatted pages are called *master pages*.

As soon as you clicked Save in the New dialog box, QuarkXPress applied the values to your document in the form of a master page. It was automatically named Master Page A. You can create additional master pages and apply them to your

51

document wherever you want. Master pages allow you to automatically add standard items like page numbers and running titles. Across the top of the Document Layout palette you will see, from left to right, a single page icon, a facing page icon that looks like a page with two dog-eared corners, a duplicate button (it's the one with the two overlapping pages), and a delete button. Below this series of icons you'll see another page icon next to the words "A-Master." This is the master page icon. Open the master page by double-clicking on the icon.

ELEMENTS OF THE MASTER PAGE

The first thing you should see when you open the master page icon is a series of lines defining the margins. These are called margin guides. Nothing unusual here. Now look up in the upper-left corner there is a symbol like the Text Linking Tool. Remember when you checked Automatic Text Box in the New dialog box? When you checked that box, a text box was set up on Master Page A that will automatically be linked to every page in the layout; hence the text linking symbol. Text will now automatically flow from page to page in order through the document.

Sometimes you may not want the text box to be linked on a particular page. To deactivate it, simply select the Unlinking Tool from the Tool palette and click on the symbol in the corner. Did the Linking Tool icon become a broken chain? Good. You just turned the automatic linking off.

CREATING A MASTER PAGE

Creating a new master page is easy. Simply click on a document page in the upper-left corner of your Document Layout palette. If you selected Facing Pages in the New dialog box, you have the option of creating a single master page or a spread with facing pages. To create a single page master, click on the icon in the upper left corner. To create facing master pages, click on the icon with the dog-eared corners. Holding the mouse button down, drag the icon into the space below Master Page A. Release the mouse button and a new master page should appear, labeled B–Master B. Double-click to open it. Now you can format it however you want. To go back to a document page, simply double-click on the page you want. This will close the master page and display the selected document page.

You can create up to 127 of these master pages within each document. There's no doubt that a name like "Master Page A" is awfully clever, but you might want to consider giving it a name of your own. If you have numerous master pages it might be less confusing to give each one a more descriptive label. And it's easy to do—click on the master page icon. This will highlight both the icon and the name in the little box beside it. Simply type the master page's new name over the default name. You can put up to 63 letters in the field.

PAGE NUMBERING

You can also use master pages to automatically number your pages. First you need to let the computer know where you want the numbered section to begin. You can start anywhere, but for now, start at Page 1. In the Document Layout palette, click on Page 1. It should say "Page 1" in the area at the bottom left of the Document Layour palette. Now click on that page number and the Section dialog box will appear. Click the box labeled Section Start, then OK. Open your master page by double-clicking on the icon. When the master page is displayed, create a new text box by selecting the text box icon from your Tool palette and dragging it on the page to make a small box. With the text box active, hold down the Command key and type 3. You should see in your text box a symbol that looks like this: <#>. This tells the computer where to place the page numbers, so be sure to drag the text box to the exact location you want it to appear on the page. Remember, this is a master page, so whatever you choose here will be repeated exactly on every page of your document. You can use the Measurements palette or the Style menu to specify the exact font, style, and size for the page numbers. Now close the master page by double-clicking on a document page in the Document Layout palette. The page numbers should now appear on your document pages and will be added automatically to any new pages.

INSERTING AND DELETING PAGES

You can also use the Document Layout palette to add and delete pages to and from your document. To add a page, simply drag one of the pages from the top of the palette into the layout below. You can drag down either a general document page or a master page. Drag it to the position you want to place it in the layout. Putting it at the end is easy—just drag the new page to the end of the string. If you want to put a new page between two existing pages, drag the new page to a point between these pages on your document layout. You'll see a symbol that looks like a line with a pointer attached. The pointer should point in the direction you want to place

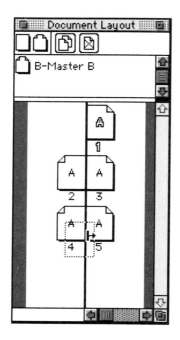

FIGURE 4.7

To insert a page, simply drag a master page to the appropriate place in your document layout.

the page. For example, if want to put it between pages 6 and 7, place the page on the center line between the pages, with the pointer pointing to the right, toward page 7. Once you have the page in the correct position, simply release the mouse button and the page will be inserted automatically (see Figure 4.7).

To delete a page, click on the page and click on the Delete button. When you click on the Delete button a dialog box will appear, asking you if you're sure you want to remove this page. If you're sure, click OK, and the computer won't remember that the page ever existed. You can use this same technique to delete a master page. Another way to insert or delete pages is to choose Insert or Delete in the Page menu. You can also move pages in the Page menu by choosing Move and typing values in the fields. (See Figure 4.8.)

WORKING WITH TOOLS AND BOXES

Open Page 1 by double-clicking on the icon in your Document Layout palette. Depending on the size of your screen, you might want to enlarge or reduce the page to a more convenient working size. There are three ways to do this. The easi-

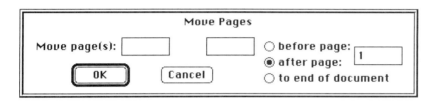

FIGURE 4.8

Another way to insert or move a page is to use the Insert and Move dialog boxes in the Page menu.

est way to enlarge the page is to use the Zoom Tool—it looks like a magnifying glass in the Tool palette. Click on the tool to select it. Put your cursor on the page. Notice how the cursor changes to the magnifying glass? Click on the page and it will zoom in 25%. (Or any other increment you've specified in Preferences.) Click again and it will zoom in another 25%. You can do this all the way up to 400%.

This is a good way to make quick jumps up or down, but what if you need to see the page at, say, 364%? In the lower-left corner of your window you'll see the percent of enlargement displayed. You can drag the cursor over that number and type in the value of any percentage you want.

You may find it more convenient to adjust the page display size by using the keyboard. Press Control-V to highlight the number in the View Percent field. Next, simply type in the desired percent value or, to display your document in Thumbnails view, type the letter T.

SHORTCUT

Another way to enlarge or reduce the size of your page is to select a size in the View menu. If you select Fit in Window, the page will automatically be scaled to the page within your window.

Lorem ipsum dolor sit amet, consectetur adipscing elit, sed diam nomumy eisusmod tempor incidunt ut labore et dolore magna aliquam erat volupat. Ut enim ad minimim veniami quis nostrud exercitation ullamcorpor suscipit laboris nisi ut aliquip ex ea commodo consequat. Duis autem vel eum irure dolor in reprehenderit in vojup-

FIGURE 4.9

Text boxes are the building blocks of your text page. You can type text into them or import text from another file. Handles on the corners and in the center of each side of the box let you resize it.

Text Boxes

Boxes are QuarkXPress's basic building blocks. There are two kinds: text boxes and picture boxes. Except for rules, anything you put on the page must be in either a text box or a picture box. Any kind of type, whether it's typed into your layout or imported from another file, must go into a text box. (See Figure 4.9.) Accordingly, any picture must go into a picture box. These boxes appear on your layout but not on the printed document.

Let's create a text box. Go to the Tool palette and select the Text Box Tool. (The Text Box Tool is the box with the letter A in it.) When the Text Box Tool is active it will be highlighted in the palette. To create a box, click anywhere on your page and, holding the mouse button down, drag diagonally across the page. Make your box approximately 2" square. When the box is about the right size, let go of the mouse button. Don't worry at this point about making it exactly the right size; it's easy to readjust it.

On the text box that you just made you will see a small square on each corner and straddling the line at the center of each side. These squares are called handles. You can "grab" a handle by placing the cursor on it and holding the mouse button down. Once you've grabbed it, you can pull or push it until the box is the size you want. You can move the entire box by clicking on it with the Item Tool and dragging it to a new location on the page. If you have more than one document open, you can even drag it to the new document. Notice the rulers at the top and right side of your document window. See what happens when you move the box? There are lines that move in the ruler to mark where you are positioning the box. This helps you align the box to an exact position on the page. For instance, if you want to place your text box (or any other element) two inches from the top of the page and one inch from the left, you could drag the box until the lines in the ruler align themselves with the 2" mark in the side ruler and 1" mark in the top ruler.

Now that you've created a text box, select the Content Tool. When the Content Tool is selected and the text box is active, a flashing cursor appears in the upper-left corner. Now type text in the box until the box is filled. When there is too much text for the box, a small box appears in the lower-right corner. This symbol lets you know that there is text in the document that wouldn't fit in the box. You can reposition the cursor by clicking anywhere within the text. To add text, place the cursor where you want the new text to begin, then type it in.

There are several ways to delete text. To delete one character at a time, place the cursor at the end of the text and press the delete key on your keyboard. To delete a block of text, place the cursor at the beginning of the text and drag across the characters you want to delete. They will become highlighted. Release the mouse button when you've selected the last character. Once the selection is highlighted, one tap of the delete key will erase the entire block.

While usually text boxes are rectangular, QuarkXPress lets you create text boxes that are irregular in shape. First, create a standard text box with the Text Box Tool. While the text box is active you have the option of choosing one of the standard shapes from the Box Shape submenu in the Item pull-down menu or you can create your own shape with the Polygon option. (The Polygon is the last shape at the bottom of the menu.) To reshape the text box, check Reshape Polygon in the Item menu, then use the cursor to drag the handles until the box is the desired size and shape. You can add additional handles to the box by holding down the Command key and clicking on the box edge.

Picture Boxes

Picture boxes are identical to text boxes, except that they have lines crossing from corner to corner to form an X. (See Figure 4.10.) You create picture boxes by using one of the Picture Box Tools. QuarkXPress is not a drawing program, and it is not set up to actually create pictures, they must always be imported from outside. (This will be discussed further in a later chapter.)

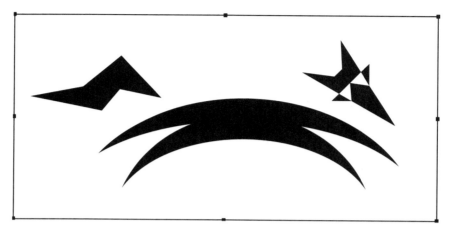

FIGURE 4.10 Picture boxes are like text boxes, but they are used for graphic elements instead of text.

Create a picture box on your page about the same size as the text box. Use any of the Picture Box Tools except for the Polygon Picture Box (the one with the irregular shape). Notice how similar the boxes look. Picture Boxes also have handles. The Polygon Picture Box is designed so that it will not have square corners. Select the Polygon Picture Box Tool from the Tool Palette and place your cursor on the page. Notice that the cursor changes from an arrow to crosshairs when it's moved over the page. Click on the page to establish the first corner point. Without holding the mouse button down, move the cursor where you want to position the second point and click the mouse button. Do this until you want to close the shape, then place the cursor over the first point again. When it's positioned properly, the cursor will change from a crosshair to a box. Click on the mouse button when your shape is complete. Just like other boxes, you can reshape a Polygon Picture Box by dragging its handles. (See Figure 4.11.)

Text and picture boxes have other uses as well. They can be filled with color or shades of color and used as shapes on the page, or they can be surrounded by a line to create an actual visual box. Double-clicking on a box will bring up its dialog box. The Text Box Specifications dialog box lets you define the dimensions of the box, the box angle, the number of columns, text alignment, and background color. Similarly, the Picture Box Specifications dialog box gives you control over the box dimensions, box angle, the size and proportion of the picture, the picture angle, and background color. You can also distort the picture by adjusting the value in the Skew field.

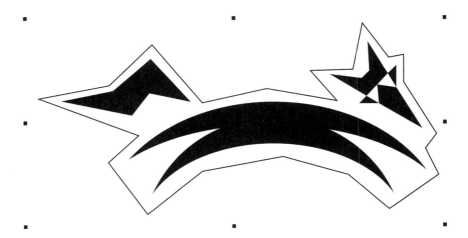

FIGURE 4.11 The Polygon Picture Box lets you create irregular shapes.

Returning to the example on your screen, double-click on the text box to bring up the dialog box. In the Background box there are two pull-down menus. The Color menu, and the Shade menu is greyed out. Pull down the Color menu and select black. Pull down the Shade menu and select 50%. Click OK and notice what has happened to your text box. It should have a 50% gray tone in it. Double-click the box again. Change the Shade value back to 0%, select None in the Color menu, and click OK. Now your box should look like it did when you started. Selecting None takes away any background color, making the box transparent. This is useful if you want to expose elements underneath the box. Double-click on the box again. Type 45 in the Box Angle field and click OK. See how easy it is to alter the angle of the box? You can also Skew the box by typing a value in the Box Skew field. Type in a value of 45, click OK and see what happens. Take a few minutes to experiment and familiarize yourself with the box tools.

The contents of both text and picture boxes can be flipped either horizontally or vertically to create a mirror image of the original by choosing Flip Horizontal or Flip Vertical from the Style pull-down menu.

LINKING TEXT BOXES

You can control the way text flows through your document by linking text boxes together. These linked text boxes are called a text chain. Text boxes can be linked in two ways. They're linked automatically if you check Automatic Text Box in the New dialog box when you open your document. Auto Page Insertion, under General Preferences in the Edit menu, will instruct the computer to automatically add pages to the end of your story, section, or document as needed. Every time you add a page to your layout it will include a text box that will be automatically linked to the last page. This specification is included in your master page. Often, however, you'll want to link and unlink text boxes manually. This is done using the Linking and Unlinking Tools.

Using the Text Box Tool, create two new text boxes on your page, each one about 2" square. From the Tool Palette, select the Linking Tool, which looks like links of chain. With the Linking Tool selected, click on the first text box. The box becomes a moving dotted line. Now click on the second box, and you'll see an arrow extend from the lower-right corner of the first box to the upper-left corner of the second box. Arrows indicate the way the text path flows from one linked box to the next. Linking text boxes is as simple as that. To unlink the boxes, select the Unlinking Tool (which looks like a broken chain). When this tool is selected, you will see all the linked boxes with the arrows. To unlink the boxes, click your cursor on the head of the arrow to break the link from the previous box, or on the tail of the arrow to break the link to the next box in the chain. (See Figure 4.12.)

WORKING WITH RULES

When designers talk about the usefulness of rules they're not expressing a reverence for the law. The term rule is printer lingo for a line. QuarkXPress lets you draw two different basic lines: orthogonal lines, which are perfectly horizontal or vertical; and angled lines. To draw a perfect horizontal or vertical line use the Orthogonal Line Tool, which looks like a plus sign. Use the Line Tool below it to draw angled lines. Take a moment to draw a horizontal, vertical, or angled line on your page. Leaving the line active (when a line is active it has handles on both ends), go to the Item menu and select Modify. This will bring up the Line Specifications dialog box. (You can also activate this box by selecting the Content Tool and double-clicking on the active rule.) This dialog box lets you specify exactly what kind of line you want. You can determine the style (solid, dotted, dashed,

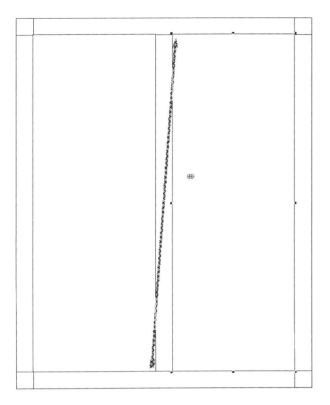

FIGURE 4.12

You create a manual text chain by using the Linking Tool to link text boxes together.

arrow, etc.), type of endcap, width, color, shade, and exact position of the rule on the page (see Figure 4.13). And remember, all of these same choices are also available in your Measurements palette, which can be left out on your desktop at all times.

You can also specify lines as a paragraph format in the Paragraph Rules dialog box. You can find this dialog box under Rules in the Style menu when a text box is active. Paragraph rules differ from lines drawn with the line tools because they remain anchored to the text and flow with it.

RULERS AND GUIDES

When you opened your document for the first time you may have noticed rulers at the top and left side of the window. The units of measurement in these rulers were probably inches, but you can change them from inches to picas, millimeters, cen-

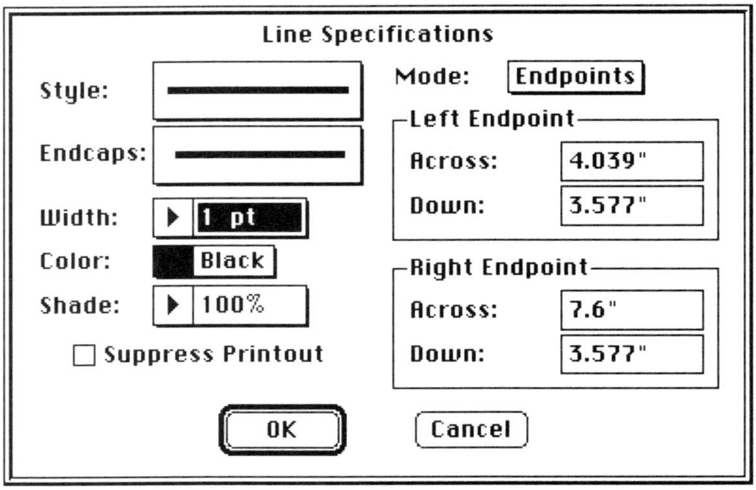

```
┌─────────────────────────────────────────────────┐
│              Line Specifications                  │
│                                                   │
│  Style:    [━━━━━━━━━━━]    Mode:  [Endpoints]    │
│                                                   │
│  Endcaps:  [━━━━━━━━━━━]   ┌─Left Endpoint──────┐ │
│                            │ Across:  [4.039"]   │ │
│  Width:   ▶ [1 pt]         │ Down:    [3.577"]   │ │
│                            └─────────────────────┘ │
│  Color:   [Black]                                 │
│  Shade:   ▶ [100%]        ┌─Right Endpoint─────┐ │
│                            │ Across:  [7.6"]     │ │
│      □ Suppress Printout   │ Down:    [3.577"]   │ │
│                            └─────────────────────┘ │
│                                                   │
│         (   OK   )        ( Cancel )              │
└─────────────────────────────────────────────────┘
```

FIGURE 4.13

The Line Specifications dialog box lets you specify style, width, color, and position of a rule.

timeters, or ciceros in the General Preferences dialog box under the Edit menu. You can put the rulers away by selecting Hide Rulers from the View menu, but I recommend leaving them out because you'll use them constantly. Open your document and place the cursor on either the top or side ruler. Holding the mouse button down, drag from the ruler out to your page. The cursor will drag a line with it. These lines are called guides, and they can be pulled out of either the horizontal or the vertical ruler. You can pull out as many as you need. They are the equivalent of a t-square and triangle and are useful for aligning elements with each other. Once placed, they can be moved or realigned by clicking and dragging. Notice that as you move them, a corresponding line moves along the ruler. This makes it easy to place them at an exact measure. For instance, if you want to align an element one inch from the left edge of the page and two inches down from the top, you can align a vertical guide to the 1" mark and a horizontal guide to the 2" mark, then drag your element to align to the guides. (See Figure 4.14)

Quark has built a convenient feature into the software that makes it easy to align elements such as boxes and rules to the guides. If it isn't already active, select Snap to Guides from the View menu. If it's active, you will see a check mark next to it. Drag a horizontal guide down from the top ruler. Using the Orthogonal Line Tool, draw a horizontal line on the page. Drag the rule to the guide. Once it's close it will "snap to" the guide, aligning itself automatically.

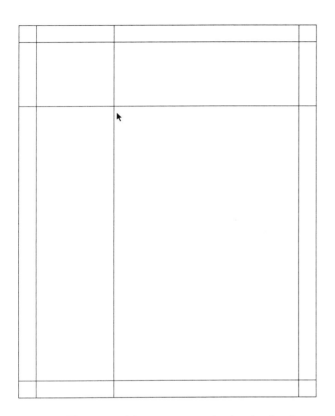

FIGURE 4.14

Guides can be pulled out of either the horizontal or vertical ruler at the top and left of your document window. They function like a t-square and triangle and are very useful for aligning items on your page.

SHORTCUT

If your guides are set to be in the background, it often becomes difficult to reposition them when numerous elements are on the page. Once you place a text box or any other element on the page you must move it to grab the guide. To avoid this, instead of dragging the guide onto the page itself, drag it outside of the page frame. This will extend the guide beyond the page frame, always leaving part of it exposed for repositioning. If you don't want your guides to be behind the page you can change the setting in the General Preferences dialog box.

SCROLL BARS

On the bottom right side of your document window you will notice a gray bar with an arrow at each end and a box in the middle. This is called the scroll bar and it is used to "scroll" to different parts of the page or to different pages in the document.

It is particularly useful if you can't see your entire page on your screen. This is common if you are working with the page enlarged or if your Macintosh has a small screen.

You can use the scroll bar in several ways. The little box is actually a slider that you can move up and down or side to side by clicking on it with the mouse and dragging it with mouse button held down. This allows you to make large, quick moves through the pages of your document. To make smaller moves, click on the gray bar. Clicking on the bar above the box will move the page up; clicking below it will move the page down. To move in very small increments, place the cursor on one of the arrows of the scroll bar and hold the mouse button down.

COPYING AND PASTING

The Copy and Paste commands under the Edit menu are not unique to QuarkXPress, but you will find them very useful. Here's how they work. When you select an item or group of items and choose Copy from the Edit menu, an exact duplicate is placed on the Clipboard. The Clipboard is a "holding area" for elements that are being moved from one location to another. You can then go to the page where you want to place the element and choose Paste. The item will automatically be moved from the Clipboard to the new location. The Cut command in the Edit menu works the same way, but instead of making a copy of the item, it deletes the item from the original position and moves it to the Clipboard. The Copy and Paste functions can be used with both graphic elements and text.

Cutting, copying, and pasting can be very useful if you want to repeat an item such as a standard headline in your layout. You may occasionally want to rearrange blocks of text or apply a graphic element to multiple places in your layout. If you don't have the element on your page, create a new text box and type the desired text into it. Add a new page to your layout by pulling down a new master page in your Document Layout palette. With the item tool selected, click on your text box to make it active and choose Copy from the Edit menu. Then click on Paste. You should see an exact duplicate of the text box on your page. Click on the text box again and choose Cut from the Edit menu. Move to the next page by double-clicking on Page 2 in your Document Layout Palette. When the new page appears, choose Paste and your element will appear.

Here's a quick way to copy and paste an object or group from one document to another. Open the document you want to copy to (QuarkXPress allows you to have up to 25 documents open at the same time), select the object you want to copy and, holding the mouse button down, drag it off of the original document and onto the new one. When you release the mouse button a copy of the original object will be placed in the new document.

SHORTCUT

REPEATING AND DUPLICATING

QuarkXPress has two features that are great time savers: the Duplicate and Step and Repeat commands under the Item menu. Suppose you want to repeat certain elements in your layout, such as the bars in a bar graph. These commands allow you to not only copy an item but to repeat multiple copies of boxes, lines, and groups, and to specify the distance between them.

To duplicate an item, select the item you want to copy and choose Duplicate from the Item menu. It will copy the item and position the new copy according to the horizontal offset and vertical offset values specified in the Step and Repeat dialog box. (The default values are .25" for both the horizontal and vertical offset, which places the new item a quarter of an inch below and to the right of the original.) You can change the default values by opening the Step and Repeat dialog box from the Item menu and typing new values in the fields. (See Figure 4.15.)

If you want to step and repeat multiple copies, choose Step and Repeat from the Item menu to again bring up the Step and Repeat dialog box. Specify the number of copies you want to make in the Repeat Count field. Remember also to specify the placement of the new items in the Horizontal Offset and Vertical Offset fields. If the items are spaced too closely they will overlap. QuarkXPress will "stack" the items on top of one another, with the first copy on the bottom and the last on the top.

GROUPING

You may sometimes find it convenient to combine multiple elements in a group. Once elements are grouped they can be treated as a single object. You can cut, paste, move, delete, or duplicate them as if they were one item. To group objects, select them to make them active and choose Group from the Item menu. The Group command is active only when multiple items are active at the same time.

You can activate more than one object at a time by choosing the Item Tool and clicking on each item while holding the Shift key down. To break up the group, activate it and choose Ungroup from the Item menu. (See Figure 4.16.)

Choosing Constrain in the Item menu enables you to contain all of your grouped items within a single box. The Constrain command is available only when a group is active and one item in the group is a box that is behind the other items and that completely contains them. However, once a group is constrained you cannot move the grouped items without moving the constraining box. When you move the box, all of the grouped items move as well.

QuarkXPress offers some ability to modify grouped items, but there are limitations. For instance, when modifying a group containing a diversity of elements such as text boxes, picture boxes, and lines, you can change only the position, angle, and background color and shade. To make these modifications, select the group and use the Measurements palette, or select Modify from the Item menu to bring up the Group Specifications box. The Group Specifications box contains fields and controls that are common to all the items in the group. If the group con-

Lorem ipsum dolor sit amet, consectetur adipscing elit, sed diam nomumy eisusmod tempor incidunt ut labore et dolore magna aliquam erat volupat. Ut enim ad minimim veniami quis nostrud exercitation ullamcorpor suscipit laboris nisi ut aliquip ex ea commodo consequat. Duis autem vel eum irure dolor in reprehenderit in vojuptate velit esse molistatie son consequat, vel illum dolore eu fugiat nulla pariature. At vero eos et accusam et justo odio dignissim qui blandit prasesent lupatum delenit aigue duos dolor et mosestais exceptur sint occaecat cupidat non provident, sinil tempor sunt in clpa qui officia desu-

FIGURE 4.16

Grouping items lets you move, cut, copy, delete, or paste them without altering their relationship to one another.

tains all picture boxes, the Modify command will bring up the Picture Box Specifications box; if the group contains all text boxes, it will activate the Text Box Specifications box.

Let's create a group. Using the appropriate tools from the Tool palette, create a picture box, a text box, and a line on your page. Select the Item Tool and, holding the Shift key down on your keyboard, click on each of the three items until they are activated. (Remember, when they are active you will see handles on them.) Now choose Group from the Item menu.

SHORTCUT

Here's a quick way to activate multiple objects: With the Item Tool selected, click and drag a rectangle around all the objects. When you release the mouse button, all the objects will be activated. To quickly deactivate them simply press the Tab key.

It's generally much easier to use the Measurements palette than the pull-down menus. If you don't already have the Measurements palette on your desktop, select Show Measurements from the View menu. You can change values in any of the fields by double clicking on the existing values and typing in a new one. Let's change the angle of the group you just created. Find the angle field in the Measurements Palette. Holding your mouse button down, double click on the numbers to select them. Type in 45. Notice that there is no OK button in the Measurements Palette. You can complete the command by clicking the mouse on the page or pressing the Return or Enter key on your keyboard.

ROTATING OBJECTS

QuarkXPress lets you rotate lines, text boxes, picture boxes to virtually any angle. To do this, you can use the Rotation Tool in your Tool Palette, the pull-down menus, or the Measurements Palette. To rotate an object with the Rotation Tool, activate the item that you want to rotate. Select the Rotation Tool from the Tool Palette and place the cursor over the object. Notice that the cursor changes to a crosshair. Place the cursor over the center point around which you want to rotate the object and click. The arrowhead pointer should be displayed. Drag the pointer in a circular motion until the object is at the desired angle. (See Figure 4.17.)

 Use your Tab key to move quickly from field to field in the Measurements Palette.

SHORTCUT

To rotate an object using the Modify command, activate the object and choose Modify from the Item menu. Depending on the type of object, the Picture Box Specifications, Text Box Specifications, or Group Specifications dialog box will be displayed. Once the box is displayed, enter a value in the Box Angle field. You can choose any value between 360° and -360°, in .001° increments. The third way to rotate an object is to type in the new value in the angle field in the Measurements Palette.

SPACING AND ALIGNING OBJECTS

The Space/Align command in the Item menu lets you control the position and space relationship of objects to one another. After activating a group of objects, choose Space/Align, which brings up the Space/Align Items dialog box. (Remember that you can activate multiple objects by holding down the Shift key

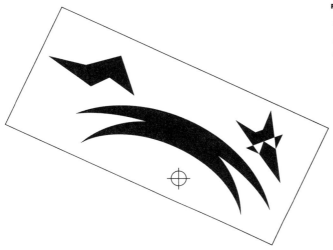

FIGURE 4.17

The Rotation Tool lets you rotate an object around a central point.

and clicking on the objects with the Item Tool.) To specify the horizontal space between the objects, click in the Horizontal box and type a value in the Horizontal Box Space field. To specify the vertical space between the objects, click in the Vertical box and type a value in the Vertical Box Space field. You can also use the pop-up menus to specify whether you want the objects aligned from the center, top, or bottom edges. Clicking the Distribute Evenly button will automatically distribute space evenly between the objects. Notice that there is a button labeled Apply in the dialog box. Clicking this button will show you what the final result will look like. When you're satisfied with the arrangement, click OK. (See Figure 4.18.)

STORING ELEMENTS IN LIBRARY PALETTES

QuarkXPress has a unique feature called Libraries, which lets you store and easily access frequently used items. This can be particularly useful for designing newsletters, magazines, and other publications that use stock items such as logos and mastheads from issue to issue. Libraries can contain text or graphics—anything that can be created in or imported into QuarkXPress, up to 2,000 entries.

Libraries are displayed as palettes on your desktop. The palette contains "thumbnail" pictures of each item so you can identify them visually. To place an item into your layout, simply reach into the palette, grab the item, and drag it onto your page. (See Figure 4.19.)

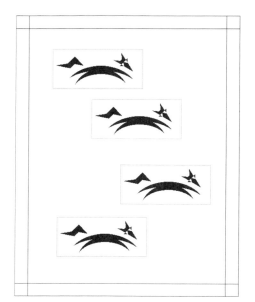
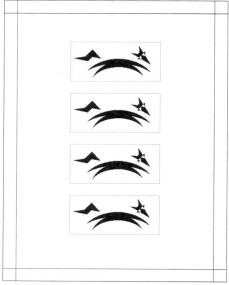

FIGURE 4.18

The objects on the left are placed randomly on the page. QuarkXPress's Space/Align feature lets you automatically space and align the objects evenly, as shown on the right.

To create a new library, choose Library from the New command under the File pull-down menu. This will bring up another dialog box. You'll need to give your new library a name, so type one into the New Library field. Use the other fields to specify where you want to store the library, then click Create.

To open a library, choose Open from the File menu. When the Open dialog box is displayed, navigate to the folder in which your library is stored. Select the library and click Open.

To store an item in the library use your mouse to drag the item, or items, from the page to the Library Palette window. When the cursor is over the Library Palette, it will change to a tiny pair of glasses. Once you've dragged the item over the palette, simply let go of the mouse button and drop it in.

It's just as easy to move an item from the library to your page. Use the scroll bars to scroll through the Library Palette until you find the item you want. Click on the item to activate it (it will become highlighted when it's active) and drag it to your

FIGURE 4.19

Frequently used items can be stored in Libraries. These items can be easily accessed through the Library Palette.

page. Release the mouse button over the place on your page where you want to position the item.

Removing an item from the library is even easier. Simply activate the item and press the delete key on your keyboard. You can also remove an item by selecting Clear from the Edit menu, but it's easier to just press Delete.

What if you actually accumulate 2,000 entries in your library? That seems like a lot of entries, but it could happen. In fact, even if you had a couple hundred, you might not want to scroll through that many pictures. That's why QuarkXPress lets you label each of your entries and view them as a list. To label an entry, double-click on the item. This will bring up the Library Entry dialog box. Enter a label in the field. Note that this is not a name, but a label. The difference is you can't confuse the computer by giving the same name to more than one item, but in a library you can use the same label for more than one item. What you're doing is putting your items into categories. This lets you create smaller libraries within the library—for instance, instead of one huge library called Amphibians, you could create subcategory labels like Bullfrogs or Bug-eyed Newts. To view only the items with the same label, simply choose the label from the top of the Library Palette. To view the entire library, select All.

SUMMARY

This chapter discussed some basic concepts of organizing information on the page. It also provided an overview of the tools and the capabilities QuarkXPress offers and described how to use QuarkXPress tools to set up the page structure. Take a moment now to consider the following questions:

1. How can you, as a designer, control the way the reader absorbs information on a page?
2. What is a *focal point*, and how is it used to create a visual path?
3. What kind of elements command the most visual attention?
4. What is a *grid* and why is it useful?
5. What are *master pages*?
6. What's the difference between a text box and a picture box?
7. How do you link text boxes?
8. What is *cutting* and *pasting*, and why are these functions useful?
9. What is the *Library Palette* and how is it used?

Working with Type

I t's hard to imagine anything more fundamental to good design than quality typography. For that reason, this chapter will explore type in some detail. In addition to general typographic fundamentals, there are some basics to learn about setting type on the computer. This chapter will address the following questions:

- How do you select the right typeface for a particular publication?

- How can you begin building a functional type library?

- How is computer type different than conventional typesetting?

- What makes one typeface more legible than another?

- Typography seems to have its own language. What is meant by terms like *leading, kerning, tracking, serif,* and *sans serif?*

- What is meant by *type color?*

- How can you creatively modify letterforms while retaining their legibility?

- Can you use QuarkXPress like a word processing program to type text into your layout?

- Do you have the option of importing text from another software program?

- How do you select *typeface, point size,* and *leading?*

- What's the easiest way to format column margins? Is it easy to change from justified to flush left or centered text?

- How do you kern the letter pairs in your document?

- How do you adjust the tracking?

- What's the easiest way to handle widows and orphans?

- How do you create an initial cap?

- How can you control the way your lines break, and how does QuarkXPress handle hyphenation?

- How can you use style sheets to make text formatting easier?

TYPESETTING OR TYPOGRAPHY?

Typography is the mechanical process of creating printed words through the arrangement of letterforms. While this definition may be accurate on a basic level, the best typography is also an art form. I tend to make a distinction between typesetters and typographers. The majority of people who set type for a living are typesetters, not typographers. The difference is this: a typesetter churns out type without regard for the details, letting the machinery do the work. This involves little more than typing and proofreading. On the other hand, the *typographer* is intimately involved with type. Everything is important: the precise spacing between letters, the amount of space between lines, the way lines break at the end of a line, the size and weight relationship between heads and body text—all of these details are crucial. The typographer typically makes numerous adjustments word by word, even letter by letter, until the entire page works together. It's very important for graphic designers to be sensitive to these kinds of refinements.

Today the computer revolution in design means that more and more designers are assuming the role of the typographer. While typographers may have spent years studying and working with type, designers have typically spent their time at a higher concept level, concerned more with the overall character of the printed piece. Although typography has always been a part of the training of designers, it is only one of many functions they must handle. Traditionally, designers have been limited to making typographic specifications and overseeing the work performed by the typographer. But now, as more and more designers use the computer as a typesetting tool, they must broaden their discipline and learn to be experts in typography as well. For the designers whose education provided them a solid working knowledge of type, this is a fairly easy and painless transition. Unfortunately, though, design education in recent years has not given the kind of attention to this area that it has in the past. As a result, even experienced and talented designers who

74

generally maintain high standards are producing type on their computers that just doesn't measure up to good traditional typography. It's sad to say, but often designers are willing to make this concession for the sake of convenience. I know of one talented and experienced traditional typographer who is unique because she is also quite involved in computer typography. She expressed a concern to me one day that many of her most demanding customers—designers who would nit-pick at the most minute details on galleys of traditionally set type—were now setting type on their computers and ignoring typographic flaws because they had neither the time nor inclination to fix them.

The fact is, setting quality type on a computer is not easy. It takes some extra work. The computer was designed for a wide variety of tasks, and publication design is only one. Even software that was designed specifically for producing printed materials was essentially created with simple desktop publishing in mind. The greatest part of the software market consists of users who want to produce something of adequate quality but who don't want to invest a lot of time to bring it up to true professional quality. As a result, software manufacturers have not been in a hurry to develop products that will easily produce professional quality type. QuarkXPress is the exception because it provides many of these capabilities, but even it falls short in some areas. Yet it is possible to get good results if you're willing to invest some extra effort.

TYPOGRAPHIC TERMINOLOGY

Typography has a language all its own. Here are some of the terms you will encounter:

Typeface

This refers to a specific letterform design that typically includes all letters of the alphabet, numbers, and punctuation. Each typeface is designed to have its own unique character.

Font

A font is a single style, size, and weight of a typeface. For example, 10-point Times Italic and 9-point Times Roman are different fonts, even though they are members of the same type family. In computer typography, a font is often considered to be a particular style within a type family, such as Times Roman, Times Bold, or Times

Italic, without regard for size. This is because computer typefaces are often scalable, which means that one type style can be scaled up or down in size electronically, eliminating the need for numerous point sizes.

Typeface Family

Type fonts are grouped in families. Families include all the fonts within a specific typeface, such as the Times family or the Helvetica family.

Serif and Sans Serif

Typefaces are generally divided into two groups: serif and sans serif (Figure 5.1). A serif is a small finishing stroke at the end of the main strokes of a letter. Many of the older traditional typefaces, such as Times, have serifs. Sans serif faces are block type letters, such as Helvetica. Sans serif in French means "without serif."

FIGURE 5.1 Most typefaces are either serif or sans serif. A serif is the tail or finishing stroke at the end of the main stroke of a letterform. It's like a visual flourish. The letter on the left is a serif face; the one on the right is sans serif.

Weight

This refers to the heaviness or boldness of the typeface. Many typefaces include several weights, such as light, medium, bold, and extra bold or heavy.

Horizontal Scaling

In QuarkXPress this refers to the relative width of the letterforms. The software lets you manipulate letters by horizontally expanding or condensing them.

Uppercase and Lowercase

Long ago when type was set by hand, letters were stored in cabinets called type cases, which were set on top of one another. The capital letters were stored in the upper case and the small letters in the lower case.

Baseline

An imaginary line on which the type in a document sits (Figure 5.2).

FIGURE 5.2 The imaginary line upon which the letters sit is called the baseline.

X-height

X-height refers to the height of the lowercase letters relative to the height of the uppercase. It is measured from the baseline to the top of the lowercase x. The point size is not an accurate indicator of the actual size of the letters. An older cut of a typeface usually has a smaller x-height than its modern counterpart (Figure 5.3).

Ascenders and Descenders

Ascenders and descenders are the parts of the letters that extend above the x-height or below the baseline, respectively.

FIGURE 5.3 Compare the x-heights of the older Century Old Style and the modern ITC Century. Older typefaces tend to have a smaller x-height.

Kerning

Often the space between individual letters must be adjusted in order to appear even. This manual adjustment of the space between a pair of letters is known as *kerning*.

Tracking

In QuarkXPress, *tracking* refers to adding or subtracting even increments of space between groups of letters.

Small Caps

Sometimes scaled-down capital letters are substituted for lowercase letters. These are called small caps.

Dingbat

A decorative typographic device inserted within a line of text.

Bullet

A dot or other device placed at the beginning of a line of text for emphasis.

Justification

This refers to a method of setting type where the side of a column of text is aligned (as opposed to ragged line breaks.)

Flush Left

Columns of type that are justified on the left side and have ragged line breaks on the right are called flush left/ragged right, or simply flush left.

Flush Right

The opposite of flush left. Columns that are set flush right are justified on the right and ragged on the left. Type set this way can be difficult to read, so it should be reserved for very short blocks of text.

Centered

Columns of type that are aligned to a center line rather than to an edge. The lines are ragged on both sides.

H&J

This stands for hyphenation and justification. QuarkXPress allows you to set specific values that control the way words are hyphenated and paragraphs are justified.

Initial Cap

You may have seen a column of type where the first letter is very large. This large letter is called an *initial cap*, or simply an initial.

Ligature

A combination of two letterforms, usually done to create a more pleasing space relationship between the two letters (Figure 5.4).

FIGURE 5.4 A ligature.

Old Style

A type style developed in the 16th and 17th centuries, characterized by bold, uniform strokes and rounded or sloping serifs. Many of these faces are still in use today. Century Old Style is a good example.

Pica

A typographic measurement. There are approximately 6 picas to an inch.

Point

A typographic unit of measure. There are 12 points in a pica.

Em

A printer's measurement that is equivalent to the spce occupied by the capital letter M. In QuarkXPress you can choose between a standard typographer's em space or an em that is based on the width of two zeros. Use the controls in the Typographic Preferences dialog box to choose one or the other.

En

Half the width of an em.

Italic Type

Letters that are slanted to the right. Italic letters are usually used for emphasis.

Roman Type

Type that is upright (as opposed to italic).

Leading

The spacing between lines of type, measured from one baseline to the next.

Widow

A markedly short line of type that appears at the top of the next column.

THE CHARACTER OF TYPE

Typefaces have personalities. Sometimes it's said that typefaces have a "voice." I know what you're thinking: If this guy thinks type is talking to him, he's been in the business way too long. But this simply means that each typeface has a different character, and that character (or voice) should match the tone of the publication. Often the actual style of the type communicates the message as much as the words themselves. Certainly the typestyle should be appropriate to the message. So the first step is to determine the "personality" of the message. Is it soft and persuasive? Bold and aggressive? Conservative or businesslike? Brash or avant-garde? Not only does an appropriate typestyle enhance the message, but an inappropriate choice of type can communicate the wrong message (Figure 5.5).

FIGURE 5.5

An inappropriate choice of typeface can create mixed signals.

Serif Type

As a rule, serif faces have a different personality than sans serif (Figure 5.6). Serif faces have been around for centuries and have a timeless quality. They tend to feel conservative and businesslike. They are also perceived as being "bookish," probably because many books are set in serif faces. Serif typefaces are also more legible than sans serif faces. Serif faces are often used for newspapers, magazines, books, and business documents. Times, Garamond, Bodoni, Caslon, and Goudy are good examples of serif faces.

Sans Serif Type

Sans serif typefaces, on the other hand, have a practical, no-nonsense feel. They tend to have a more forthright kind of personality, sometimes to the point of being brash. A bold sans serif head can appear to scream. Because they lack the refinement of serifs, sans serif have a very streamlined look. Sans serif faces are not quite as legible for lengthy documents, but they are used quite effectively for shorter items like heads and captions. They often provide a nice contrast to serif faces. Some common sans serif faces include Helvetica, Futura, Univers, and Avant Garde.

AaBbCcDdEeFf

AaBbCcDdEeFf

AaBbCcDdEeFf

AaBbCcDdEeFf

FIGURE 5.6

Note how these common typefaces differ in personality.

CLASSIC TYPEFACES

In just the past ten or twenty years I've seen numerous typefaces introduced, become trendy, and fall out of favor. Using one of these faces is a sure way to make a publication look dated. However, there are a number of typefaces that have become classic. These are primarily styles that have been used for centuries and possess a timeless quality. Over years and years they have been used in all kinds of applications and have proven themselves to be just as appropriate today as when they were first designed. Every type collection should contain a number of these versatile "workhorse" faces. These include Century, Goudy, Helvetica, Times, Bodoni, Garamond, Franklin Gothic, Futura, Caslon, and Univers, to name just a few (Figure 5.7).

BUILDING A TYPE LIBRARY

You will want to build a personal type library by gradually adding typefaces to the collection that came with your computer. There's no need to run out and buy dozens of typefaces; you probably won't use them all and they take up a lot of memory space in your computer. I've found that I can get by very nicely with just a handful of "classic" faces. I strongly recommend that you start with a solid foundation made up of some of the classics listed above, then add others as you need them. Over time you will find which typefaces you use the most.

ABCDEFGHIJKLMNOPQRSTUVWXYZ
abcdefghijklmnopqrstuvwxyz

ABCDEFGHIJKLMNOPQRSTUVWXYZ
abcdefghijklmnopqrstuvwxyz

ABCDEFGHIJKLMNOPQRSTUVWXYZ
abcdefghijklmnopqrstuvwxyz

ABCDEFGHIJKLMNOPQRSTUVWXYZ
abcdefghijklmnopqrstuvwxyz

ABCDEFGHIJKLMNOPQRSTUVWXYZ
abcdefghijklmnopqrstuvwxyz

ABCDEFGHIJKLMNOPQRSTUVWXYZ
abcdefghijklmnopqrstuvwxyz

ABCDEFGHIJKLMNOPQRSTUVWXYZ
abcdefghijklmnopqrstuvwxyz

FIGURE 5.7 These are examples of classic fonts.

Be careful about being attracted to trendy or decorative typefaces. While many of these decorative faces are visually interesting, you'll find that it's difficult to find appropriate uses for them. Once you've chosen the typefaces that you want to include in your personal library, get to know them. Look at the details of every letter—set them large, small, tightly leaded, widely leaded, in bold, italic, and in reverse, and use them in every combination and configuration you can think of. Developing this kind of familiarity is the first step in learning to use type skillfully.

COMPUTER TYPE

In addition to gaining an understanding of typography in general, there are a few things you should know about setting type on a computer. All the same principles apply to both traditional and electronic methods, but there are technical considerations that are inherent to working electronically.

First, let's look at how the computer generates type. Computer typefaces are not really type at all, but software that is designed to "draw" the type characters both on your screen and through output devices such as printers and imagesetters. Computer fonts can be divided into two categories. The first, fixed-size or bitmapped fonts, contain character sets of one size only—for example, 10-point Helvetica Bold or 12-point Times Roman. PostScript fonts fall into this category. In order to have access to all the point sizes you must install all the sizes in your computer. Unfortunately, this takes up a lot of memory.

Indispensable Type Software

However, there is software available to help you get around the memory problem. Two programs that I strongly recommend, particularly if you are using PostScript fonts, are Fifth Generation Systems' Suitcase, and Adobe Systems' Type Manager. Suitcase was developed in response to the number and variety of fonts being marketed for the Macintosh. As you add more and more fonts to your system, problems begin to occur. For starters, the system folder can hold only 800 fonts at one time. This may seem like a lot, but remember that each size, weight, and style of each typeface is a different font. To make matters worse, font ID conflicts can occur. Each font has a number. You may know a particular font as 10-point Century Schoolbook Italic, but the computer may know it as 183. Every once in a while, two fonts from different manufacturers have the same ID number, and when a font is specified the computer becomes confused. You might select Helvetica and get

Blippo Bold. Suitcase lets you store your fonts in "suitcases" and even keep them outside of your system folder. You can selectively open the font or fonts that you want access to at any given time. This not only reduces the memory burden in your system file, but it also allows you to manage ID conflicts.

The other indispensable software program, Adobe Systems' Type Manager (ATM), reduces your computer's memory burden by allowing you to install only one point size of each typestyle in your system. But the main benefit of ATM is the way it displays the type on your screen. Until ATM came along, screen fonts were subject to the "jaggies." When you install a PostScript font, you actually install two font files: a *screen font* and a *printer font*. The printer font is designed to give you a precise, accurate drawing of the font when you output it on a printer or an image-setter. The screen font is a representation of the printer font but is bitmapped, which means it's made up of tiny squares or blocks. Sometimes these bitmapped fonts can look very rough on your screen. ATM smooths out the jaggies and pre-sents a clear, accurate screen representation at any point size. If you use fixed-size fonts in your system, both Suitcase and ATM will save you a lot of frustration.

The other kind of fonts you can add to your system are scalable or outline fonts. These are based on a technology developed by Apple and are called TrueType fonts. Scalable fonts differ from bitmapped fonts in that they require only one font for each typestyle to be installed in your system. That font is then "scaled" up or down to any point size with no degradation of quality. This technology is so new, however, that scalable fonts work only with Macintosh system software version 6.0.4 or later.

WYSIWYG

One of the unique features of the Macintosh is the accuracy of what you see on the screen. In the industry this is referred to as *WYSIWYG* (pronounced "wizziwig") and stands for What You See Is What You Get. This is tremendous for designers who like to know that what they design on the screen is going to bear some resem-blance to what is finally printed. (Designers can be very fussy about things like that.) Unfortunately, when it comes to typography WYSIWYG is still not entirely possible. ATM has made the screen representation of the type much more accu-rate, but with smaller point sizes the screen image may not exactly match the out-put. And accuracy of the printed type can vary dramatically, depending on the kind of output device that is used. A dot-matrix printer will give you only a very crude representation of type, especially at small point sizes, and letterspacing will not be accurate. A laser printer is better—it will typically reproduce the letters at a resolution of 300 or 600 dots per inch, which is a fair representation. But the best quality will come from an imagesetter, which can achieve a resolution of 2,540 dots per inch. This is true typesetting quality. Keep in mind that you can expect only a rough representation of the type on your screen, and it may look different than what is produced on your printer. For this reason it's important to proof your type after it's printed, and for most people a laser printer is the most practical option. The resolution is adequate for proofing. Trying to proof type on a dot matrix printer is a waste of time, and an imagesetter can be prohibitively expensive.

USING DECORATIVE TYPEFACES

I generally define decorative faces as any that fall outside of the classic or mainstream styles. This covers a lot of territory. Some decorative faces are fairly close in style to the old standards but have a unique character that sets them apart. Avant Garde is a good example of a decorative typeface (Figure 5.8). It's a simple sans serif face, but its letterforms are very distinctive.

ABCDEFGHIJKLMNOPQRSTUVWXYZ
abcdefghijklmnopqrstuvwxyz1234567890

FIGURE 5.8 Avant Garde is a typeface with a very distinctive character.

Most decorative faces are not as subtle as Avant Garde. Many are downright outlandish and should be used with a good deal of caution. I don't say this because I'm a hopelessly conservative old fuddyduddy—there are some very practical considerations that should dictate how you use decorative fonts. Inexperienced designers tend to be attracted to them because they have lots of character. They're unique and often quite beautiful. But because they have so much character, they should be used sparingly, to add zest to the page. Just as you can ruin a recipe by adding too much seasoning, you can ruin a layout by adding too much decoration.

Decorative faces are most effective when you want to add special emphasis, such as in initial caps or pull quotes (Figure 5.9). When a typeface has a distinct character it's often less legible when set as body text because the character itself can become a distraction. A good example of this is script type. It's very beautiful and can be appropriate for applications like wedding announcements, where a strong sense of formality is required. In these kinds of applications, however, the text is usually short. It would be very difficult to read long passages of text in a script face (Figure 5.10).

OLOR SIT AMET, CONSECTETUR

ADIPSCING ELIT, SED DIAM

NOMUMY EISUSMOD TEMPOR INCIDUNT

UT LABORE ET DOLORE MAGNA ALIQUAM ERAT VOLU-

PAT. UT ENIM AD MINIMIM VENIAMI QUIS NOSTRUD

EXERCITATION ULLAMCORPOR SUSCIPIT LABORIS NISI

UT ALIQUIP EX EA COMMODO CONSEQUAT.

FIGURE 5.9 Decorative typefaces are often used effectively as initial caps.

TYPE SHOULD BE EASY TO READ

Type can perform numerous functions. It can be used as decoration or illustration and it can give a certain character to the page, but its most important function is to be read. If it isn't legible, it doesn't live up to its primary purpose. As we have seen, the choice of typeface can have a great influence on legibility, but how the type is set can also affect the ease with which it is read.

The choice of type font can have a profound effect on legibility. This block of text was set in Garamond, a classic typeface. It was designed to be easy to read. Decorative typefaces are to designed to be decorative. Often legibility is sacrificed for style.

This block of text was set in a decorative typeface called Caslon Open Face. While Caslon is a very legible classic face, this version is a variation intended to be decorative. Can you see how it is more difficult to read than the text above?

This example is set in Shelley Allegro Script. Script type is great for short blocks of text and can add character to a formal announcement or invitation but it can be very difficult to read..

FIGURE 5.10 The text block at the top is set in Garamond, a classic typeface. The others are set in decorative typefaces. Notice the difference in legibility.

CAPS OR UPPER- AND LOWERCASE?

When type was first invented, the alphabet consisted entirely of capital letters. In fact, in the grand scheme of history, lowercase letters are a fairly recent innovation. But lowercase letters are much more legible than caps, for a couple of reasons. First, lines set in all caps create an unbroken visual line at both the top and the bottom, creating very little differentiation between words. When the eye scans words on a page, the mind searches for visual clues that will help it identify words quickly. The shape of words provides the mind with a means to separate one word from another without deciphering it letter by letter. When words are set in upper- and lowercase, they have a more distinctive shape and as a result are easier to recognize (Figure 5.11).

Another reason type set in upper- and lowercase is easier to read is simply because we're used to it. From the time we first learn to read, we are presented with text set primarily in upper- and lowercase. We're more conditioned to read text set in this manner.

FIGURE 5.11 Setting type in upper- and lowercase give words a more distinctive shape and makes them easier to read.

I'm not suggesting that you set everything in upper- and lowercase letters, but I do urge you to use caps sparingly. Setting long passages in all caps will certainly adversely affect legibility, but there may be instances when you want to use caps in short sections of type like captions or heads to set them apart.

TYPE SIZE VERSUS COLUMN WIDTH

For maximum legibility, it's important to create a proper ratio between the size of the type and the length of line. If there are too few characters in a line, the reader's eye spends too much time jumping from one line to the next. Too long a line can tire the eyes and make it difficult to jump to the beginning of the next line. A good rule of thumb is to set your column width and point size so that you have 8 to 10 words per line. This isn't a very accurate method, though, because word lengths can vary so dramatically. A better way to determine the ratio is by formula. Take your point size and use that number to determine the minimum line width in picas. In other words, if your type size is 12 points, the minimum line width would be 12 picas. Double the minimum line width to determine the maximum. In this case the maximum line width would be 24 picas.

LEADING

Leading is the measurement of vertical space between the lines. Too much or too little leading can affect legibility. QuarkXPress has an autoleading feature, but don't trust it to always give you proper leading. It's based on a mathematical formula that gives you pretty good results in the mid-size range—say from 10- to 14-point type—but it will lead small sizes too tightly and large type will have far too much space between the lines.

Leading is largely a visual judgment. I haven't found a formula that works reliably in all cases because so much depends on factors such as the style, weight, and size of the typeface. There are also stylistic considerations. There may be times when it's appropriate to "force" the leading to be overly tight or loose to achieve a particular effect. For most applications and for optimum readability, however, the lines of type should be spaced so that there is a small amount of space separating the top of the ascenders from the bottom of the descenders in the line above (Figure 5.12).

TYPE COLOR

When typographers talk about type color, it really has nothing to do with color at all. What they're referring to is the unique "texture" of a type page created by the distinctive irregular pattern formed by the letter combinations of each font. Some of the factors that contribute to type color are the style and weight of the type, the leading, width, and number of columns, and the variety of typefaces used. Type color is important because it can affect the impact of the page and emphasize the personality or emotion of the content.

Optimal type leading should be wide enough so that the ascenders and descenders don't touch but not so wide that the eye has to search for the beginning of the next line. These examples show the range of optimal leading.

Optimal type leading should be wide enough so that the ascenders and descenders don't touch but not so wide that the eye has to search for the beginning of the next line. These examples show the range of optimal leading.

Optimal type leading should be wide enough so that the ascenders and descenders don't touch but not so wide that the eye has to search for the beginning of the next line. These examples show the range of optimal leading.

FIGURE 5.12

These are examples of proper type leading.

KERNING

Kerning refers to the adjustment of space between pairs of letters. Proper kerning is the hallmark of fine typography. Professional typographers, when proofing galleys of set type, will not only look for things like misspelled words and poor line breaks but also for poor letterspacing. This is important because it has a profound affect on legibility. Ideally, a word set in type should be a perfectly balanced unit. It should be an object in its own right, not just a collection of letters. When a person learns to read, he or she first begins to "sound out" words by finding phonetic clues in individual letters and groups of letters within words. As the reader becomes more proficient, the words cease to be an assortment of letters to be deciphered, they become symbols themselves. Experienced readers do not read letter by letter, but rather word by word. That's why it's important to legibility that words work as symbols or objects. If letters are spaced unevenly or if there are big gaps of space between letters, the eye tends to stumble. If the eye does not recognize a word as a symbol it reverts to deciphering it letter by letter. Granted, all this happens in a fraction of a second, but if you multiply this by thousands of words it definitely takes its toll.

The fundamental rule to remember about kerning is that the negative space between the letters is as important as the positive space occupied by the letters themselves. If you were to space letters mathematically—that is, by carefully equalizing the space between the letters—you would find that the resulting spacing would look uneven (Figure 5.13). This is due to the irregular shape of the letterforms. Because each letter has a distinctive shape, the letterspacing will vary depending on the letter positioned next to it. Each letter combination must be adjusted visually.

The trick to kerning is equalizing the negative space between the letters. Think of the negative space as having volume. You want to equalize the volume between each letter in the word. Rounded letters tend to create more negative space around them. Letters such as W and V, which take up more space at the top, create extra negative space at the bottom that must be compensated for (Figure 5.14).

Typography

FIGURE 5.13 Mathematically spaced letters tend to look uneven.

Typography

FIGURE 5.14 This word has been properly kerned. Notice how the letterforms tuck into one another to equalize the negative space between the letters.

Most computer fonts have built in automatic kerning of problematic letter combinations. While fonts used by professional typesetters may have thousands of built-in kerning pairs, the typical computer font has between 200 and 400. This means that the type you get right off the computer will be full of awkwardly spaced letter pairs. In order to bring your computer typesetting up to professional standards, you'll need to either go back into your document and manually adjust the kerning or build extra kerning pairs into your system.

The main reason I've chosen to use this software over the competition is because it offers so much more kerning control. There are several ways to kern text in QuarkXPress. The easiest (and most tedious) is to use menu commands to add or delete increments of space between the letters.

Here's how you do it: using the Content Tool, click the cursor between the letters that you want to adjust. You'll see the flashing Text Insertion bar. Next, choose Kern from the Style menu. When you see the Kern Amount dialog box you'll see 0 displayed in the field. Type a new value in the dialog box. A positive value will increase the space between the letters, and a negative value will decrease it. Entering a 1 will add a 1/200-em space. You can enter any value between -500 and 500. You can perform these same functions using the keyboard and you will probably find doing it that way much quicker and easier. Once you have the Text Insertion bar positioned, hold down the Command, Option and Shift keys at the same time and then tap the { key to decrease the space by 1/200-em. To increase the space by 1/200-em do the same thing but use the } key. You can also make adjustments in 1/20-em increments by using the same commands but don't use the Option key, for example Command-Shift-} will increase the space by 1/20-em. Kerning can also be adjusted in the Measurements Palette. You do this by clicking on the kerning arrows. Clicking on the left arrow decreases space while the right arrow increases space.

These methods are quick and easy if you're kerning a headline, but to go letter-by-letter through an entire document can be very time-consuming. I used to do this routinely with all my work. I would enlarge the page to 400% and scroll across each line adjusting letter pairs manually in every line, page after page after page. When I adopted this method I had 20/20 vision and now I wear glasses with lenses as thick as the bottom of Coke bottles…OK, I'm lying about the glasses but it really will give you eyestrain and I don't recommend it. There's a better way to do it, but it's not quick and easy, at least not at first.

If you find yourself routinely using the same fonts you may want to consider making adjustments to the fonts' built-in kerning pairs by using the Kerning Table Edit utility (Figure 5.15). Kerning tables are where the information is stored for automatic kerning, so modifying the spacing here will apply it to all QuarkXPress documents where that particular font is used. For example, let's say your favorite font is Modern Oldstyle. You use it all the time. The trouble is there's always a mile of open space between the W and O. Using Kerning Table Edit you can respace the W and O and, once it's just the way you like it, you can save it and make that new spacing a permanent value (that is, until you change it again). From now on, every time you use Modern Oldstyle in QuarkXPress, the W and O will be properly spaced. Now doesn't that sound better than kerning letter by letter?

Kerning Values for B BauerBodoni Bold «Plain»

Kerning Values:

AT	-10	Pair: [ ]	[ ]	[OK]
AU	-17			
AW	-17	Value: [ ]	[ ]	[Cancel]
AY	-17			
Av	-10		[ ]	
Aw	-10			
Ay	-10		[Import]	[Export]

FIGURE 5.15 You can make "permanent" kerning adjustments in the Kerning Values dialog box.

Be sure to leave Auto Kern in the Typographic Preferences dialog box turned on. This will automatically activate any kerning pairs built into your fonts and automatically take care of a lot of your kerning problems. You can still alter kerning pairs manually with Auto Kern activated.

To edit or kern a letter pair using the kerning tables, choose Kerning Table Edit from the Utilities menu. When you see the Kerning Table Edit dialog box, you'll notice a list of all the available fonts. Select the font you want to work on and click Edit. Now you'll see the Kerning Values dialog box. On the left is a list of all the kern pairs with their kerning values currently resident in the font. To add a new pair to the table, simply type the letters into the Pair field and a kerning value into the Value field. A negative value takes out space, and a positive value adds space. You can specify a kerning value between -500 and 500. To adjust an existing kern-ing pair, select it from the list on the left. Once selected, the pair will be displayed in the Pair field and the kerning value will be displayed in the Value field, where the value can be adjusted. Now, here's the fun part. When you edit a value in the Value field, you don't just stick in a number and hope for the best. You can actually see the letter pair displayed in the big box below the Value field and every time you delete or add space you can see the letters move closer together or farther apart. This is very important because kerning is a visual judgment, not a mathe-matical one. You need to actually see how changing the value changes the spacing.

You can also utilize the QuarkXPress Kern to Space feature to specify kerning pairs consisting of a character-word combination or a character and an en space. This works just like kerning two characters with an exception: to put an en space in the Pair field of the Kerning Values dialog box, you must first enter an en space in a text box, then copy and paste it into the Pair field.

Here's something important to keep in mind when modifying kerning tables. Kerning edits to a font don't affect all styles of the typeface. Remember that each style is a font and each must be edited individually. So kerning edits made to Modern Oldstyle won't affect Modern Oldstyle Italic.

NOTE

TRACKING

Tracking refers to the equal adjustment of space between groups of letters such as between words, sentences, or paragraphs (Figure 5.16). QuarkXPress's tracking capability can be particularly useful if you want to make an overall change in the letterspacing. For example, sometimes large point sizes appear to be too loosely spaced and very small point sizes may need to be opened up a bit for maximum legibility. Tracking is sometimes used for creative effect as well. You may have seen designs where words are very widely spaced. This can be an interesting technique, but use it with caution. Words with an inordinate amount of space between the letters are not easily read. If you employ this technique, limit it to one or two words.

Typography

FIGURE 5.16 Tracking refers to the even adjustment of space between groups of letters.

Making small adjustments to a paragraph's tracking value is a quick and easy way to pull up widows.

SHORTCUT

ADJUSTING TRACKING IN QUARKXPRESS

Just beneath the leading control in the Measurements Palette is the control for tracking. It also has a number value with two arrows, but these arrows point to the left and the right. To evenly increase or decrease the space between the letters, select the type to be adjusted and type in a new value. A positive number increases the tracking, and a negative number decreases it. You can select any number between -500 and 500. You can also use the arrows to adjust the tracking. Clicking on the left arrows decreases the tracking in increments of 1/20 of an em. Clicking on the right arrows increases the tracking by the same increment. Holding down the Option key while clicking the arrows increases or decreases the tracking in 1/200-em increments.

CREATING A HIERARCHY

When setting large amounts of text such as in a book, magazine, or newsletter, it's very important to establish a *typographic hierarchy*. This is really a typographic application of the visual path discussed in Chapter 4. The goal of the typographic hierarchy is to control the way the reader absorbs the information. I always try to design in such a way that the reader can pick up the publication and browse through it (Figure 5.17). Even if the reader chooses not to read every word, the publication's message should come through. This is done by strategically organizing the information through the effective use of heads, subheads, captions, size and weight of type, by positioning type relative to illustrations, and by using techniques such as initial caps to draw the reader's eye. Much of this is just common sense. It's hard to imagine anyone typesetting a publication with heads, subheads, captions, and body text all the same style, size and weight. There are, however, some typographic guidelines that can make your hierarchy more effective.

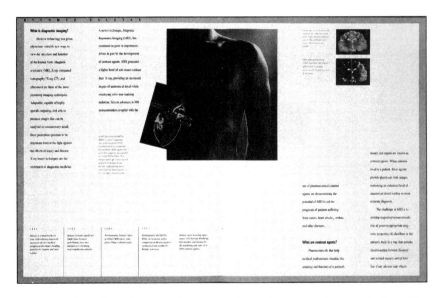

FIGURE 5.17 Notice how the designer used space to enhance the typographic organization of the page.

TYPE SIZE AND WEIGHT

As discussed earlier, the eye tends to be attracted to bigger and bolder objects first. We can easily apply this principle to our typographic hierarchy. Main heads should logically be the most prominent typographic element. This can be achieved most effectively by making the point size of the head larger than the body text, making it bolder than the body text, or both. Subheads should have less importance, so they should be set smaller or lighter in weight. Captions are generally set smaller than body text, but since they are strategically important they are sometimes set off by bold face or italic. The rule of thumb: The more important an element, the bigger or bolder it should be.

USING SPACE TO ORGANIZE INFORMATION

Sometimes using space to separate typographic elements contributes to the visual hierarchy. It's usually a good idea to add space for visual relief above a head that is buried within the text page. Adding extra space under a main head to set it off can make it more effective. Even paragraphs can be separated by space, whether by an indent or an entire line.

USING INITIAL CAPS

An initial cap is a large capital letter at the beginning of a section of text. It's usually used to draw the eye to the beginning of an article or story. This can be an important hierarchical element because it creates a strong focal point (Figure 5.18). Be careful, however, about using too many initial caps. Using them in every paragraph, for instance, would create too many distractions and would actually make the typographic hierarchy less effective.

Often a large initial cap at the beginning of a block of text can add character to the design and create a strong focal point for the page. Creating pleasing initials, however, takes some practice.

FIGURE 5.18 An initial cap can provide a strong focal point on the page.

Initial cap letters can be aligned in different ways. Most common is a drop cap, where the large capital letter is actually "buried" or inset into the first few lines of text. Other options include hanging it out to the side or setting it above the top line of type, but however you choose to align your initial, there are a few rules you should follow. First, since the initial is actually the first letter of the first line of text, it must be placed closely in front of the next letter. Don't leave a big gap between the initial and the first line—there must be a visual connection. This may require that the text follow the contour of the letter (Figure 5.19).

The initial cap can be set to various depths within the text, (up to 16 lines deep) but the baseline of the initial should always align with the baseline of one of the lines of text.

Consider setting the first line after an initial in caps. This creates a smoother visual transition from the large letter to the small ones.

Often a large initial cap at the beginning of a block of text can add character to the design and create a strong focal point for the page. Creating pleasing initials, however, takes some practice.

Often a large initial cap at the beginning of a block of text can add character to the design and create a strong focal point for the page. Creating pleasing initials, however, takes some practice.

FIGURE 5.19 In the intitial cap on the left, the letterform creates a gap between the initial and the first line of text. Notice how much better it looks when the type is realigned to follow the contour of the letter.

When the initial is preceded by a quotation mark, keep the quotation mark small. Usually a size or two larger than the body text is appropriate, and it usually looks better if you hang the quotation mark out in the margin and leave the initial aligned to the left margin (Figure 5.20).

"Often a large initial cap at the beginning of a block of text can add character to the design and create a strong focal point for the page. Creating pleasing initials, however, takes some practice.

FIGURE 5.20 This illustration shows the special alignment required for round letters and quotation marks.

Rounded letters like O and Q need special consideration when they're used as initials. Because they curve in so radically at the top and bottom, they appear to be misaligned and look better if they hang out into margin slightly. Cheating them to the left compensates for this illusion.

CREATING INITIAL CAPS IN QUARKXPRESS

Earlier we talked about the usefulness of initial caps, or initials, as a focal point at the beginning of a block of text. In QuarkXPress you can create several kinds of initials and you can even set them up as paragraph formats. Let's try creating a drop initial cap using the Paragraph Formats dialog box (Figure 5.21). First, open a document and select a paragraph. Next, choose Formats from the Style menu. When you see the Paragraph Formats dialog box, click on the box labeled Drop Caps. The dialog box will expand to include Character Count and Line Count fields. Indicate the number of characters you want to make drop caps in the Character Count field. You can specify any number between 1 and 8, but in this case type in the number 1. Now go to the Line Count field. This is where you decide how many lines deep you want your initial to be, from 2 to 8 lines. Let's make a large initial by entering the maximum, 8. Click OK and your initial cap will be automatically sized and placed into position. If you want to change the size, select the character you want to resize and choose Other from the Size submenu under Style. When the Font Size dialog box is displayed you can enter a percentage of enlargement or reduction in the field. Even simpler, highlight the character and use the Measurements Palette to change the size.

Another way to create an initial cap is to anchor a text box containing the initial to the beginning of a paragraph (Figure 5.22). First, create a text box and type in the character you want to use as an initial. Now select the Item Tool from the tool box and use it to activate the text box. Now choose Cut or Copy from the Edit menu. With the Content Tool activated, place the Text Insertion bar at the point in the text where you want to insert the initial. Choose Paste from the Edit menu. Now the box with the initial cap is placed and anchored in position. Since it's anchored it will "flow" with the text. (By the way, if you want to import a character as a piece of art, you can follow this same procedure using a picture box instead of a text box). You can make alterations to the initial cap by activating the text box and selecting Modify from the Item menu. When the Anchored Text Box Specifications dialog box appears, you can select Baseline to align the initial to the baseline of the associated line of text or you can select Ascent to align the text box to the tallest ascenders of the top line of text in your paragraph. Take a few minutes to try these options and see how they change the style.

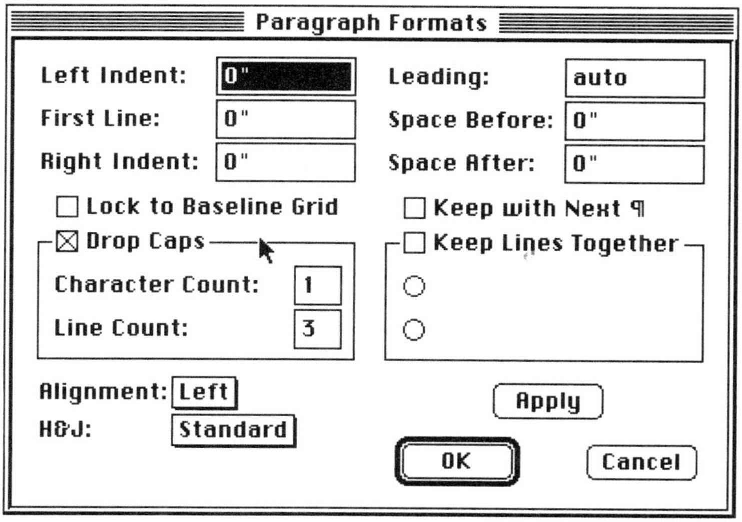

FIGURE 5.21 You can create initial caps in the Paragraph Formats dialog box.

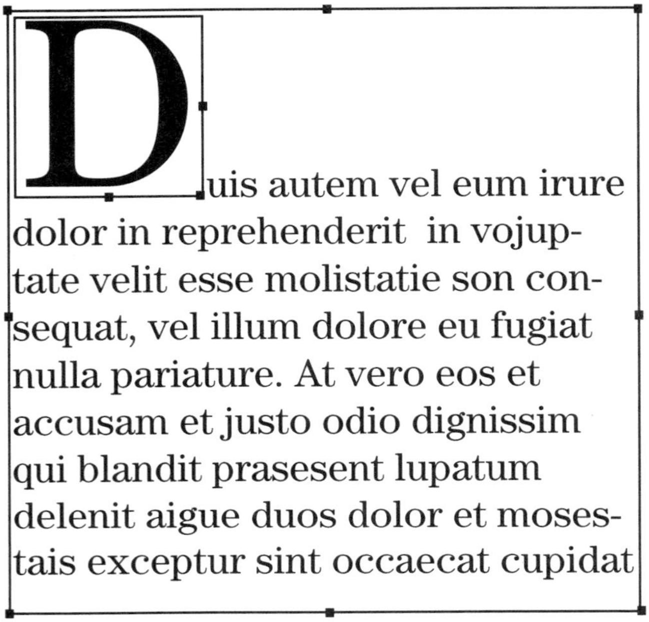

FIGURE 5.22

Use an anchored text box to position an initial cap.

Duis autem vel eum irure dolor in reprehenderit in vojuptate velit esse molistatie son consequat, vel illum dolore eu fugiat nulla pariature. At vero eos et accusam et justo odio dignissim qui blandit prasesent lupatum delenit aigue duos dolor et mosestais exceptur sint occaecat cupidat

ALIGNING MARGINS

The way the margins are formatted can dramatically affect the style of the page as well as its readability. When you're setting text in columns, there are several ways you can format the margins. QuarkXpress offers six margin formatting options, only two of which are practical for long blocks of text. Let's look at these options one by one, from the most practical to the least.

Flush Left/Ragged Right

This is probably the most common and most readable way to set type (Figure 5.23). In this form the lines of type are aligned on the left margin and allowed to break in an apparently random fashion on the right (although typographers generally take great care to balance the ragged right edge).

Justified

Justified text is aligned on both the right and left edges of the column (Figure 5.24). This is traditionally a very popular way to set columns, although in recent years the popularity of this form has given way to flush left/ragged right. Justified

Lorem ipsum dolor sit amet, consectetur adipscing elit, sed diam nomumy eisusmod tempor incidunt ut labore et dolore magna aliquam erat volupat. Ut enim ad minimim veniami quis nostrud exercitation ullamcorpor suscipit laboris nisi ut aliquip ex ea commodo consequat. Duis autem vel eum irure dolor in reprehenderit in vojuptate velit esse molistatie son consequat, vel illum dolore eu fugiat nulla pariature. At vero eos et accusam et justo odio dignissim qui blandit prasesent lupatum delenit aigue duos dolor et mosestais exceptur sint occaecat cupidat non provident, sinil tempor sunt in clpa qui officia desurunt mollit anum id est laborum et dolor fugai.

FIGURE 5.23

This block of text is set flush left/ragged right.

text looks very neat and formal but is slightly less legible than flush left, largely because forcing justification on both ends of the line tends to make wordspacing uneven from line to line. Another advantage to justified text is that it allows you to fit more information in less space. For this reason it is the preferred style for newspapers and magazines.

Force Justified

In justified text, both the right and left ends of the line are aligned to the edge of the text box but the last line of the paragraph is left short. Force justification makes the last line of the paragraph conform to the margins as well.

Centered

Centered text is aligned to a centerline and ragged on both the left and right sides (Figure 5.25). Use this form only for very short blocks of text. It's commonly used for advertisements or invitations.

Flush Right

Flush-right text is aligned on the right side and ragged on the left (Figure 5.26). Type set in this style is very hard to read because the eye has to search for the beginning of each line. This is used only for stylistic reasons and should be limited to very short blocks of text.

Freeform Alignment

Frankly, I hesitate to even mention this form of alignment because there really isn't any alignment (Figure 5.27). This is purely stylistic and for the most part impractical, but I mention it because it's becoming fairly common in contemporary design. This form is the most difficult to read since the lines are placed randomly. To do this effectively requires experience and skill.

Lorem ipsum dolor sit amet, consectetur adipscing elit, sed diam nomumy eisusmod tempor incidunt ut labore et dolore magna aliquam erat volupat. Ut enim ad minimim veniami quis nostrud exercitation ullamcorpor suscipit laboris nisi ut aliquip ex ea commodo consequat. Duis autem vel eum irure dolor in reprehenderit in vojuptate velit esse molistatie son consequat, vel illum dolore eu fugiat nulla pariature. At vero eos et accusam et justo odio dignissim qui blandit prasesent lupatum delenit duos dolor et mosestais exceptur sint occaecat cupidat non provident, sinil tempor sunt in clpa qui officia desurunt mollit anum id est laborum et dolor fugai.

FIGURE 5.24

Justified text is aligned on both the right and left edges of the column.

Lorem ipsum dolor sit amet, consectetur adipscing elit, sed diam nomumy eisusmod tempor incidunt ut labore et dolore magna aliquam erat volupat. Ut enim ad minimim veniami quis nostrud exercition ullamcorpor suscipit laboris nisi ut aliquip ex ea commodo consequat. Duis autem vel eum irure dolor in reprehenderit in vojuptate velit esse molistatie son consequat, vel illum dolore eu fugiat nulla pariature. At vero eos et accusam et justo odio dignissim qui blandit prasesent lupatum delenit duos dolor et mosestais exceptur sint occaecat cupidat non provident, sinil tempor sunt in clpa qui

FIGURE 5.25

Centered text has ragged edges on both sides.

Lorem ipsum dolor sit amet, consectetur adipscing elit, sed diam nomumy eisusmod tempor incidunt ut labore et dolore magna aliquam erat volupat. Ut enimad minimim veniami quis nostrud exercition ullamcorpor suscipit laboris nisi ut aliquip ex ea commodo consequat. Duis autem vel eumirure dolor in reprehenderit in vojuptate velit esse molistatie son consequat, vel illum dolore eu fugiat nulla pariature. At vero eos et accusam et justo odio dignissim qui blandit prasesent lupatum delenit duos dolor et mosetais exceptur sint occaecat cupidat non provident, sinil tempor sunt in clpa qui officia desurunt mollit id est laborum et dolor fugai.

FIGURE 5.26

Long blocks of flush-right text is very difficult to read.

Lorem ipsum dolor sit amet, consectetur

adipscing elit, sed diam nomumy eisusmod

mpor incidunt ut labore et dolore magna

aliquam erat volupat. Ut enimad minimim veniami

quis nostrud exercitation ullamcorpor

suscipit laboris nisi ut aliquip ex ea commodo

consequat. Duis autem vel eumirure dolor

reprehenderit in vojuptate velit esse

molistatie son consequat, vel illum dolore

eu fugiat nulla pariature.

FIGURE 5.27

Freeform alignment is not really alignment at all, but the seemingly random placement of lines of type.

A Few Words About Hyphenation

Hyphenation refers to the way a word breaks at the end of a line. Often the maximum number of characters that can fit on a line is reached somewhere in the middle of a word. When this happens, you have two options: you can break the line at the end of the last full word, or you can break the last word between syllables and add a hyphen. Hyphenation decisions always require editorial judgment. Hyphenated words at the end of a line make a paragraph more difficult to read, but if you choose not to hyphenate words you often end up with an awkward rag in flush-left format, or large gaps between words if the margins are justified. These can also make a paragraph hard to read. It may seem like a no-win situation, but it's really just a matter of finding a point of balance. Here are a few guidelines that might help:

- Always hyphenate on short line measures or narrow columns.

- Space out your line breaks and use as few as possible. Never more than two or three in a row.

- Don't hyphenate capitalized words, which are usually things like names of companies, products, people, or places.

- Don't hyphenate headlines.

It takes a little more work, but if you follow these simple rules the result will be a more readable document.

You can let QuarkXPress do the hyphenating for you by turning on Auto Hyphenation in the H&J dialog box and applying your own H&J values. This saves you the trouble of manually hyphenating your entire document, which would be prohibitively time-consuming. It's still a good idea, however, to visually check the line breaks while you're proofing your text. Even with Auto Hyphenation some awkward line breaks can occur.

HYPHENATING IN QUARKXPRESS

H&J is a typographers' term for Hyphenation and Justification. You'll find the option under the Edit menu. This is a paragraph format that enables you to apply hyphenation and justification rules to single paragraphs, groups of paragraphs, or your entire document. What's more, you can create different formats for different applications. For example, you might establish one set of hyphenation rules for the main text and another for captions. You can also append hyphenation specifications from another QuarkXPress document.

To create a new set of QuarkXPress H&J specifications, open your document and choose H&Js from the Edit menu. (You can create a new set of H&J specifications without opening your document first, but this will change the default settings and the new ones will be applied automatically to any document you open in the future.) Once the H&Js dialog box appears, you have a couple of options. (See Figure 5.28.) You can either create a new H&J specification, or you can modify the Standard. To create a new specification, click New. To modify existing specifications for the open document, click Edit. In either case, the Edit Hyphenation & Justification dialog box will appear.

Once you've entered a name for your new specification in the Name field, you can fill in the other fields. Notice the box labeled Auto Hyphenation. Auto Hyphenation is a feature that uses an algorithm built into QuarkXPress to determine where words should be hyphenated. When Auto Hyphenation is turned on it will automatically hyphenate words and determine the rag at the edge of your column. To turn on this feature, click on the Auto Hyphenation check box. Within the Auto Hyphenation box are three fields. The first is labeled Smallest Word. Type the number of characters of the smallest word to be hyphenated into that field. In the second field, Minimum Before, enter the number of the fewest characters allowable to appear before a hyphen. In the third field, Minimum After, enter the fewest number of characters allowable to appear after a hyphen. When everything is filled in, click OK. You'll see the H&J dialog box again. To activate your new specifications, click Save.

Suppose you want to apply H&J specifications that were created for another QuarkXPress document. When the H&J dialog box appears, click Append instead of New or Edit. The Append H&J dialog box will appear. Use the controls to find the document whose H&J specifications you want to append. When you've selected the document, click OK. The H&J specifications from that document will be added to your current document when you click Save in the H&J dialog box.

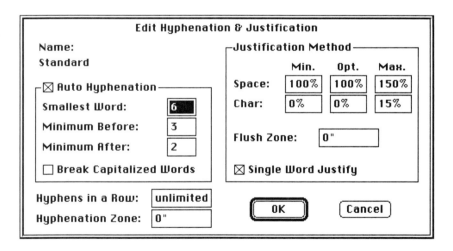

FIGURE 5.28 Use the Edit Hyphenation & Justification dialog box to create or edit hyphenation and justification values in your document.

A word of caution: be sure to proof your document carefully. Because QuarkXPress uses an algorithm rather than a dictionary to determine where words should be broken, it occasionally hyphenates words in strange places. It would be wise to look your document over carefully.

What if you're changing the rag and want to insert a hyphen manually? You can insert a hyphen by typing one in, but be careful. The H&J specifications don't apply to manually inserted hyphens. If for any reason the hyphenated word moves, the hyphen will move with it, just like any other character. You might find hyphens buried in the middle of words throughout your document—another strong case for careful proofreading. But you can get around this by inserting a discretionary hyphen. This is a hyphen that will disappear if the text moves and it is no longer needed. You can insert a discretionary hyphen by holding down the Command key while typing your hyphen.

A word of caution to users of QuarkXPress version 3.1: If you have upgraded your software from version 3.0 to 3.1 or later, be aware that the default H&Js have been changed. When you open the Hyphenation Method pop-up menu in 3.1, you have a choice between Standard and Enhanced. Standard is the same default used in 3.0. Enhanced is 3.1's new and improved default version. If you don't specifically choose Standard, any documents that were created using Standard Auto Hyphenation in version 3.0 will be converted to Enhanced, and the text will be reflowed. This could mess up your document, but you can easily fix it by changing the specification back to Standard in Typographic Preferences.

GETTING A GOOD RAG

Rag is an abbreviated term for the ragged edge of an unjustified column. It's not a good idea to let the lines break randomly. Your objective is to get a ragged edge that makes an even and balanced pattern along the edge of the text column. When you allow the computer to rag your column automatically, you'll occasionally end up with some strange negative shapes created by the edge formed by the line endings (Figure 5.29). These can be distracting for the reader and should be re-ragged manually to create a more pleasing pattern.

CONSIDER THE BACKGROUND

Type is most legible when it's set in very black letters on a white background. Any deviation from this risks a loss of legibility. Use caution when setting type against backgrounds that have any kind of visual tone or texture. Sometimes setting black type against a colored background can add dramatic impact to a design, but be sure that the color is light enough to provide contrast for the type. The narrower

Lorem ipsum dolor sit amet, consectetur adipscing elit, sed diam nomumy eisusmod tempor incidunt ut labore et dolore magna aliquam erat volupat. Ut enimad minimim veniam quis nostrud exercition ullamcorpor suscipit laboris nisi ut aliquip ex ea commodo consequat. Duis autem vel eumirure dolor in reprehenderit in vojuptate velit esse molistatie son consequat, vel illum dolore eu fugiat nulla pariature.

FIGURE 5.29

This is not a good rag. See how the line endings form an awkward shape?

Lorem ipsum dolor sit amet, consectetur adipscing elit, sed diam nomumy eisusmod tempor incidunt ut labore et dolore magna aliquam erat volupat. Ut enimad minimim veniam quis nostrud exercition ullamcorpor suscipit laboris nisi ut aliquip ex ea commodo consequat. Duis autem vel eumirure dolor in reprehenderit in vojuptate velit esse molistatie son consequat, vel illum dolore eu fugiat nulla pariature.

This is a better rag.

the contrast range, the less legible the type. Similarly, be careful about using white type on a colored or black background. White type on any color background will have less contrast than white type on a black background, and any of these unusual color combinations should be used sparingly and only for short blocks of type. Avoid at all costs putting type against a texture (Figure 5.30). Type is recognized because the eye is able to read the shapes of the letters. A texture applied to the background can camouflage the letter shapes and make them difficult to read. There may be instances when you'll want to print type over a photo or reverse type to white in a dark area of a photo. This can be a very effective graphic treatment, but always be sensitive to the values in the photo. Contrast can vary greatly from one part of a photo to another. Type placed over a photo can read well in one part but be nearly invisible in another.

FIGURE 5.30 Use caution when applying type over a toned or textured background. In some cases it can adversely affect readability.

MIXING TYPEFACES

Using two or more typefaces in a layout can add interest and can visually separate different kinds of information. Choosing the right stylistic combinations, however, takes skill. It's a little like mixing and matching clothes—some people have a knack for coordinating various colors and textures. They can grab this and that out of their closets, put them on, and look stylish. Other people try the same thing and look like they got dressed in the dark. Usually this ability requires both an intuitive sense of style and a good deal of experience. The same holds true when it comes to mixing typefaces. I usually recommend that beginners try to be as consistent as possible. Try to add variety by using different styles of the same face, such as bold and italic. Then try adding a second face, but use it sparingly and consistently. For instance, use a serif face for body text and a bold sans serif for heads and captions.

MODIFYING LETTERFORMS

The computer has given us the ability to alter letterforms, and as a result we see all kinds of crazy things in modern design. We see letters that are stretched, squashed, skewed, and spun. Some programs even allow you to make your own letterforms or change existing ones. For all the creativity these programs have fostered, the result has been, for the most part, a lot of very strange and impractical type treatments.

Type design is both an art and a science. Type designers spend years studying their craft and painstakingly drawing the letterforms of an alphabet so that all letter combinations work together harmoniously and gracefully. Effective typographic design requires great skill, and even the alteration of letterforms should be exercised with caution. In the hands of a skilled designer with a thorough understanding of type, however, modified letterforms can be a very effective form of communication (Figure 5.31). Type can be an art form, particularly in the design of logotypes where letters are altered to create a unique treatment of a word or name.

Design: Mark Galarneau

FIGURE 5.31 In the hands of a skilled designer, letterforms can be altered to create an artistic statement that enhances communication.

In QuarkXPress, letterforms can be altered in a couple of ways. Horizontal scaling lets you expand or contract letterforms horizontally; that is, to squash them to be narrower or pull them out to be wider (Figure 5.32). The problem is that altering letters this way distorts them, and the more you stretch them the more distorted they become. Since this can adversely affect legibility, I suggest staying within a range of 80 to 120%. This will let you create interesting effects without drastically changing the proportion and balance of the letters.

FIGURE 5.32

In QuarkXPress you can horizontally condense or expand letters using the Horizontal Scaling option in the Style menu. The letter on the left is condensed to 80 percent, while the one on the right is expanded to 120 percent.

QuarkXPress also lets you rotate text to any angle so you can run it vertically, at an oblique angle, or even upside down. While this affords some interesting layout options, remember that people are used to reading horizontally from left to right, so deviating from the norm will, to some degree, sacrifice readability.

WIDOWS AND ORPHANS

Typographers are always looking out for widows and orphans. This might sound like charity work, but it actually refers to the beginnings and endings of columns of type. A *widow* is the last line of a paragraph that happens to fall at the top of a column. These are often very short and look awkward. An *orphan* is the first line of a paragraph that happens to fall at the last line of the column. It's not uncommon for these to happen numerous times in a document, particularly if it's large. Widows and orphans can sometimes be fixed typographically by re-ragging the margin to lose or gain a line, but often they need to be resolved by editing the text.

WIDOW AND ORPHAN CONTROL IN QUARKXPRESS

QuarkXPress's Keep Lines Together controls in the Paragraph Formats dialog box automatically eliminates widows and orphans (Figure 5.33). This function is a paragraph format that forces the lines of a paragraph to stay together. You can specify that if an entire paragraph won't fit at the bottom of a column, the entire paragraph will move to the top of the next column. You can also specify how many lines you want to move to the top of the next column, and how many you want to stay at the bottom of a column.

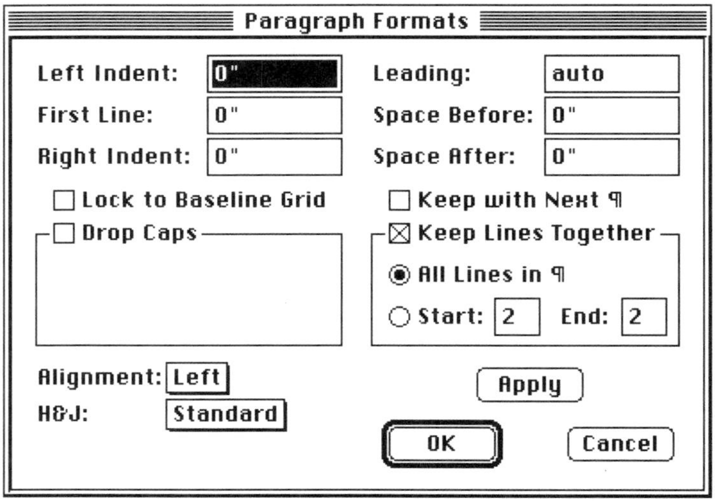

```
╔═══════════════ Paragraph Formats ═══════════════╗
║                                                  ║
║   Left Indent:  [0"        ]   Leading:   [auto] ║
║   First Line:   [0"        ]   Space Before: [0"]║
║   Right Indent: [0"        ]   Space After:  [0"]║
║   □ Lock to Baseline Grid    □ Keep with Next ¶  ║
║   ┌─□ Drop Caps──────────┐  ┌⊠ Keep Lines Together─┐║
║   │                      │  │ ● All Lines in ¶      │║
║   │                      │  │ ○ Start: [2]  End: [2]│║
║   └──────────────────────┘  └───────────────────────┘║
║   Alignment:[Left]              [ Apply ]         ║
║   H&J:    [Standard]                              ║
║                       [  OK  ]   [ Cancel ]       ║
╚══════════════════════════════════════════════════╝
```

FIGURE 5.33 Use the Paragraph Formats dialog box to control widows and orphans.

To specify how lines are to be kept together, choose Formats from the Style menu. When the Paragraph Formats dialog box appears, click the check box next to Keep Lines Together. Notice that there are two radio buttons. One says All Lines in ¶; the other says Start and End. Clicking the All Lines in ¶ button will force entire paragraphs or strings of paragraphs to stay together as a unit. If you click on the button by Start you can specify in the fields the number of lines to be left at the beginning or end of a paragraph.

Above the Keep Lines Together check box is another box, labeled Keep with Next ¶. This is used primarily to ensure that heads run over the paragraphs that follow them. If you select a head and paragraph, then check Keep with Next ¶, you'll prevent the head from appearing as the last line in a paragraph.

You can also use these controls on subheads as long as they are at least two lines deep.

USING QUARKXPRESS AS A WORD PROCESSOR

QuarkXPress allows you to enter text just as you would in any word processing program. If you don't already have a text box open, create one using the Text Box

Tool. With the text box activated, switch to the Content Tool. You should see the text cursor blinking in the upper-left corner of the text box. You can now begin typing text into the box just as if your computer was a typewriter. If you are both writing and designing your publication, you can save a few steps by typing your text directly into the page layout rather than typing it in a word processing program and importing it into your document. Once text is entered into your document you can use all of the standard word processing and editing functions such as cut, copy, and paste.

IMPORTING TEXT

Often designers get their text from writers or editors who have used another word processing program to create it. Obviously, retyping the text into your layout is not an attractive option and it usually isn't necessary. QuarkXPress includes import/export filters for most of the commonly used word processing software, allowing you to grab text from another document and pull it back into QuarkXPress. To import text, first activate the text box where you want the text to be placed. With the Content tool selected, pull down the File menu and select Get Text. This will bring up the Get Text dialog box. (See Figure 5.34.)

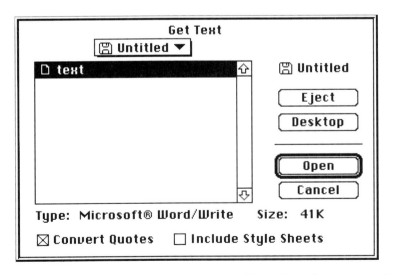

FIGURE 5.34 Use the Get Text dialog box to import text created in another software program into a QuarkXPress document.

Use the controls in the dialog box to find the text file you want to import. Before you click Open, notice the check boxes at the bottom of the dialog box. One says Convert Quotes, and the other says Include Style Sheets. If the Convert Quotes box is checked it will automatically convert double hyphens to em dashes and foot and inch marks to typesetter's apostrophes and quotation marks. You'll generally want to check this box. Checking the Include Style Sheets box will do two things. First, if you're importing a file created in Microsoft Word, it will append all of the style sheets with which the text was formatted. (If the box isn't checked, it will import the file as raw text. Unless you're sure you want to keep the style sheets in place, leave the box unchecked—you can always format the text once you import it into QuarkXPress.) Second, checking the Include Style Sheets box will retain the style tag codes embedded in an ASCII file. *ASCII* (pronounced ASKEE) is an industry-standard file exchange format. Files saved in this format can be read by almost any software program. Again, it's generally easier to leave the styles out so you can customize the formatting to fit your design.

NOTE *QuarkXPress provides a number of import/export filters with the program software. Storing them all in the same folder with QuarkXPress uses a lot of memory, even if they are not all being used. You might consider storing them in a separate folder within the QuarkXPress folder when they're not being used. But you must have the appropriate filter in the QuarkXPress folder when you start the program.*

Click Open, and the file will appear in your text box like magic. If there is more text than will fit in your text box, one of two things will happen. If you have Auto Page Insertion turned on, pages with text boxes will be added to your layout until all the new text is accommodated. If Auto Page Insertion is not turned on, the text will fill the text box and a little box will appear in the lower-right corner indicating that there is more text that wouldn't fit in the box. You will now need to create more text boxes and link them using the Linking Tool.

EXPORTING TEXT

QuarkXPress's import/export filters let you export text in a form that can be read by other word processing programs. Suppose you want to save a block of text created in QuarkXPress in a Microsoft Word format. First, be sure that the Microsoft Word filter is in your QuarkXPress folder when you start the program. Next, with the Content Tool, select the text you want to export by highlighting it with your cursor. Choose Save Text from the File menu to bring up the Save Text dialog box. (See Figure 5.35.)

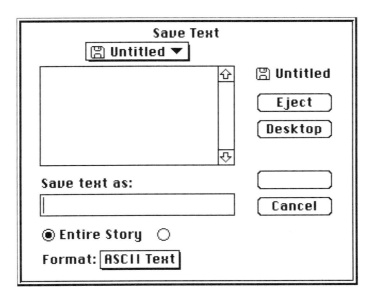

FIGURE 5.35 Use the Save Text dialog box to export text in a format that can be read by other word processing software.

At the bottom of the box is a pop-up menu labeled Format. This menu lists all of the active filters. Select the Microsoft Word format. Now type a name for the file in the Save Text As field. Use the controls in the dialog box to select the folder in which you want to save the file, and click Save. The copied and formatted file will automatically be placed in the selected folder.

This is a very handy feature if you need to exchange files with writers or editors who don't have QuarkXPress.

XPRESS TAGS

When saving text in ASCII format, you can retain formatting information such as character attributes, indents, spacing, and rules by using XPress Tags. XPress

Tags is a QuarkXPress XTension included with your software. It embeds codes in your file that contain formatting information. If you select XPress Tags from the Format pop-up menu in the Save Text dialog box, your text file will be saved as an ASCII file with XPress Tags in place. When the file is opened by a software program that supports XPress Tags, the codes will be translated and the text will appear just as you formatted it in QuarkXPress. A number of popular software programs support XPress Tags. These include MacWrite, Microsoft Word, Microsoft Works, WordPerfect, and WriteNow.

EDITING TEXT

Editing text is fast and easy in QuarkXPress. Once your text is in place you can add, delete, or rearrange portions of it in seconds. Type a few lines of text into your text box. You can add text anywhere within the body of text by moving the cursor and typing. Using the Content Tool, move the cursor over your text box. Notice how the cursor changes to look like the letter I once it's over the text box. It's called the I-beam pointer. Place the I-beam pointer where you want to add text and click. The I-beam pointer changes to a flashing cursor called the Text Insertion Bar. Now simply type in the new text.

What if you want to take text out? That's even easier. Place the I-beam pointer at the beginning of the text you want to delete. Click and while holding the mouse button down, drag the cursor across the text to highlight it. When you come to the end of the section to be deleted, lift up on the mouse button and punch the delete key. Presto! Your text is gone. (By the way, if you ever delete something you didn't mean to delete, before you do anything else, choose Undo Typing from the Edit menu. The deleted text will reappear.)

Rearranging blocks of text is accomplished in one of two ways. First, you can use the Cut and Paste commands in the Edit menu. Simply highlight the text you want to move and choose Cut. The highlighted text will disappear. Place the Text Insertion Bar where you want to insert the text and click. Choose Paste and the text will reappear in its new location. The second method is even easier. It's called drag and drop editing. Highlight the text you want to move then, hold the mouse button down and drag the cursor to the new location and release the mouse button. The text will be moved to the new location in one simple step.

USING THE MEASUREMENTS PALETTE

There are several ways to initiate commands in QuarkXPress. You can use pull-down menus, keyboard commands, or palettes. We'll start by using the Measurements Palette to format text because it's the easiest.

If your Measurements Palette isn't already on your desktop, go to the View menu and select Show Measurements. (See Figure 5.36.) When a text box is active, the Measurements Palette places most of the typographic controls at your fingertips. You have control over the position and angle of your text box, type font and style, margin alignment, leading, and tracking, and it's as easy as pointing and clicking. The Measurements Palette contains several kinds of controls, including fields, pop-up menus, and buttons. To change the values in a field, drag the cursor over the value to highlight it and type in a new value. To make a change using a button, simply click on it. The pop-up menus will display a number of options, simply click on the one you want. Using the Measurements Palette not only saves steps, it also lets you see all of your text formatting at a glance.

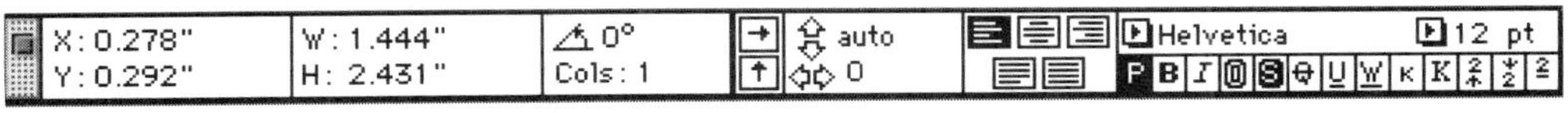

FIGURE 5.36 The Measurements Palette lets you easily specify typographic formats.

CHANGING TYPEFACES

When you enter or import text into a text box, QuarkXPress automatically imposes the default typeface. To change to a different font, select the section of text to be changed by highlighting it, then go to the Measurements Palette. Near the upper-right corner the name of the current font will be displayed. Next to the name is a button with an arrow in it. Pressing this button will display the pop-up menu listing all the available fonts. Hold your mouse button down and run down the list until the desired type font is highlighted, then let go of the mouse button. Your type will be displayed in the new style.

That's pretty simple, but believe it or not, there's an even easier way to do it. If you know which font you want, highlight the name of the existing font in the Measurements Palette and type in the first few letters of the new font. QuarkXPress will search the font library to find one that begins with those letters. Be careful, though, often several typefaces can begin with the same letters and you

119

must know the precise name of the font. Then tap the Return key or click on your page to activate the change.

CHANGING POINT SIZE

You can change point size the same way. Highlight the text to be changed, then go to the Measurements Palette. In the upper-right corner the current type size is displayed. You can either click on the button and make the change in the pop-up menu, or simply type over the existing value. One of the convenient features inherent in computer typography is that you have more size options for type. In traditional typesetting you are often limited to specific point sizes (typically 6, 7, 8, 9, 10, 12, 14, 16, 18, 24, 36, 48, 60, and 72 points). While modern typography has expanded that range, the computer has opened even more options. You can specify virtually any point size you want, between 2 and 720 points. You could specify 3.75 point or 632.97 point type. This kind of versatility is helpful, especially when you're trying to make type fit precisely into a limited space.

CHANGING TYPE STYLE

In the bottom-right corner of the Measurements Palette you'll see a long row of boxes or buttons with letters and numbers in them. Each of these boxes corresponds to a type style command under the Style menu. You can select a type style by clicking on one of the boxes.

Let's take a look at these boxes one by one, moving from left to right. The box with the P represents Plain text. The box with the B stands for Bold. The I is for Italic. The O is for Outline text. The S is for Shadow text. The Q with the line through it represents Strike Thru text. The U with the line under it is Underlined text. The W with the line under it lets you underscore words. The box with a small capital K in it specifies Small Caps. The box with the large capital K sets All Caps. The next box, which contains a small 2 with upward pointing arrow under it, specifies Superscript. The box next to it is similar, but the arrow is above the 2 and points down—this box specifies Subscript. Finally, the last box has a small 2 in it as well, but there's a line under it. This is for Superior type.

Select an item of text in your text box and experiment with the type style boxes. Click on the various boxes and see how they change your text.

CHANGING TEXT ALIGNMENT

You can also use the Measurements Palette to change the way your text columns are aligned. As discussed earlier, alignment choices include flush left, justified, flush right, centered, and freeform. The Measurements Palette includes controls for all but the freeform style, which is always based on visual judgment.

To change the alignment of your text, place the cursor anywhere within the paragraph or, for multiple paragraphs, highlight the section of text you want to change. Often you'll want to apply an overall format change. You can select all of your text by activating the text box and choosing Select All from the Edit menu. This will select all of the text in the activated text box and all others linked to it. Once the text is selected, go to the Measurements Palette. About two-thirds of the way to the right you'll see a box with four small rectangles containing rows of horizontal lines. These lines represent lines of text within a text page. Notice how the lines are configured. In one rectangle the lines are positioned flush left, in the second they're centered, in the third they're flush right, and in the final box they're justified. Simply click on the box that represents the style you want and your text will be automatically realigned.

CHANGING THE LEADING

In the middle and at the top of the Measurements Palette you'll see a number next to two arrows, one arrow pointing up and the other pointing down. This is the control for leading lines of type. Again, there are two ways to adjust this value. You can type a new value over the old one, but the easiest way is to click on the arrows (which are really buttons). Clicking on the upward arrow increases the line leading in 1-point increments. Clicking on the downward arrow decreases the leading in 1-point increments. If you want to make more minute adjustments to your leading, hold down the Option key while clicking the arrows—this increases or decreases the leading in .1-point increments.

There are actually three types of leading used in QuarkXPress: absolute leading, incremental leading, and auto leading. *Absolute leading* refers to what you just did with the Measurements Palette. You specified a standard distance between lines of type, to be applied consistently regardless of size. For example, if you specify 10-point leading, every line will measure 10 points from baseline to baseline. *Incremental leading*, on the other hand, is designed to add an incremental space to the measure of the largest character on each line. In other words, if you specify +2 points of incremental leading, two extra points will be added to the measure of the largest character in the line. *Auto leading* is based on the value placed in the Auto Leading field in the Typographic Preferences dialog box in the Edit menu. It works in much the same way as incremental leading, but you can choose between adding an incremental space or a percentage. For instance, you can specify that no matter what size the type, QuarkXPress should automatically add 25% extra space between the lines.

CHANGING THE NUMBER OF COLUMNS

You can set up or change columns within a text box by using the columns control in the Measurements Palette. The default is 1 column, but you can change the number by replacing the existing value with a new one. You can also use the Modify command to change the values in the Box Specifications dialog box.

SETTING UP TABS

Tabs make setting columnar material easy and consistent. This is a very convenient feature for things like tables and charts or the financial information in an annual report. In QuarkXPress there are six kinds of tab stops: Left, Right, Center, Comma, Align On (Character), and Decimal. You can set tabs for an entire document or a single paragraph. Since tabs are a paragraph format, you can't set tabs for a single line.

First, select the paragraph or paragraphs for which you want to set up tabs. Next, choose Tabs from the Style menu to display the Paragraph Tabs dialog box. When the dialog box appears you'll also see a ruler above the active text box in your document. Take a look at the dialog box. At the top there's a menu box called Alignment with six choices: Left, Center, Right, Decimal, Comma, and Align On. You choose the kind of tab stop you want by highlighting one of the menu choices. Choosing Left will create a tab on which the characters will align themselves on the left. Choosing Center will create a tab that centers the column, and Right will align the column on the right. Decimal or Comma will align numbers at their decimal points or commas, respectively. Align On will align each line to a selected character.

You can set tabs two different ways. First, you can enter a value in the Position field. For instance, if you want to set up a tab one inch from the left margin of your column, enter 1" in the Position field. But there's an easier way to do it. Take another look at the ruler sitting on top of your text box. You can click anywhere on this ruler, and an arrow will be placed where you clicked. These arrows represent the type and position of the tab. You can reposition these tab stops by clicking on the little arrow and dragging it right or left to a new position.

There's one more field in the dialog box that I haven't mentioned. It's called Fill Character. QuarkXPress allows you to specify a typographic character to fill the space between tab stops by typing it into the field. This will literally fill the space between the tab columns with a series of characters. Any character can be inserted, but this feature is most commonly used to create a dot leader by inserting a period into the Fill Character field. Dot leaders are often used in tables of contents or price lists. You can enter up to two characters in the field. This is handy if you want to add a little more space between the periods. You can accomplish this by simply typing a space after the period in the Fill Character field.

Once you've specified your tab values you can click the Apply button to see what they look like in your layout or click OK to apply them and quit the dialog box.

POSITIONING BASELINES

When working on a page layout with multiple columns, it's important that the baselines are aligned from column to column across the page. Remember that a baseline is the imaginary line upon which a line of text sits. This can be done manually, of course, by shifting the text boxes up and down until everything lines up, but QuarkXPress lets the computer to do this precisely. Here's how it works: In the Typographic Preferences dialog box under the Edit menu, you can set up an underlying horizontal grid to which the baselines will align automatically. (See Figure 5.37.) If you open the dialog box you'll notice a section called Baseline Grid. You can specify how far down from the top of the page you want to place the first baseline by typing a value in the Start box. This value can be any number between 0 and 13.889 inches. Type a value in the Increment field to specify the distance between grid lines. Choose Show Baseline Grid from the View menu to display the baseline.

While using the baseline grid is a great way to ensure that your text will align properly, there are some little idiosyncrasies that you might find annoying. First, the baseline grid is applied to the entire document. This is all well and good, except that you have to plan all of your text formatting and spacing around it. If you create a grid with 12-point increments, and lock your baselines to it, all of your spacing must be in multiples of 12 points. For instance, you couldn't have a 15-point space between the end of a line and a footnote—since everything snaps to the next available grid line, your 15.point space would automatically become 24 points. Accordingly, you could specify leading only in 12-point increments, which could be very difficult to work around in some circumstances. Remember that you can always pull a grid line down from your ruler and use the Snap to Guides command to align the top of your text box to that.

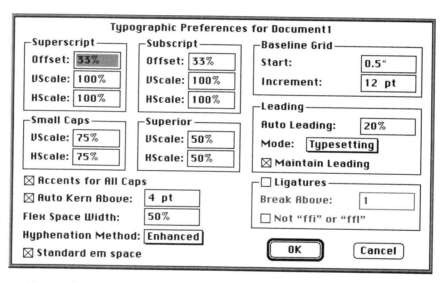

FIGURE 5.37 You can align baselines automatically to a grid by placing values in the Baseline Grid area of the Typographic Preferences dialog box.

You can also automatically align baselines of text within the text box itself. To do this, determine where the baseline of the first text line should be placed in relation to the top of the text box. With your text box active, select Modify from the Item menu. This will bring up the Text Box Specifications dialog box. (See Figure 5.38.) In the field labeled Offset, type a value to specify the distance from the top of the box to the first baseline. For example, if you type .5 in the field, the first baseline will be positioned one half inch below the top edge of the text box.

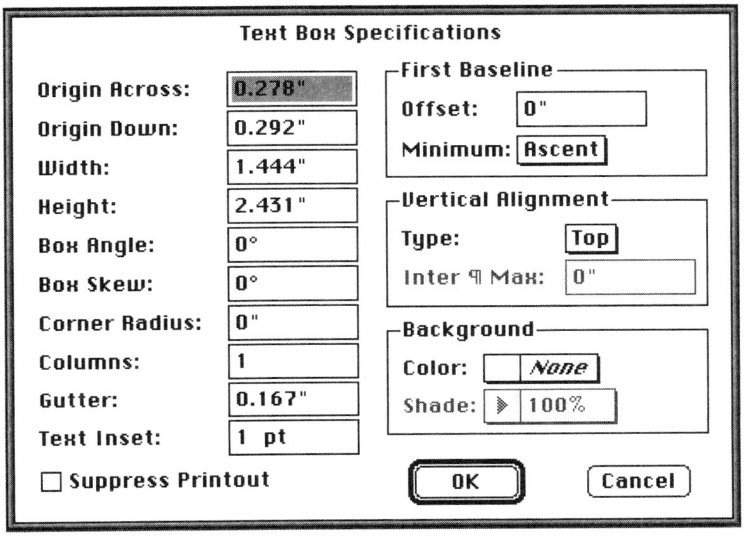

Text Box Specifications

Origin Across: `0.278"`
Origin Down: `0.292"`
Width: `1.444"`
Height: `2.431"`
Box Angle: `0°`
Box Skew: `0°`
Corner Radius: `0"`
Columns: `1`
Gutter: `0.167"`
Text Inset: `1 pt`
☐ Suppress Printout

First Baseline
Offset: `0"`
Minimum: `Ascent`

Vertical Alignment
Type: `Top`
Inter ¶ Max: `0"`

Background
Color: `None`
Shade: `100%`

`OK`   `Cancel`

FIGURE 5.38 To standardize the position of the first baseline in a text box, use the First Baseline area of the Text Box Specifications dialog box.

Just below the Offset field you'll see a pop-up menu called Minimum. This menu lets you set the minimum amount of space between the inside edge of the top of the text box and the first baseline. Don't type in a value here, instead you have three choices: You can choose Cap Height, which is the height of the letter O in the largest font on the first line of text; Cap + Accent, which is the same thing but with a little more space added to make room for an accent mark; or Ascent, which is the height of the ascender of the largest character on the first line. When QuarkXPress positions the first line of text, it chooses between the Offset distance and the Minimum setting, selecting whichever is larger.

SHIFTING BASELINES MANUALLY

Characters can be shifted up or down by using the Baseline Shift command in the Style menu. This doesn't actually shift the baseline, but rather the character above or below the baseline. With the Content Tool selected, highlight the character you want to shift. Select Baseline Shift from the Style menu. When you see the Baseline Shift dialog box, type a value into the field. (A positive value shifts the character up and a negative value shifts it down.) You can enter a value up to three times the point size; for example, you could shift a 10-point character as high as 30 points or as low as -30 points. This feature comes in handy when you want to adjust the alignment of such things as punctuation marks, asterisks, or trademark symbols. Be aware, though, that changing the point size of a character after Baseline Shift has been applied will proportionately alter the amount of the shift. For example, a 12-point character shifted 3 points above the baseline would shift to 6 points above the baseline if it were changed to 24 points.

CHARACTER AND WORD SPACING

Justified text is too often characterized by strange word and letterspacing within the lines. This happens because there are never the same number of characters in all lines. Since the lines are stretched or compressed to align evenly at both ends, each line has an unequal amount of negative space. This space must be distributed evenly throughout the line, or the reader's eye will tend to stumble over the irregular gaps. With QuarkXPress you can specify how this space is distributed.

To set rules for space distribution within justified columns, bring up the H&Js dialog box by choosing H&Js from the Edit menu. Select an H&J specification and click Edit. The Edit Hyphenation & Justification box will be displayed. On the right side of the box you'll see an area called Justification Method. In the Word Spacing area, type a value in the Minimum field. This specifies the minimum amount of space that can be placed between words of a justified paragraph. Now type a value in the Optimum field to specify the ideal amount of space, and a value in the Maximum field to specify the maximum space you will allow. You can make the same specifications for letterspacing in the Character Spacing area below.

At the very bottom is a field labeled Flush Zone. This is the area at the end of a line into which the last word must fall in order to be justified. Therefore, if you enter .5" in the Flush Zone field, any word falling into the last half inch of the line will be justified.

By default, when you type in quotation marks you get those funny-looking inch marks. By checking the Smart Quotes check box in the Application Preferences dialog box, QuarkXPress will automatically substitute real typographer's quotation marks.

NOTE

LIGATURES

A *ligature* is a typographic device where two letters are combined into one. (See Figure 5.39.) Most Macintosh fonts contain ligatures in their alphabets for characters such as "f" followed by "i" or "l". Since some people like to use ligatures and others don't, QuarkXPress gives you an option. You can specify how ligatures are to be used in Typographic Preferences under Preferences in the Edit menu. In the dialog box you'll see a Ligatures pop-up menu in the lower left. The Ligatures menu gives you three choices: Select Off if you don't want to use ligatures at all. Selecting On will incorporate all ligatures in the font. On (not ffi or ffl) will allow for ligatures except where preceded by another "f" (as in office).

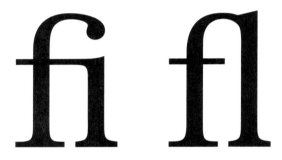

FIGURE 5.39

These are ligatures commonly incorporated into Macintosh fonts.

SCALING TYPE

You can expand or condense letters in QuarkXPress using the Horizontal Scale command in the Style menu. This offers a couple of advantages. First, having the ability to condense type slightly can be useful if you need to fit more words into a document. Since condensed letters take up less room you can increase your document's word count by condensing the letters. The other advantage is purely stylistic. Sometimes condensing or expanding the letterforms can create some interesting effects. But be careful. It's easy to overdo it. Horizontal Scaling doesn't scale the letters uniformly but rather, it distorts them. (See Figure 5.40.) Extremes in scaling will have a bizarre effect. A good rule of thumb is to confine your scaling range between 80% and 120%.

FIGURE 5.40

The letters at the top are condensed to 25% using Horizontal Scale in the Style menu. The letters in the middle are expanded to 400%. The letters at the bottom are normal. Notice how extremes in scaling can distort the letterforms.

To scale letters, select the type in your document that you want to modify. Choose Horizontal Scale from the Style menu. (See Figure 5.41.) When you see the dialog box type a value between 25% and 400%, remembering that 100% is normal. A smaller percentage will condense the letters and a larger percentage will expand them.

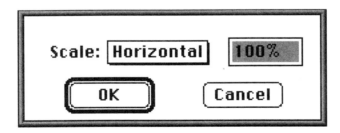

FIGURE 5.41 Use the Horizontal Scale dialog box to condense or expand letterforms.

NOTE *Here's a shortcut that allows you to scale text interactively but it only works if you want to scale all of the text within a text box. It works great for ad headlines. Simply hold down the Command key and drag the handles on the text box. In addition to resizing the box, the characters are scaled proportionally.*

FONT CREATOR

If you use Adobe's Multiple Master fonts you can use Font Creator from within QuarkXPress to create custom stylistic variations of your fonts. To use Font Creator you must have ATM (Adobe Type Manager) version 3.0 or later and you must have the Multiple Masters INIT installed in your system. For more information on how to create Multiple Master font instances refer to the documentation that came with your Multiple Master fonts.

ANCHORING RULES AND BOXES TO TEXT

While creating an initial cap in the section above, you "anchored" a text box to a paragraph. QuarkXPress gives you the option of anchoring text boxes, picture boxes and rules within a text document. Why would you want to go to the trouble? Let's say that your design calls for a rule at the top of every subhead. You could use the line tool to draw them in and space them manually, but it would take a lot of time and the lines wouldn't move with the text if it reflows. Fortunately, there's a better way. In QuarkXPress you can actually anchor the rule to a paragraph so that it moves with the text.

To anchor a rule to text, select a paragraph or range of paragraphs and choose Rules from the Style menu to display the Paragraph Rules dialog box. (See Figure 5.42.) To place a rule at the top of the selected paragraph, check the box labeled Rule Above. To place the rule under the paragraph, check Rule Below. Once you've checked the appropriate box you'll need to specify how long the rule should be and exactly where it should be positioned. In the Length pop-up menu you have two choices. Selecting Text will set the length of the rule based on the length of the first or last line of the paragraph (depending on whether the rule is above or below the paragraph). Choosing Indent will extend the rule from the left indent of the paragraph to the right indent. If you don't like the result of either of these options, you can lengthen or shorten the rule. To move the right endpoint of the rule out further to the right, enter a value in the From Right field. For example, if you'd like to see the rule extend one quarter of an inch on the right end enter .25" in the field. Adjust the left endpoint the same way by using the From Left field. In the Offset field you can specify how much space you want to leave between the baseline of the closest line and the rule. Entering .25" in this field would put one quarter of an inch between the baseline and the rule. You can also indicate this space as a percentage of the total space between the paragraphs.

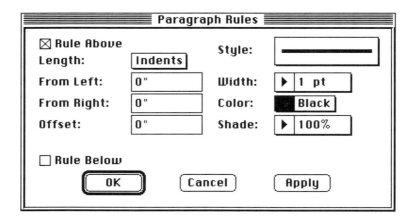

FIGURE 5.42 Rules can be anchored to a paragraph of text by using the Paragraph Rules dialog box.

NOTE

Even though the Paragraph Rules dialog box allows you to apply a shade to a rule, it's important to note that shades are created by breaking the color up into tiny dots. Very narrow rules can become broken and indistinct when shaded. Always leave narrow rules at 100% and reserve shading for rules at least 6 points wide.

Now that you have your rule positioned correctly you need to decide what style of rule you want. On the right hand side of the dialog box you'll see menus that allow you to choose not only the style of the rule but the width, color and shade as well.

RUNNING TYPE AROUND AN OBJECT

Type that conforms to the shape of an object is called a *runaround*. This is a typographic technique that's an effective way to visually integrate type and image as well as lend informality to the page. (See Figure 5.43.)

Actually, text will automatically run around an object. If you drag a picture box, for instance, into a column of text the type will wrap itself around the object. The trouble is, initially it may not look all that great. But you can exercise control over how that text conforms to the object by using the Runaround Specifications dialog box. First, activate the object by clicking on it. Now choose Runaround from the Item menu. When the Runaround Specifications dialog box appears, pop up the Mode menu and look at the choices. (See Figure 5.44.) Selecting None will flow the text behind the object. (See Figure 5.45.) Essentially, the text pretends the object isn't there. This is a good choice if you want the text to overprint a very light object but you should still send the object to the back using the Send to Back command in the Item menu. Otherwise, the light image will overprint the text. Choosing Item makes the text "see" the picture box (or text box) as an object and the type will then run around the edges of the box itself rather than the object in it. (See Figure 5.46.) Auto Image will automatically sense the shape of the object within the box and run the text around the contour. (See Figure 5.47.) Now, here's the tricky one, choosing Manual Image creates a line around the object with handles. (See Figure 5.48.) The text conforms to the line rather than the image itself. Pulling or pushing the handles allows you to reshape the contour of the runaround. This option is the most versatile and gives you a lot of control over exactly how the rag is shaped.

Lorem ipsum dolor sit amet, consectetur adipscing elit, sed diam nomumy eisusmod tempor incidunt ut labore et dolore magna aliquam erat volupat. Ut enim ad minimim veniami quis nostrud exercitation ullamcorpor suscipit laboris nisi ut aliquip ex ea commodo consequat. Duis autem vel eum irure dolor in reprehenderit in vojuptate velit esse molistatie son consequat, vel illum dolore eu fugiat nulla

FIGURE 5.43

This is a typical runaround. Running type around an object adds informality to the page and breaks up the linear feel created by straight columns of text and square-cut photos.

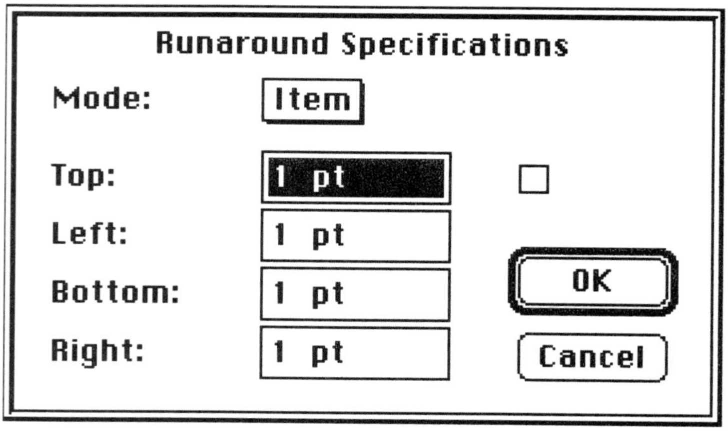

Runaround Specifications

Mode: | Item |

Top: | 1 pt | ☐

Left: | 1 pt |

Bottom: | 1 pt | | OK |

Right: | 1 pt | | Cancel |

FIGURE 5.44

Runarounds are created in the Runaround Specifications dialog box.

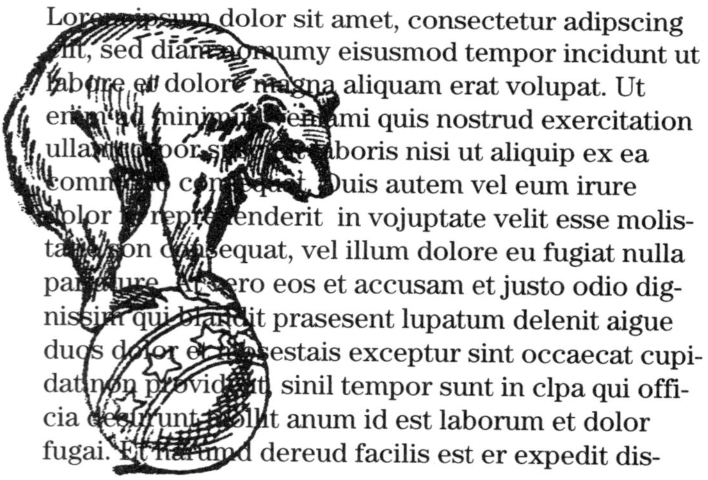

Lorem ipsum dolor sit amet, consectetur adipscing lit, sed diam nomumy eisusmod tempor incidunt ut labore et dolore magna aliquam erat volupat. Ut enim ad minim Geniami quis nostrud exercitation ullam corpor s boris nisi ut aliquip ex ea commro corport Quis autem vel eum irure dolor repre enderit in vojuptate velit esse molistan con dequat, vel illum dolore eu fugiat nulla pari ure ero eos et accusam et justo odio dignissim qui blandit prasesent lupatum delenit aigue duos dolor et molestais exceptur sint occaecat cupidatnon provident sinil tempor sunt in clpa qui officia deserunt mollit anum id est laborum et dolor fugai. Et harumd dereud facilis est er expedit dis-

FIGURE 5.45

The text runs behind the object when you choose None in the Mode pop-up menu.

Lorem ipsum dolor sit amet, consectetur adipscing elit, sed diam nomumy eisusmod tempor incidunt ut labore et dolore magna aliquam erat volupat. Ut enim ad minimim veniami quis nostrud exercitation ullamcorpor suscipit laboris nisi ut aliquip ex ea commodo consequat. Duis autem vel eum irure dolor in reprehenderit in vojuptate velit esse molistatie

FIGURE 5.46

Choosing Item mode will conform the text to the edges of the picture box.

Lorem ipsum dolor sit amet, consectetur adipscing elit, sed diam nomumy eisusmod tempor incidunt ut labore et dolore magna aliquam erat volupat. Ut enim ad minimim veniami quis nostrud exercitation ullamcorpor suscipit laboris nisi ut aliquip ex ea commodo consequat. Duis autem vel eum irure dolor in reprehenderit in vojuptate velit esse molistatie son consequat, vel illum dolore eu fugiat nulla

FIGURE 5.47

Auto Image conforms the text to the contour of the object.

133

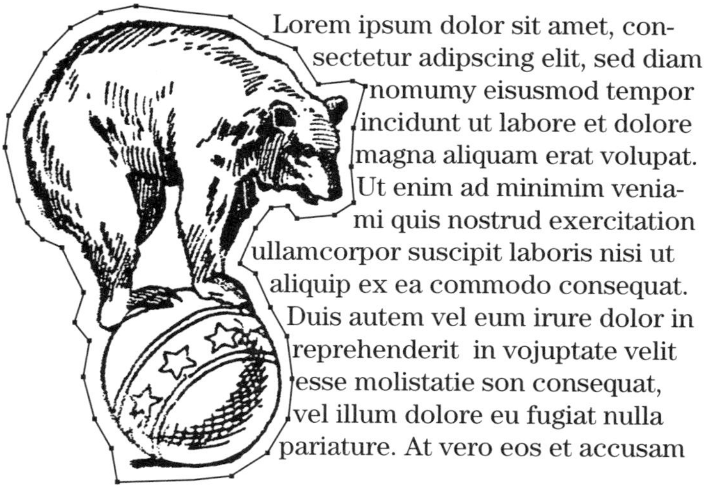

Lorem ipsum dolor sit amet, consectetur adipscing elit, sed diam nomumy eisusmod tempor incidunt ut labore et dolore magna aliquam erat volupat. Ut enim ad minimim veniami quis nostrud exercitation ullamcorpor suscipit laboris nisi ut aliquip ex ea commodo consequat. Duis autem vel eum irure dolor in reprehenderit in vojuptate velit esse molistatie son consequat, vel illum dolore eu fugiat nulla pariature. At vero eos et accusam

FIGURE 5.48

Manual Image also conforms the text to the object but also creates a line around the object with handles. Use the handles to change the text contour.

No matter which mode you choose, you'll want to watch how closely the type hugs the object. If you are in the Item mode, you can adjust the distance by typing values into the fields labeled Top, Left, Bottom, and Right. Since the object is a box you can adjust all four sides separately, or specify different values for the top, left, bottom and right sides of the box. If you chose Auto Image or Manual image, you can enter a value in the Text Outset field to space the text an even distance away from the contour of the object.

CHECKING SPELLING

I hate to admit it, but graphic designers are not often sought out for their spelling prowess. In fact, I can think of a couple of my designer friends who would have great difficulty putting two accurate sentences together without a dictionary by their side. The thought of these guys actually proofreading…well anyway, like it or not, designers are ultimately responsible for the accuracy of every word in the documents they create. QuarkXPress makes it possible for you to check the accuracy of your document by single word, an active story, an entire document, or individual text blocks included in master pages.

Here's how it works: QuarkXPress uses an internal dictionary that has more words than you'll ever want to know, somewhere around 80,000. And, if that isn't enough, you can create a customized auxiliary dictionary. To check the spelling of an individual word within a document, select the word and choose Check Spelling from the Utilities menu. Choose Word from the submenu and the Check Word dialog box pops up. To check a story, choose Story from Check Spelling. (A story is defined as all the text within a text box or a series of linked text boxes.) To check the entire document choose Document. Now you'll see the Word Count dialog box. QuarkXPress will scan the text and compare each word to those in the dictionary. The Word Count dialog box will list the total number of words, the number of unique words found, and the number of questionable words. Words listed as Suspect are any that are not found in the main or auxiliary dictionaries. If there are no suspect words, your document is probably free of misspelled words. Click OK to return to the document.

If there are suspect words, clicking OK will display the Check Story or Check Document dialog box. (See Figure 5.49.) QuarkXPress will scan through the document displaying the suspect words one at a time in the Suspect Word field. Sometimes the word may be correct, it just isn't in the dictionary. If so, click Skip to move on to the next word. If you want to add the word to the auxiliary dictionary so you won't have to see it pop up over and over, click Keep. Now, here's the best part. What if a word is displayed in the Suspect Word field but it looks OK to you? You can check it by clicking Lookup. QuarkXPress will display any similar words in the scroll list. If you see the correct spelling of the word in the list, click on the word and then click Replace. The incorrectly spelled word will automatically be corrected every place that it appears in your document. What if a word appears in the Suspect Word field that's obviously wrong? A typo. Rather than look it up you may want to just correct it yourself. Just type the correct spelling in the Replace With field and then click Replace.

Often documents contain words that are not in the XPress Dictionary. QuarkXPress lets you create your own auxiliary dictionary and add any words that you like. Choose Auxiliary Dictionary from the Utilities menu. (See Figure 5.50.) You can create an auxiliary dictionary for a particular document or a general default dictionary. If no document is open when you choose Auxiliary Dictionary it will automatically be a default dictionary. If the document is open you can create a dictionary specific to that document. When the dialog box appears, give the new dictionary a name and select a folder in which to keep it. To select an existing auxiliary dictionary click Open in the Auxiliary Dictionary dialog box.

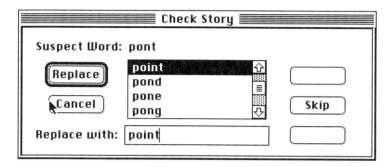

FIGURE 5.49 The Check Story dialog box will display suspect words and even look up alternatives. Once an alternative is found you can automatically correct it throughout your document.

In order for QuarkXPress to check spelling, the XPress Dictionary file must be in either the System Folder, or the same folder as the QuarkXPress program. If it isn't, you can find the dictionary on the Utilities disk.

NOTE

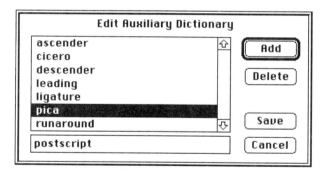

FIGURE 5.50 Add words to an auxiliary dictionary in the Edit Auxiliary Dictionary dialog box.

To add words to an auxiliary dictionary choose Edit Auxiliary from the Utilities menu and the Edit Auxiliary Dictionary dialog box will appear. Simply type in the word to be added in the field below the scroll list and click Add. After you've finished entering the new words click Save.

FINDING AND REPLACING TEXT

What if you're working with a very long document and you need to find a specific section of text? Or a specific word? In the Edit menu you'll find a very useful item called Find/Change. (See Figure 5.51.) This command not only finds text for you but lets you make changes to it that can be applied to all occurrences throughout the document. You could change all occurrences of a misspelled word for instance. Or you can change the character attributes of a word or phrase—say from 10 pt. roman to 11 pt. italic throughout the document.

To begin the search, activate the text box and place the Text Insertion bar at the beginning of the text that you want to search. Next, choose Find/Change from the Edit menu. When you see the Find/Change dialog box you'll notice two fields, one labeled Find What and the other Change To. Enter the word or words that you want to find in the Find What field. (Both the Find What and the Change To fields will handle up to 80 characters.) Do you see the series of check boxes under the Find What and Change To fields? Check the one labeled Document to have QuarkXPress search through the entire document. (Remember how you activated a text box before selecting Find/Change? That told QuarkXPress that you were only interested in searching that text box and those linked to it. If you want to search the entire document, be sure to open Find/Change with no text boxes activated.) The next check box is labeled Whole Word. Check that box when you want to search only for the word typed into the Find What box. Check Ignore Case if you want to find all instances of the specified word regardless of whether they are capitalized, caps & lower case, or all caps. Ignore Attributes is already checked when you open the dialog box. When this box is checked it ignores such things as typeface, size, and style. If you want you can search with these attributes in mind. When you uncheck the Ignore Attributes box a new expanded dialog box appears. (See Figure 5.52.) On both the Find What and the Change To sides you can get very specific about character attributes. What this means is you can not only search for a word based upon the characters it contains but also what it looks like.

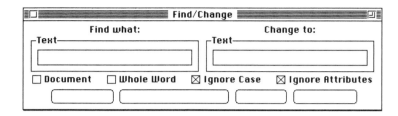

FIGURE 5.51 The Find/Change command in the Edit menu makes finding and changing text in long documents easy.

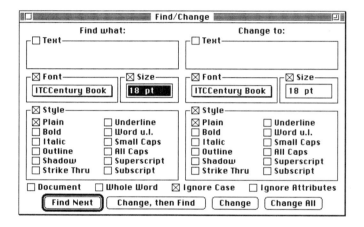

FIGURE 5.52 An expanded Find/Change dialog box lets you use character attributes as search criteria.

When using the Find/Change dialog box, holding down the Option key changes the Find Next button to Find First. When utilizing this option QuarkXPress will automatically go back to the beginning of the document to search for the selected word.

No matter which search option you choose, the next step is to actually do the searching. When you type your word or words in the Find What field and are ready to search, click Find Next. When the word appears, click Change to replace it with the word in the Change to field. Now can click Find Next again or, if you want to speed things up, you can click the Change, then Find button to automatically make changes and move on to the next occurrence. Or you can click Change All to immediately change all occurrences of the word throughout the document.

USING STYLE SHEETS

Using Style Sheets is a real time saver. Style Sheets "remember" character attributes for such things as body text, captions, heads, subheads and pull quotes. Using Style Sheets also ensures typographic consistency throughout your publication. To create, edit, or append a style sheet, open your document and choose Style Sheets from the Edit menu. When the Style Sheets dialog box appears you'll notice a scroll list on the left side listing all style sheets currently set up for your document. Since you probably haven't created any yet, none will be listed except the default, Normal.

To create a new style sheet click New. Now the Edit Style Sheet dialog box appears. (See Figure 5.53.) Type a name for the new style sheet in the Name field. Just below the Name field there's a field called Keyboard Equivalent that lets you type in a keyboard shortcut for a particular style. In other words, you can activate the style by tapping a couple of keys on your keyboard instead of using the menus. You can use any combination of the Command, Shift, Control, and Option keys along with a keypad or function key. Under the Keyboard Equivalent field there's a pop-up menu labeled Based On. You can use this to base your new style on one that you've already created.

On the right side of the dialog box you'll see four buttons. The one on the top is labeled Character. When you click on Character you'll get a new dialog box called Character Attributes. (See Figure 5.54.) This is where you specify the typographic characteristics of your new style. For instance, if you're setting up a new headline style you might want to use the Character Attributes dialog to make this headline 24-point. Helvetica Bold with a horizontal scale of 80% and tracked open to 40. Enter all of your specifications, then click OK.

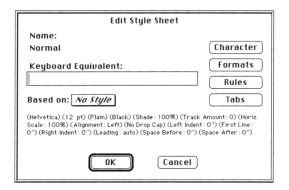

FIGURE 5.53

Creating style sheets is a real time saver. To create a new style sheet or edit an existing one, use the Edit Style Sheet dialog box.

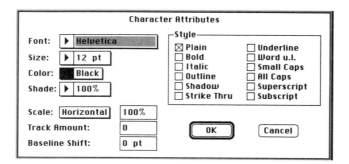

FIGURE 5.54

Use the Character Attributes dialog box to specify typographic characteristics.

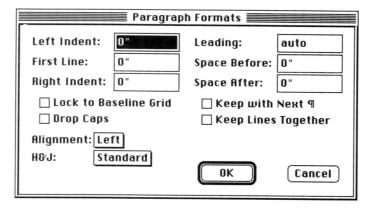

FIGURE 5.55

The Paragraph Formats dialog box is used to specify paragraph attributes for your style sheet.

The next button is called Formats. Clicking this button will display yet another dialog box. This one is called Paragraph Formats and is used to specify things like indents, leading, hyphenation, margin alignment, and widow and orphan control. (See Figure 5.55.) Again, it's pretty much a matter of filling in the blanks and click-

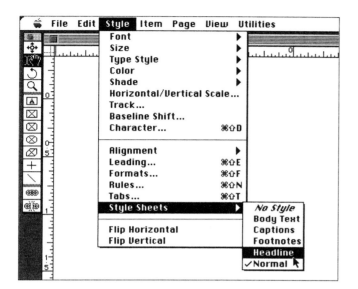

FIGURE 5.56

To apply styles to your document, select the text, then use the Style Sheets pop-up menu under Style.

ing OK.

Under Formats there are two more buttons. One is called Rules and the other is called Tabs. Clicking these buttons will display the Paragraph Rules and Paragraph Tabs dialog boxes. The Paragraph Rules dialog box lets you specify rule formats and the Paragraph Tabs dialog box lets you standardize tab settings for things like charts and tabular material.

Now that you've set up your style sheets you'll probably want to know how to actually apply them to your document. Let's say that you're beginning to format your document and you come across a headline that's set just like the body text. You want to apply a style that you've created called Headline. Select the headline in your text and choose Style Sheets from the Style menu. (See Figure 5.56.) Style Sheets is actually a pop-up menu that lists all of your styles. Simply click the one called Headline and the style will be applied to your text. Or, if you set up a keyboard equivalent for your Headline style you can just type the keyboard command. If you have QuarkXPress version 3.1 or later you have a Style Sheet palette that you can leave out on your desktop. It includes a scroll list of all your styles and gives you easy access to them at all times. You'll find it in the View menu.

But what if you apply your styles and then think afterward, "Geez, those headlines look way too big"? No problem. You can easily edit any style sheet by going back to Style Sheets in the Edit menu. Once the dialog box appears click Edit. Now you can go back in and change any of the attributes. When you're finished be sure to click Save before you click OK. If you don't, none of your changes will be saved.

Let's say you're working on a document that's the second in a series. All of the formatting must be consistent. You've already set up all the styles for document 1. Do you have to recreate all of those styles for document 2? In the Style Sheets dialog box is a button labeled Append. This lets you import the style sheets already created in another QuarkXPress document. When you click Append, a new dialog box will appear asking you to locate the document from which you want to append the styles. Use the controls to locate the document and click Open This will open a dialog listing the style sheets. Click Save and the styles will be added to your new document.

SUMMARY

We've covered a lot of ground in this chapter. We discussed some fundamental rules of typography. The most important thing to remember is that type is to be read, and every typographic decision you make should be evaluated on the basis of whether or not it will improve communication. Since this book is designed to be both an overview of QuarkXPress and a reference book, don't hesitate to go back over the material whenever a question comes up. And speaking of questions, see if you know the answers to these:

1. All type has an *inherent character*. What exactly does this mean?

2. What's the difference between a classic typeface and a decorative typeface?

3. What's the difference between fixed-sized fonts and scalable fonts?

4. What is meant by *type color*?

5. What is *kerning* and why is it important?

6. What is meant by *typographic hierarchy*?

7. What form of text alignment is the easiest to read?

8. What are some of the considerations when mixing typefaces?

9. In what ways does QuarkXPress let you modify letterforms?

10. What are *widows* and *orphans*?

11. How does QuarkXPress import text from another document?

12. What's the easiest way to change type attributes like typeface, style, leading,

tracking, and alignment?

13. What is meant by *H&Js?*

14. How does QuarkXPress control widows and orphans?

15. What's the *Kern Table Edit* and what is it used for?

16. What is meant by Horizontal Scale?

17. What's a *ligature?*

18. What's the advantage of anchoring rules to text?

19. What is a *runaround* and how is one created with QuarkXPress?

20. How does QuarkXPress check spelling?

21. What are *Style Sheets* and why should you use them?

CHAPTER SIX

Working with Pictures

Chapter 2 discussed the importance of visual elements to the success of a design. While the purpose of any publication is to communicate information, often a picture communicates more information than words. Good visuals set the emotional tone of a publication. They create a mood or define the aesthetic quality of a design. With this in mind, QuarkXPress has developed a number of tools intended to make working with pictures easier for the designer. This chapter will answer these questions:

- How can you tell a good picture from a poor one?

- How do you get the best results from a photographer or illustrator?

- How does the computer translate a picture into a form that QuarkXPress can use?

- How do picture boxes differ from text boxes?

- How do you import a picture into QuarkXPress?

- What can you do to make a picture bigger or smaller?

- How can good cropping make a picture more dramatic?

- What's the difference between line art and continuous tone art?

- What can you do to make a boring picture look interesting?

HOW TO TELL A GOOD PICTURE FROM A BAD ONE

Pictures are so powerful within the context of a layout that even those of poor quality will attract attention. The problem is you don't want bad pictures to attract attention. Poor-quality pictures will raise doubts about the quality of your entire publication. It's better to use no pictures than to use poor ones.

This statement assumes—probably inaccurately—that you have complete control over choosing your visuals. Some designers do, and they have a distinct advantage. But most designers have only marginal authority in this area and are constantly fighting to get more. If you're working on a newsletter, for instance, you may inherit pictures from numerous sources, and many of them may look like they were snapped by a chimpanzee with an Instamatic. There's not much you can do under these circumstances except use what you have wisely. But if you are able to pick and choose your visuals—or better yet, actually create them—there are a few guidelines to follow. The best pictures possess these characteristics:

1. *Impact*—A good picture gets your attention; a great picture jumps off the page and grabs you. Let's face it—that's what the picture is there for. If it isn't good enough to demand attention, it's a waste of space. Unfortunately, many publications are peppered with visuals that are just not very interesting. Often they're nothing more than visual clichés. How many newsletters have you seen that feature a picture of two executives holding an award, shaking hands, and smiling at the camera? Or the picture of the businessperson sitting in front of the computer, staring intently into the screen? These kinds of pictures are so pedestrian that few people bother to look at them. They have little or no impact. In contrast, look at the photograph in Figure 6.1. It's interesting because it treats the subject in an unusual way. These are the kinds of pictures you should strive for in your publications.

2. *A candid quality*—Pictures of people can be very compelling. We have a natural curiosity about other people and pictures that give us a glimpse into someone else's life are very effective. (See Figure 6-2) But pictures of people that are obviously contrived are not only uninteresting—they're insulting to the viewer. For example, consider the two executives holding the award and shaking hands...do you really believe they're overcome with happiness just because they're smiling at the camera? Of course not! Everyone who looks at that picture knows that the photographer said, "OK, everybody smile on the count of three...."

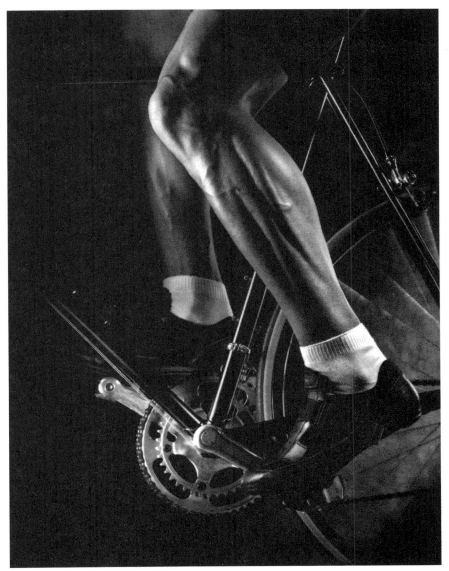

Photo by Mel Lindstrom

FIGURE 6.1 Always look for photos that have impact.

FIGURE 6.2 Candid photos of people are much more interesting than those that are posed. Can you sense the human drama in this picture?

But what if the photographer had been at the awards ceremony and snapped a picture just as the winner's name was announced? You could see the surprise and happiness in the winner's face as he or she goes to the podium to accept the award. Don't you think that would be a more interesting picture? Journalists say this is like being a "fly on the wall." Taking photographs without being observed takes a certain amount of skill. Obviously, you can't just march up to someone and blast a flashbulb in their face. If you're taking your own pictures, try using a film with a high ASA number. This will let you shoot without flash in low-light situations. You might also try using a telephoto lens so that you can photograph people surreptitiously from across the room.

3. *Simplicity*—The best pictures are simple ones. Try to edit out anything that isn't essential to what the picture is attempting to communicate. Avoid placing subjects against complicated backgrounds. A consistent hallmark of amateur photography is an overemphasis of background. Consider the picture your Uncle Harry took of Aunt Martha at Disneyland. You know Aunt Martha is in there somewhere, but all you see is a crowd watching a parade, with the Matterhorn in the background. It's always better to keep the background simple. A sense of setting can certainly add a lot to a picture, but it should serve only to give the picture context. The viewer should be looking at the subject of the picture, not at what's going on in the background.

4. *A strong focal point*—A good picture always has a clear focal point. One element should always dominate the composition. This is the same principle as the visual path discussed in Chapter 2.

How do you determine if a picture has a strong focal point? A good test is to look quickly at the picture and see how easily your eye finds a place to land. In a good composition, your eye will immediately be riveted to one spot and then go on to take in the rest of the picture. (See Figure 6.3.)

There are several ways to create a focal point. One way is to use a dramatic difference in scale, with one element of the picture clearly larger and dominating the composition. Another method is to use contrast. Perhaps the focal point is very light in value against a predominantly dark background. Sometimes color can also create a focal point, such as a bright red carnation in the lapel of a dark suit.

5. *Lighting*—Good lighting is characteristic of all quality pictures. In fact, photography is by definition the graphic representation of light. Effective lighting can infuse a sense of drama or mood to a picture, while poor lighting can make it dull and life-

less. Unfortunately, amateur photos are often characterized by poor lighting. This is due primarily to the use of flash photography. While a flash is often necessary in low light, it has a tendency to blast all detail out of the highlights and create dark, distracting shadows. Effective flash photography takes skill. Professional photographers have ways of manipulating the flash to create more natural lighting effects. By and large, the goal of photography should be a natural sense of lighting. People are very good at sensing anything artificial in a picture, and if something is unnatural, it's distracting.

FIGURE 6.3 Can you find the focal point in this picture?

But let's face it, often a photographer is faced with situations where the lighting must be created. Lighting is artificial. The trick is to make artificial lighting appear natural. If you've had experience working with professional photographers in a studio, you know to what lengths the photographer will go to create the impression of natural light in an artificial environment. Most people would be amazed if they could see all the paraphernalia outside the edges of a photo. Typically, a photographic subject is surrounded by strobe lights with diffusers, white umbrellas to bounce light indirectly at the subject, white cards on the shadow side of the subject to reflect "fill" light into the shadows and keep them from becoming too dark, mirrors, baffles, and a host of other tools to help create an illusion of natural light.

6. Contrast—The best pictures have a good range of contrast, from a good clean white in the highlights to a strong black in the deepest shadows. It's the middle tones, however, that are the most important. Good differentiation of gray tones is critical to successful reproduction. This is especially important to black-and-white

MarketShare

U.S. Central Area Gets Ready for Commercial Campaign

BY CATHY GUTHRIE

The U.S. central area is meeting the commercial markets challenge by planning SunExclusives direct marketing campaigns for Q3 of this year. Likely target industries include banking and insurance, with other key areas under consideration.

SunExclusives is a new lead-generation program developed by the Catalyst group in conjunction with the Sun field to help bring in qualified leads from a target market for sales. The program involves a direct mail campaign, with call to

INSIDE

Enabling Technologies

Sun's CASE Strategy

Teamwork Wins at Chemical Bank

Special Deal on SunCD

COLOR FIGURE 1
Use color sparingly. In this example, color was used only to call attention to the most important elements on the page. Since color is a powerful lure for the eye, use it only where you want to draw the reader's attention.

THE GUARANTEED PATH TO ENTERPRISE ATM

There's no question that Asynchronous Transfer Mode (ATM) technology is the wave of the future when it comes to the evolution of today's networks. Initially viewed as a carrier technology for broadband ISDN, today ATM is generally acknowledged as the universal technology that enables the creation of end-to-end networks that encompass LANs, WANs, and carriers. In other words, ATM eliminates the boundaries between different types of networks.

N.E.T.'s ATM solutions go beyond concepts, or visions. We offer real products that support ATM in the LAN today, and platforms that pave a path to ATM in the WAN. We provide superior solutions for incorporating ATM into the fabric of your existing and expanding global enterprise network.

Whether you start with an ATM LAN backbone or an ATM carrier service, N.E.T. can put you on the road to enterprise ATM. No matter how you look at it, all roads lead to ATM. And we're helping to pave them. Guaranteed.

ADAPTIVE ATMX: THE WORLD'S FIRST ATM LAN SOLUTION

Introduced in 1992, the ADAPTIVE™ ATMX™ switch is the first commercial product to use ATM technology to solve today's LAN performance and complexity issues. Even more impressive is the fact that shortly after its introduction, the ATMX was recognized as *LAN Magazine's* "Product of the Year."

The ATMX offers significant software capabilities that were pioneered by N.E.T.'s ADAPTIVE division:

- Virtual LAN (VLAN) allows your organization to flatten its LAN backbone to reduce the management complexities caused by today's hierarchical hub/router networks.

- ATM LAN emulation allows existing LAN applications and protocols to operate transparently over an ATM network.

- The ATMX congestion management system provides consistent end-to-end network performance.

These software capabilities are an integral part of the ATMX architecture, and with the addition of Ethernet and token-ring connectivity in the coming year, the benefits of VLAN will be extended to existing desktops, enabling you to incorporate legacy LANs into an ATM infrastructure.

RE-ARCHITECTING THE LAN

The ATMX VLAN capability changes the way LANs are built. Instead of playing by the physical and geographical rules of hubs, bridges, and routers, now LANs can be defined based on your business and organizational needs.

ATMX VLAN advantages include:

- Software-defined LANs for greater flexibility and ease of management.

- Broadcast domains defined by software, rather than by physical router ports, for increased flexibility.

- Automated network administration—VLAN membership follows stations' "moves and changes."

- Centralized server placement and trouble-shooting greatly simplify LAN management.

- Separation of switching and routing functions in the LAN backbone, to provide you with better performance and a lower price than router-FDDI-based backbone architectures.

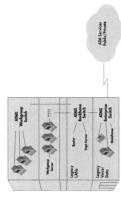

COLOR FIGURE 3
Use color to create mood. Note the difference in mood between these two pictures. The one composed of cool colors tends to be passive while the same photo, when warm colors are applied, seems more active and energetic.

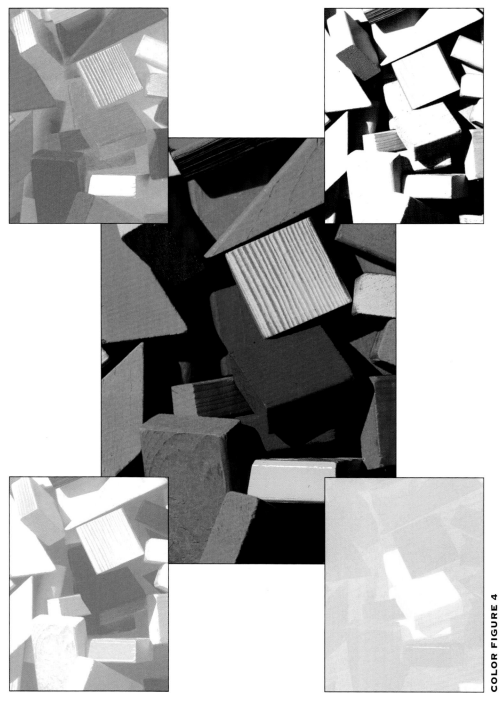

COLOR FIGURE 4

Color pictures are reproduced by "separating" them into varying densities of cyan, magenta, yellow, and black (CMYK). This example shows the separated color plates.

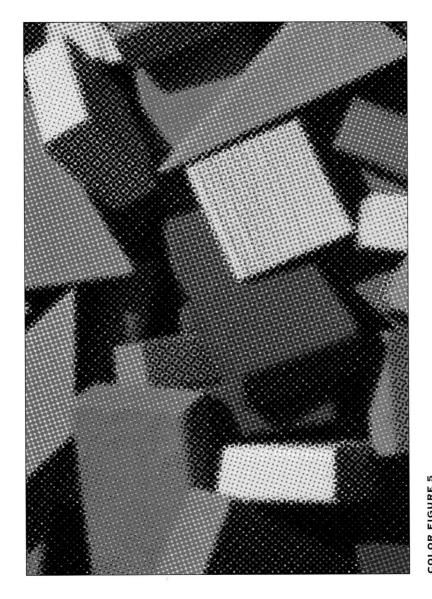

COLOR FIGURE 5
Before a color image can be printed, halftones of each color are created and superimposed one on top of another.

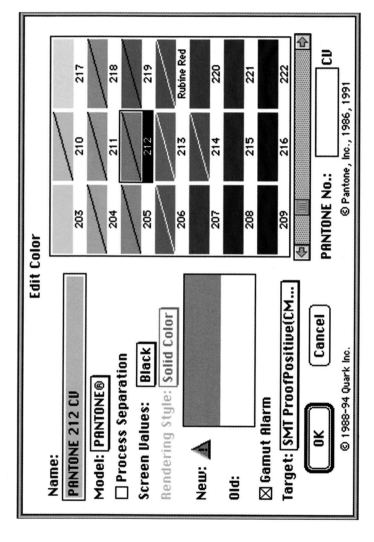

COLOR FIGURE 6

Not all colors can be accurately reproduced on every printer. EfiColor's gamut alarm warns you when a color is outside of the color range achievable with your device. The dialog box at the top shows a color selected from the PANTONE color system. Note the little triangle with the exclamation mark. This symbol alerts you that the color you've chosen is outside the gamut.

COLOR FIGURE 7

QuarkXPress eliminates the need for creating conventional mechanicals, or pasteups. What's more, QuarkXPress is capable of producing very high-quality full color publications. For example, this brochure was created entirely within the computer. The images were scanned as high-resolution EPS files, then color corrected and retouched in Adobe's Photoshop. The page layouts were created in QuarkXPress then the file was turned over to the printer for processing. Film and plates were created directly from QuarkXPress.

COLOR FIGURE 8

When creating a series of publications that must all have the same basic "look," QuarkXPress makes the job much easier. This series of brochures were created for a company that was producing a steady stream of publications, and they all had to appear as if they were part of the same family. Once the basic format was designed, a template was created along with typographic styles. These standards could then easily be applied to any new brochure ensuring consistency.

images because there is no color to provide other visual clues for the viewer.

7. *Clarity of detail*—This should be obvious. It's always better if your pictures are in focus! It's amazing how often fuzzy pictures seem to make their way into the pages of publications. Also, it's especially important that images to be printed start out having exceptional clarity of detail because the printing process will certainly do nothing to improve them. We'll discuss this in more detail later, but the quality of the paper, the type of printing process, and the way in which the pictures are prepared for reproduction can often degrade the quality of the image. For this reason, the clarity of the original image must be exceptional.

ILLUSTRATION OR PHOTOGRAPHY?

Pictures fall into two general categories: *illustrations* and *photographs*. While the term illustration is broad and can encompass all kinds of visuals, I will use it to refer to pictures created by an artist, and the term photography to refer to pictures created with a camera.

Both kinds of visuals are routinely used in professional publications, and both have their strengths. Photography, for instance, creates an illusion of realism. A photograph, even if it's contrived, seems somehow more believable than an illustration. Illustration, on the other hand, offers opportunities that aren't normally afforded by photography. While photography is documentary in nature, illustration tends to be more interpretive. The camera records only what it sees, but illustration can capture virtually anything that exists in the mind of the artist. This makes illustration the medium of choice for symbolism. Illustration can transcend reality. It can exaggerate the familiar, making romance seem more romantic or a dangerous situation more frightening.

The type of media you choose should be dictated by the story or article you're designing. For example, a news story or documentary is usually better served by photography because it lends a sense of realism and accuracy to the presentation. Fiction, on the other hand, is usually illustrated because illustration can more effectively capture the romanticism and drama of the story.

Advertising often makes use of photography because advertisers want an accurate representation of their product. However, some kinds of products can't be photographed effectively. A good example is computer software like QuarkXPress. You can photograph the package, but you can't photograph the functionality of software because it's abstract. In such cases, you might choose to symbolize the abstract using illustration.

A Few Words about Cropping

To a designer, the crop is the way a picture is visually "trimmed." *Cropping* is essentially a visual editing process, and effective cropping can actually save a poorly composed picture. To crop a picture, you use your judgment to determine which elements are essential and which are superfluous and should be left out. Don't be afraid to trim off a busy background or crop a picture tightly to make one element dominate, thereby creating a strong focal point. (See Figures 6.4 and 6.5.)

Working with Photographers and Illustrators

You may encounter situations in your work where you'll need to commission work from a professional photographer or illustrator. When selecting an artist, the most important rule is don't let your fingers do the walking. The phone book is full of listings for professional photographers and artists with widely varying degrees of talent and expertise. You wouldn't want to hire a photographer to shoot your company's annual report only to find that his only professional experience involved taking pictures of kids on ponies at birthday parties. Similarly, you wouldn't want to hire an artist who creates paintings by squirting paint on canvas from ketchup bottles to illustrate a children's story. Every reputable professional, whether a photographer or an illustrator, has a portfolio that includes samples of his or her work (many also have printed promotional materials they can send you). Never hire anyone without seeing their portfolio.

Imagine that you've arranged an appointment to meet with an illustrator. You're paging through the samples in his portfolio, and they look good. But how do you know if this particular artist is right for the job? What are some of the things you should consider when evaluating his work? Here are a few things to keep in mind.

1. *Evaluate the style*—All artists have a particular approach to their work that is unique to them. This is more apparent with some artists than others. Try to find a common stylistic thread that runs through all the work in the portfolio. Some artists and photographers swear that they don't have a unique style at all, insisting that they are extremely versatile and can create any style that's necessary. That may be partially true, but you can usually see something of the artist's personal

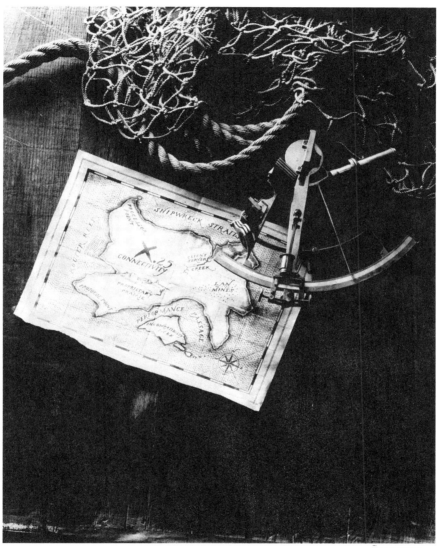

Photo by Mel Lindstrom

FIGURE 6.4 Original photo

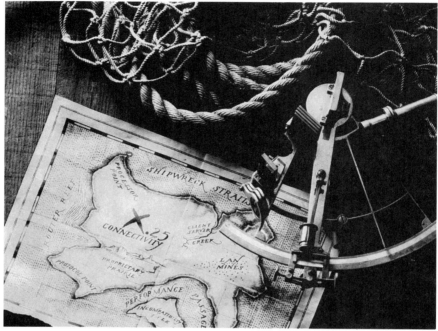

Photo by Mel Lindstrom

FIGURE 6.5 The same photo cropped to create a stronger composition.

taste showing through. In fact, you may be more aware of it than they are. The trick is to match the style of the work to the tone of the article or story. Even if the work is technically of a high quality, don't use it if the style isn't appropriate.

2. *What you see isn't necessarily what you get*—Always judge the quality of a portfolio by the worst piece in it. Think about it—any professional who's been in business for a few years should be able to collect enough good samples to make up a presentable portfolio. The examples you're looking at represent the best work the artist has done, not necessarily what he or she produces every day.

3. *Personality*—What's the artist like personally? Is he or she personable? Professional? Remember, you're going to have to actually work with this person. Look for artists who are professional, courteous, and willing to work with you to achieve your objectives, not just their own.

There are basically two kinds of commercial artists. One sees their role as a problem solver. Their concern is to evaluate your problem and apply their creative skills toward solving it. The second kind sees themselves as a fine artist. It's their job to be a creative genius and yours to send them money. Who would you rather work with?

4. *Talk about money*—Get this out of the way up front. The pricing of illustration and photography is extremely subjective. For the same shot you could have three photographers quote prices ranging from $500 to $2,500. There are a lot of factors that go into pricing this sort of thing, but often it's somewhat like reading tea leaves. Make certain that the artist can work within your budget and that there won't be any extra charges for expenses tacked on at the end.

5. *Look for imagination*—Always look for work that's conceptually imaginative. Some artists are purely technicians, while others can add a lot of creativity to a project. The type of artist you select depends on the assignment. If you simply need a nicely lit photograph of a product package sitting on a table, a technician may be able to produce acceptable results for a good price. But more often, you might look for someone who can contribute some imagination. A creative artist can make the difference between an adequate picture and a great one. Often this caliber of professional doesn't come cheap, but remember—the quality of the pictures is crucial to the success of a publication. If you are fortunate enough to work with a creative professional, give him or her some room to do the job. Explain your objectives in broad terms and allow the artist to suggest ideas. Don't be overly dogmatic about what you want. Often a cooperative effort can produce ideas you would never have thought of on your own.

WORKING WITH PICTURES IN QUARKXPRESS

Just as the basic building block for text is the text box, QuarkXPress uses picture boxes to handle pictures. In traditional graphic design, incorporating pictures into a document involves a photographic process. The printer makes a negative of the original art and physically places it into position on the page. Now, the computer makes it possible to import pictures into your document electronically. This method not only saves time for the printer, but it also lets you see the assembled page on your computer screen—pictures and all. You also can resize the picture, change the crop, adjust color or contrast, and otherwise manipulate it until it's exactly what you want.

But how does the picture get into the computer? Usually the picture is converted to electronic form by a scanner. The scanner quite literally scans over the surface of the picture and reads the relative densities of values and/or colors. Converting these densities to electronic data, the scanner then translates the data into one of several standardized file formats. These files can then be imported into QuarkXPress or other computer programs. Once imported, the information is translated back into a visual image for the screen. The same information can be used by the printer to reproduce the image on paper.

FILE FORMATS

There are three types of images that can be imported into QuarkXPress. Line art refers to high-contrast, black-and-white art, such as type, logos, or line drawings. (See Figure 6-6.) There are no grays in line art—only pure black and pure white. A grayscale image, on the other hand, is made up of a range of tonal values, from black to white. (See Figure 6-7.) It includes a full spectrum of grays. Black-and-

Photo by Mel Lindstrom

FIGURE 6.6 A typical line art image.

white photographs are grayscale images. A color image, like a grayscale image, generally has a range of values but also includes a full range of colors. Color photographs fall into this category.

All images, regardless of type, must be converted to an electronic file format. File formats that can be imported into a QuarkXPress file are Bitmap (or Paint), TIFF, and RIFF (which can include both line art and grayscale images), TIFF color,

Photo by Mel Lindstrom

FIGURE 6.7 A typical grayscale image.

PICT, JPEG, PhotoCD, BMP, PCX, Windows metafile and EPS, which can include both black-and-white and color images. Of these choices, the most commonly used are probably TIFF, PICT and EPS formats. TIFF, RIFF, and Paint files have the advantage of being more flexible. Once they're imported, you can edit these files, adjusting colors, contrast, and size. EPS files are encapsulated, which means you can't get into them. You can resize them, but you can't adjust color or contrast.

CREATING PICTURE BOXES

If you don't have QuarkXPress up and running on your computer, load it now. Let's take a few minutes to create some picture boxes. Open a QuarkXPress document, and open the Tool palette. The Tool palette has four different picture box tools and each one creates a different kind of box. The first one looks like a rectangle with an X across it. This is called the Rectangle Picture Box Tool. Beneath that is a similar box but with rounded corners. This is the Rounded-corner Picture Box Tool.

Beneath that is the Oval Picture Box Tool, and finally, beneath that is the Polygon Picture Box Tool. You create a picture box in much the same way that you would create a text box. Click on one of the picture box tools. Then click on the page and drag the crosshair pointer diagonally across the page. When the box is the size and shape you want, let go of the mouse button. You can resize the picture box by pushing or pulling on the handles (the little boxes on the corners and in the middle of each side of the box). You can drag the box to another location on the page by selecting the Item Tool, clicking on the box, and dragging it with the mouse button held down. When you have it in the correct position, release the mouse button. Use the picture box tools to create different kinds of picture boxes, but don't try to create a polygon picture box yet. That tool works a bit differently, and we'll get to it in a minute.

In the Item menu there's an entry called Box Shape. While the Tool palette offers you four different kind of text boxes, this menu gives you six choices. In addition to the rectangle, rounded-corner, oval, and polygon picture boxes, you can choose an angled-corner picture box and a concave-corner picture box. Use this menu to change the shape of any active picture box.

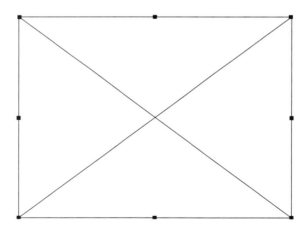

FIGURE 6.8 A rectangle picture box

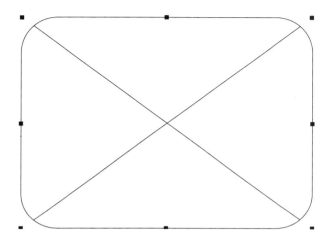

FIGURE 6.9 A round-corner picture box.

THE RECTANGLE PICTURE BOX TOOL

The Rectangle Picture Box Tool is probably the most commonly used Picture Box Tool. It can be used to create square-cornered pictures of all shapes and sizes as well as square boxes. (See Figure 6.8.) To create a rectangle box, click on the tool and then drag the pointer until the box is the correct size and shape. To create a square box, hold down the Shift key while you drag.

THE ROUNDED-CORNER PICTURE BOX TOOL

You can create a rounded-corner picture box in the same way. The corner radius for an active picture box can be adjusted by selecting Modify from the Item menu. When the Picture Box Specifications dialog box appears, type a value in the Corner Radius field. (See Figure 6.9.)

THE OVAL PICTURE BOX TOOL

The Oval Picture Box Tool is used to make both ovals and circles. (See Figure 6.10.) To create an oval shape, click on the tool and drag the pointer until the picture box is the desired size and shape. Create a perfect circle by holding down the Shift key while you drag the pointer.

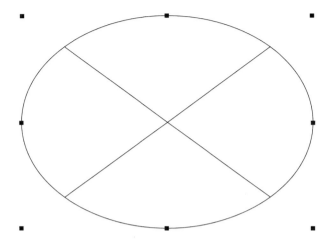

FIGURE 6.10 A oval picture box.

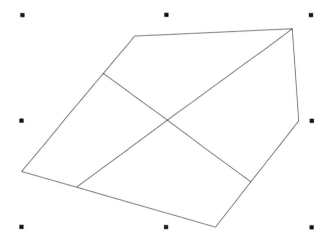

FIGURE 6.11 A polygon picture box.

THE POLYGON PICTURE BOX TOOL

If you select the Polygon Picture Box Tool, you can't drag the cursor to create a box; you must actually draw the sides of the box to create the desired shape. Let's try it. Select the Polygon Picture Box Tool from the Tool palette, then click and release the crosshair pointer at the point on the page where you want to position

your first corner point. Once you've positioned the first corner point, move the crosshair pointer to the second corner point. Notice that as you move the pointer a line is created. When you move the pointer, the line moves as well. Click the pointer where you want the second corner point, then the third, fourth, fifth, etc. (a polygon picture box must have at least three sides). Finally, when you're ready to close up the shape, pull the pointer back to first corner point. When the pointer is positioned over the top of the first point and the polygon is completed, you will see a small box appear. This box is called the Handle Creation Pointer. When you see the Handle Creation Pointer, click the mouse button and the box will be completed.

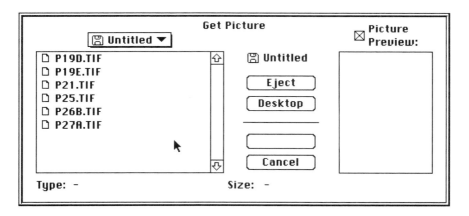

FIGURE 6.12 Pictures are imported into QuarkXPress using the Get Picture dialog box.

IMPORTING PICTURES

Importing pictures into a picture box is easy. Select the Content Tool from the Tool palette and activate the picture box. Then choose Get Picture from the File menu. When the Get Picture dialog box appears, you'll need to locate the file name of the picture you want to import. (See Figure 6-12.) Once you've found it, either click

Open or double-click on the file name in the scroll list. Presto! The picture materi-alizes in the picture box. Unlike other similar software programs, QuarkXPress let's you preview a picture before you import it. This is very handy if you're work-ing on a long document with numerous pictures. Under such circumstances, it's often difficult to remember the names of each picture file. Click on Picture Preview in the Get Picture dialog box. Then you select a picture file in the scroll list, you can see what it looks like in the box in the upper-right corner.

Notice that the box in the lower-left corner that normally contains the page num-ber changes to a percentage when you import a picture into a text box. This per-centage refers to the portion of the file that has been imported. Depending on how large the image is the box may display only a portion of the picture. You can repo-sition the picture in the box by selecting the Content Tool and using the little hand to "push" the image around until you find the portion you want.

Sometimes the picture box appears to be blank after you import a picture. This is usually because a blank part of the picture is showing. If this happens, you'll need to use the Content Tool to move the picture around in the box until you find the rest of it. You can also try to enlarge the box temporarily to expose a part of the elusive picture.

There are keyboard commands that you can use to modify a picture as you import it. For example, to convert a TIFF grayscale picture to TIFF line art, hold down the Command key while you click Open in the Get Picture dialog box. Similarly, you can use the same keyboard command to automatically convert a TIFF color picture to TIFF grayscale.

If the picture box appears empty after you've imported a picture, it may be that the image has been positioned somewhere outside the view defined by the box. Try holding the Command and the Shift keys down at the same time and typing M. This should center the picture in the box. If that doesn't work, try Command-Shift-F to force the picture to conform to the box—but be aware that this technique can also distort the picture.

N O T E

Pictures are displayed in QuarkXPress at fairly low resolution. The default is 36 dpi (dots per inch). This is pretty coarse, and frankly, it can be annoying if you want to see an accurate representation of the picture in your layout. You can double the resolution by holding down the Shift key while you click Open in the Get Picture dialog box. The only drawback to this is that it takes a lot more memory for QuarkXPress to display these higher-resolution images, and if you have a lot of pictures in your document you can end up with a very large file. For this reason, consider increasing resolution only if you have a lot of memory available in your system.

Some page layout software programs include pictures with document files. For example, if a picture is actually resident within a file, you can transport that file to a different computer to be printed and it will print just fine—pictures and all. QuarkXPress is different in that it includes a screen representation of the picture but when printing, it refers back to the data in the original picture file. That means that you must keep the original TIFF, EPS, JPEG, PCX, PICT, RIFF, PhotoCD, or Paint files with the document in order for them to print properly.

MISSING OR MODIFIED PICTURES

To complicate matters further, you can confuse QuarkXPress by moving or modifying the original picture file. Even if the file name doesn't change, QuarkXPress will sense that the picture file has been modified and won't be able to find it when you try to print. If you attempt to print a document containing a picture file that has been in some way modified, you'll see a dialog box that lets you reestablish the link to the file. There's a similar idiosyncrasy concerning EPS files. If an EPS file includes type as a part of the picture, you must include the original type font with the file in order for it to print properly.

You can simplify this process by using a feature called Auto Picture Import, found under General Preferences in the Edit menu. When you select On in the Auto Picture Import pop-up menu, QuarkXPress will automatically check all imported pictures against their original files each time a document is opened. If it detects that a file has been modified it will automatically reimport the modified picture file as it opens the document.

Keep in mind that displaying pictures in a document can require a lot of memory, as picture files are often quite large. Occasionally you may get a message telling you that there is not enough memory to display the picture. When this happens the picture will actually be imported, but not displayed, on your screen. It will print, but you won't be able to see it to position or crop it. If you're using MultiFinder or are running System 7, try quitting any other open applications. If this doesn't work, try quitting QuarkXPress and increasing the amount of memory allocated to it. You can do this by clicking on the QuarkXPress icon and selecting Get Info from the File menu. In the bottom-right corner is a box showing both the recommended and the actual memory allocation. To change the amount of memory allocated to QuarkXPress, simply type in a new value. Keep in mind, though, that increasing the amount of memory allocated to QuarkXPress will limit the memory available for the system and for other applications you may want to have running at the same time.

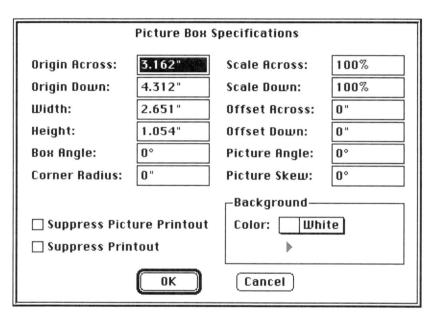

FIGURE 6.13 The Picture Box Specifications dialog box lets you resize, reposition, rotate, or slant a picture within a picture box.

IMPORTING PHOTOCD IMAGES

PhotoCD technology was developed by Kodak as a consumer product. The idea was to provide a convenient way to store and view pictures. If you have a CD-ROM drive connected to your TV or computer you can take your 35mm slides to a photo processor where they will be scanned onto a CD. You can then slip the CD into your drive and look at your baby pictures or Aunt Helen's wedding. What Kodak didn't count on was the immediate appeal of PhotoCD to the graphics industry. It's not too hard to figure out why. A PhotoCD scan costs a fraction of a commercial scan. The downside is that, in general, the quality is not as good as a scan produced on a high-end commercial scanner. Nonetheless, these scans have become very popular especially for low budget publications. Since PhotoCD is it's own file format, with the release of version 3.2, Quark added a filter that lets QuarkXPress recognize this new format. As long as the PhotoCD Xtension is installed in your QuarkXPress folder you can import these images just as if they were EPS, TIFF, or another common file format.

RESIZING PICTURES

When a picture is imported into a QuarkXPress document, it's placed in a picture box at the picture's original size. Usually the picture will need to be resized to fit the layout. There are a couple of ways to do this. One way is to activate the picture box and choose Modify from the Item menu. When the Picture Box Specifications dialog box is displayed, look in the upper-right corner. (See Figure 6.13.) The first two fields are labeled Scale Across and Scale Down. You can change the size of the picture by entering a new value in these fields (any value between 10% and 1000%, in .1% increments). For example, a value of 50% in both fields will resize the picture uniformly to half its original size. Keep in mind that to resize the picture uniformly—that is without proportional distortion—you must enter the same value in both fields.

Another way to resize photos is to use the Measurements Palette. You may find this method a time saver since you can keep the palette on your desktop where it's easy to access. To resize the photo, simply activate a picture box and enter new values in the X% and Y% fields.

UPDATING PICTURES

When you make changes to a picture, QuarkXPress will sense that the picture has been modified and will ask you to update it. For example, let's say you create an illustration with Adobe Illustrator, save it as an EPS file, then import it into your Quark document. Later in the day your client calls and asks you to change all the red colors in the illustration to blue. Now you have to go into the Illustrator document and make the changes and save it. The next time you try to print your Quark document a dialog appears telling you that some of your graphic files have been modified or are missing. Even though you saved the illustration with the same name, Quark senses that there's something different about it. Fortunately, this is a simple problem to fix. Choose Picture Usage from the Utilities menu and the Picture Usage dialog box will appear listing all the graphic files in your document and their current status. Most will probably be OK but one or more will be labeled "modified" or "missing." If the file has been modified, the dialog will ask you if you want to update it. If you do, simply click on the Update button and QuarkXPress will automatically reimport that particular file. If some pictures are missing, follow the same procedure. If multiple missing files are located in the same folder Quark will update them all at once.

NOTE

If you have a lot of pictures in your document it can become quite large. Large files can take a long time to print. If you want to print a rough draft, and don't need to see the pictures, you can check either the Suppress Picture Printout or the Suppress Printout boxes in the Picture Box Specifications dialog box. Checking Suppress Picture Printout will cause the currently active picture box to print with any frame or tint but without the picture. Suppress Printout will cause both the box and the picture not to be printed. You can also choose to print a low resolution or rough draft from the Output pop-up menu in the Print dialog box. This will print the entire document with pictures at low-resolution or without pictures.

Picture Usage				
Name	**Page**	**Type**	**Status**	**Print**
Hammer :Phone Receiver	1	EPS	OK	√
Hammer :Galileo :Galileo Signature	1	TIFF	OK	√
Hammer :San Francisco Scan	1	TIFF	OK	√

Update   Show Me

FIGURE 6.14 Use the Picture Usage dialog box to update modified or missing graphic files.

REPOSITIONING THE PICTURE

As we discussed earlier, an easy way to reposition a picture within a picture box is to use the little hand to push it around. Besides being intuitive, this method lets you experiment with the composition. But if you have a more mathematical orientation, you may be more comfortable with other methods. You can use the Picture Box Specifications dialog box (choose Modify from the Item menu) and enter a new value in the Origin Across and the Origin Down fields. The trouble with this approach is, since there's no Apply option to show you a preview, you have no choice but to click OK, then go back to the document page to see the result. If you don't like it, you must go through the procedure all over again. This can be very cumbersome and time consuming. Using the Measurements palette is much easier. Notice that the Measurements palette for pictures is divided in the middle. This can be confusing because there are two sets of X and Y coordinates and two angle fields, one on each side. But it's really simple—just remember that the controls in the right half modify a picture within an active picture box. The controls in the left half modify the box itself. Simply activate the picture box and type new values in the fields next to the X+ and Y+ fields. Easier still, click on the arrows to move the picture within the box in 1-point increments. For finer adjustments, hold down the Option key while clicking the arrows to move the picture in .1-point increments.

ROTATING PICTURES

QuarkXPress lets you to rotate a picture within a picture box. Why would you want to change the angle of a picture? For one thing, it gives you some creative options. There may be times when you want to alter the angle of a picture to create a particular effect. But even if you like your pictures straight up and down, there's a very practical reason for this feature. When a picture is scanned, it may not be aligned perfectly on the scanner bed. If it's scanned crooked, it will be imported into your document crooked. The rotation feature lets you straighten pictures that are imported at odd angles.

To change the angle of a picture, you can use either the pull-down menu or the Measurements palette. In the pull-down menu, choose Modify from the Item menu and use the Picture Box Specifications box. You'll see a field called Picture Angle on the right side of the box. (Don't confuse this with Box Angle, which we'll discuss later). Enter a value for the new angle in the box and click OK.

Photo by Mel Lindstrom

FIGURE 6.15 A high-contrast picture.

In the Measurements palette you simply type a new value in the Angle field (it will probably be set at 0 degrees before you enter a new value).

CHANGING THE BOX ANGLE

You can also alter the angle of the box itself, either by typing a new angle in the field in the left half of the Measurements palette or by typing a new value in the Box Angle field in the Picture Box Specifications dialog box.

SKEWING THE PICTURE

QuarkXPress has an interesting feature that lets you skew or slant a picture within a picture box. (You might not use this feature often, but it's kind of fun to play with.) Again, you can do this using either the pull-down menu or the Measurements palette. In the Picture Box Specifications dialog box, type a value in

Photo by Mel Lindstrom

FIGURE 6.16 A low-contrast picture.

the Picture Skew field. In the Measurements palette, type a new value between -75 and 75 in the Skew field. (In the Measurements palette the Skew field is symbolized by a little parallelogram in the lower-right corner).

Take a few minutes to play with this feature and see what it does. Import a picture into a picture box and make sure the picture box is active. (If you don't have a picture to import, import one from the exercise disk that came with the book). Try typing different values into the Skew Field to see how they affect the picture.

ADJUSTING PICTURE CONTRAST

Contrast refers to the relative values of darks and lights in a picture. A high-contrast picture is characterized by the extreme ends of the value spectrum—strong blacks and whites without much in the middle tones. (See Figure 6.14.) A low-contrast picture, on the other hand, is relatively flat in appearance and emphasizes

Photo by Mel Lindstrom

FIGURE 6.17 A picture with a normal contrast range.

middle tone values. (See Figure 6.15.) As we discussed earlier, pictures being pre-pared for reproduction should have a wide range of tones, with especially strong clarity in the middle tones. When a picture is printed its contrast range tends to be compressed, generally giving up detail in the extreme highlights and shadows. For that reason it's important to make sure that your original has a good range. When you import a picture in QuarkXPress, Normal Contrast is applied automatically. If you have a good original scan, this will probably be just fine. But sometimes scans need some enhancement. QuarkXPress provides a number of controls that let you modify the contrast and create special effects.

Remember, not all file formats allow modifications. You can't edit EPS or PICT files, so if you are scanning your own pictures and want to edit them in QuarkXPress, always save them as TIFF, RIFF, or bitmap files.

NOTE

Photo by Mel Lindstrom

FIGURE 6.18 Posterizing a picture creates a very graphic effect by limiting the tonal range to black, white, and shades of gray.

To adjust a picture's contrast, activate a picture box and pull down the Style menu. If the picture box contains a TIFF, RIFF, or bitmap picture you have several options. Normal Contrast should have a check mark next to it. This means that Normal Contrast has already been applied to the picture. (See Figure 6-16.) High Contrast applies the predefined high contrast settings to the picture. Posterized applies a special contrast effect created by limiting a grayscale picture to six tonal levels: black, white, and four shades of gray. This isn't something you should do to every picture, but it is an interesting effect that can sometimes save a poor picture by adding some graphic interest. (See Figure 6.17.)

The Other Contrast option lets you customize the contrast of your picture. Choosing Other Contrast from the Style menu will display the Picture Contrast Specifications dialog box. (See Figure 6-18.) In the dialog box you'll see several

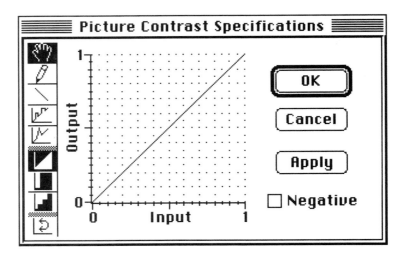

FIGURE 6.19 The Picture Contrast specifications dialog box lets you customize a picture's contrast range.

strange symbols and a graph. The graph displays the contrast curve of the picture. When the picture has normal contrast, the line will be a straight diagonal stretching from the lower-left to the upper-right corner of the graph. Changing this graph line changes the contrast values in your picture.You'll notice a tool palette along the left edge of the dialog box. The first tool is the Hand Tool, which you use to push the line on the graph up or down. This makes sweeping, uniform changes to the contrast, making the entire picture lighter or darker. The Pencil Tool lets you adjust the curve by drawing. The Line Tool is for making linear modifications to the curve. The Posterizer Tool makes custom posterization possible. The default posterization settings are set at 0%, 20%, 40%, 60%, 80%, and 100%, but you can apply different values to create different effects. Clicking on the Posterizer Tool will place handles on the curve at 10% intervals. By pulling the handles up or down you can alter the individual tonal values.

The next tool is called the Spike Tool. It works in a fashion similar to the Posterizer Tool in that it adds handles at 10% increments, but it allows a wider range of tonal adjustments.

The next three tools in the palette represent the three default settings. Sometimes after adjusting a picture's contrast you may decide you aren't crazy about the result and wish you could start over. Clicking on the Normal Contrast Tool (with the diagonal line) will automatically reset the picture to normal contrast. The High Contrast Tool will automatically apply the high contrast setting, and the Posterized Contrast Tool will apply the default posterization values. The last tool, which looks like a curved arrow, is called the Inversion Tool. It is used to turn the contrast curve upside down, reversing all the values. While this creates the effect of a negative image, it shouldn't be confused with the Negative setting in the Style menu. The effects are similar, but the Inversion tool creates a negative image based on the customized contrast curve, while the Negative setting in the Style menu inverts the values based on the picture's original contrast.

Working with these controls takes some experimentation. Take some time to play with all the tools and see what each one does to your picture. After each change

you make to the curve, you can click on the Apply button to see the effect. Modifying pictures affects only the picture in QuarkXPress, not the original picture file, so don't worry about ruining your original scan.

GHOSTING PICTURES

Ghosting is a popular technique in publication design. It's often used to decrease the picture contrast so type can be printed over the top. You can add shading to grayscale pictures within QuarkXPress provided they are in the TIFF format. Simply use the Shade command in the Style menu to apply any shade between 0% and 100%.

SUMMARY

QuarkXPress provides greater control over pictures than any other general-purpose desktop publishing software program. In this chapter you explored the techniques for controlling pictures in QuarkXPress and considered some general principles that can improve the quality of the pictures in your publications. Take a few minutes to review the content of this chapter by answering the following questions:

1. Name three characteristics of a good picture.

2. What are the advantages of using photography over illustration? Illustration over photography?

3. What is cropping?

4. List three factors to consider when selecting a photographer or illustrator.

5. What's the difference between a TIFF file format and EPS, and why should it matter to you?

6. What are the six types of picture boxes available to you in QuarkXPress?

7. Name three ways you can modify a picture using the Picture Box Specifications dialog box.

8. What is different about a picture that's been posterized?

CHAPTER SEVEN

Using Color

This chapter explores the use of color in design, focusing on some practical considerations of applying color in printed publications. It addresses the following fundamental questions.

- You can't apply color to everything. How do you decide when and where to use color?

- Once you've chosen a color, how do you tell the printer exactly what color ink to use?

- What's the difference between spot color and process color?

- How do you use QuarkXPress to apply color to your publications?

- Can you use QuarkXPress to apply color to pictures?

- What is *process color*?

- What is *color trapping*?

- How can you achieve consistent color from scan to printer?

- How can you achieve the effect of multiple colors on a limited budget?

USING COLOR WISELY

Color is a very powerful element in design. When used properly, color enhances the effectiveness of the printed page. Used improperly, color can be a distraction. Effective use of color is a skill that takes time to develop. Unfortunately, many beginning designers tend to misuse color. Here are a few simple guidelines to help you make good decisions concerning color.

1. *Use color sparingly*—When it comes to color, less is more. Color on a black-and-white page is so powerful you don't need to use a lot of it. It's far better to under-use color than to overuse it.

Color is a very powerful element in design. When used properly, color enhances the effectiveness of the printed page. Used improperly, color can be a distraction.

2. *Put color where it counts*—When you're using color for accent, remember that even the most subtle color will attract the eye more quickly than black will. With that in mind, it's important to apply color where you want to create visual emphasis. Color is very useful for creating a focal point on a page. It's also good for headlines, subheads, and captions, since these are generally the typographic elements that the reader scans first while browsing through a publication. Using color in illustrative elements such as drawings and photos is also effective.

3. *Use color to create mood*—Color can add emotional impact to a page layout. "Hot" colors such as red, orange, and yellow are action colors—they create visual excitement. These colors might be used to create a mood for an article on a circus or a chili cookoff. Conversely, "cool" colors like blue, green, and purple tend to be tranquil and passive. You might use them to set the tone for a book of meditative poetry or a new age album cover.

The hue and shade of color can influence mood as well. For example, pastel colors tend to be soft and "feminine." Pure, clear colors are generally more active, while muted or grayed colors tend to be conservative and passive.

Creators of advertising have long studied color psychology. They know how important color is in influencing the consumer's opinion of a product. For example, you won't see an ad for menthol cigarettes sporting vibrant orange or flaming red. That kind of ad will always use a blue or green color scheme to emphasize the coolness of the product. Similarly, the next time you stroll through the aisles of your supermarket, notice how many packages feature bright colors such as yellow and red. These colors are arresting; they command your attention in a very competitive environment. There have even been studies that conclude that these active colors enhance one's appetite.

Professional designers and art directors never take color for granted. Selecting colors should not be a capricious decision, but should be based on strategy and a sense of what's appropriate.

"Hot" colors create visual excitement,
while "cool" colors tend to be tranquil and passive.

4. *Use color to organize*—Color can also be useful in organizing information. For example, you might use different colors to separate elements such as bars in a graph, or to color-code sections of a book or catalog. You might put a block of text against a color field to tell the reader that the text is separate from the main body of an article. You might use a color rule to highlight the beginning of a new section of text or apply color to emphasize important elements such as subheads.

HOW YOUR COMPUTER HANDLES COLOR

Let's imagine for a moment that you create a color document on your computer, then send it off to a commercial printer. When the printed documents are delivered, you discover to your dismay that the colors you created on your computer screen don't bear much resemblance to those on the printed page. Unfortunately, this is not an uncommon experience for desktop publishers. While technology has gone a long way toward solving this problem, the underlying cause remains the same: each device in your computer system displays color in a different way. For example, your computer monitor is an RGB device. Your monitor displays color by transmitting colored light and mixes color by varying the intensities of three colors: red, green, and blue (R,G & B). Because you're viewing pure colored light on your monitor, colors tend to look pure and bright. The printing press uses a different color model entirely. It's based on four colors: cyan, magenta, yellow, and black (CMYK). (Seems like it should be CMYB, doesn't it? But to printers, K stands for black.) To print a four-color photograph, colors are applied one on top of another in varying shades until the desired color is achieved. Since what you view on your screen and what you see on the printed page are based on entirely different color models, there is bound to be a difference in the way color is perceived. But it gets even worse. Each printing device—color copiers, color laserwriters, printing presses—use different methods to apply color to a page. You could print your document several different way and get several different results.

This might not be a big deal for some kinds of publications but for those that require accurate color it can be a disaster. In response to this problem, a variety of color management tools have been developed, some hardware and some software. These tools are designed to even out the color variation as your document proceeds through the publishing process.

Perhaps the most widely embraced color management system is EfiColor developed by EFI. EfiColor translates the color characteristics of one device to another, for example between your particular monitor and your particular brand of color printer. EFI has developed color profiles for the most popular computer devices. When you specify your monitor and printer type, the EfiColor software makes allowances for any inaccuracies inherent in the translation of color information between these devices. EfiColor software is built into QuarkXPress (versions 3.2 or later). With Eficolor you can feel reasonably confident that the colors you see on your monitor in QuarkXPress will be what you get on the printed page. This system is by no means foolproof but it is a big improvement.

USING EFICOLOR

Using EfiColor isn't particularly complicated unless you're using a lot of different devices. If you consistently use the same monitor and color printer, it's fairly simple. The first step is to let EfiColor know which monitor and printer you're using. In the Applications Preferences dialog box you'll see a checkbox labeled Display Correction. When this box is checked, it activates a pop-up menu that displays a wide choice of monitors. Find your monitor in the list and select it. If you don't see your monitor listed you can probably add a profile for your device at a nominal cost. A profile is simply a software module that contains color data for a particular printer. EFI profiles can be purchased separately from the EfiColor software. Contact Quark or EFI for more information.

Next, you need to select a printer. You'll need to remember to do this when you're ready to print. In the Page Setup dialog box, there is a pop-up menu labeled Printer Type. Find your printer in the list and select it. Just under the Printer Type menu there's another menu labeled EfiColor Profile. Select the printing device's profile from the list.

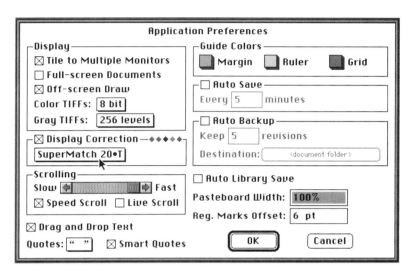

FIGURE 7.1   Select an EfiColor profile for your monitor in the Application Preferences dialog box.

Under the EfiColor Profile menu is yet another menu labeled GCR. GCR stands for Gray Component Removal. GCR is a process by which neutral grays that are made up of combinations of cyan, magenta, and yellow in a color image are replaced by tints of black in order to reduce the amount of ink on the page. If you're a real pre-press expert and want to specify GCR values before color separations are made, this is where you do it. Be sure to check with your printer first. He will have some definite ideas about how to set this up for his printing equipment.

Finally, if you're creating color separations directly from QuarkXPress, you have the option of selecting EFI's screen values over Quark's default values. Just check the box in the lower right corner labeled Use EfiColor Screen Values. Screen values are the angle, frequency, and dot shapes within a halftone screen. This only applies if you're outputting pictures as film halftones or color separations. Both Quark and EFI have built-in screen values and they are slightly different. I've found the EFI screen values to be excellent so I leave this box checked but you may want to experiment to see if you prefer one over the other.

You'll also need to tell EfiColor about the pictures you're importing into your QuarkXPress document. At the bottom of the Get Picture dialog box there are two pop-up menus. One is labeled EfiColor Profile and the other is labeled Rendering Style. In the EfiColor Profile menu, select a profile that best describes how the file was saved. For example, if the picture is an RGB image, select RGB profile, for CMYK choose SWOP-coated. For the most part, EfiColor senses the kind of image you're importing and offers appropriate choices in the list.

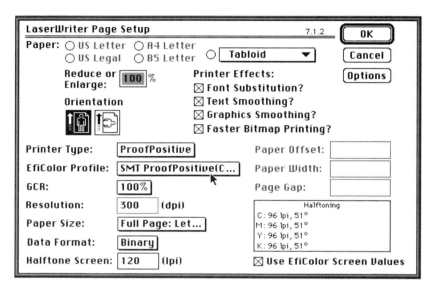

FIGURE 7.2 Select a printing device and EfiColor profile in the Page Setup dialog box.

You also have two choices of rendering style. Choose Photographic for scanned photos and other continuous tone images. Solid Color is for art that is composed of primarily flat even colors such as a color logo or type.

APPLYING COLOR WITH QUARKXPRESS

In QuarkXPress you can apply color to type, to rules and boxes, and to black-and-white pictures. You can also import color pictures into your document and, if you have a color monitor and printer, view and print them in color.

Before we discuss applying color in QuarkXPress, it's important to understand the difference between *spot color* and *process color*. Spot color is a single solid color or a tint of one color that you apply to elements of your layout. Process color is color that is created by using combinations of magenta, cyan, yellow, and black. Process color can be used in color tints or art or photos that are imported into your document; the common factor is that all process color must be separated into its four components in order to print accurately.

Each time you open a document in QuarkXPress, you'll see a color palette that contains all the colors used in that document. You can add to the palette or edit it at any time. To make changes to a document's color palette, use the Colors dialog box, found under the Edit menu. Take a moment now to open the Colors dialog box. You'll see a palette of default colors along the left side. (See Figure 7.3.)

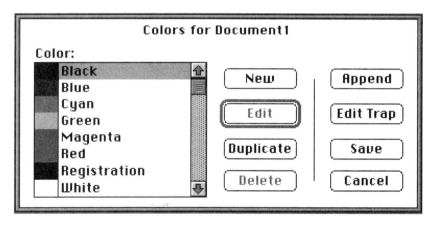

FIGURE 7.3 You can edit, add, or append colors to the document color palette in the Colors dialog box.

In the Colors dialog box, there is a series of buttons that let you create new colors, edit existing colors, duplicate and delete colors, and append them from another QuarkXPress document.

Click the New button to bring up the Edit Color dialog box. This box offers even more choices. When working with color in QuarkXpress, you can simulate different kinds of color models. The Model menu offers the following choices.

- *HSB*—This color model lets you mix color, similar to the way artists mix paint. Hue refers to the pigment color. Saturation is the amount of pigment in the color. Brightness is the amount of black mixed with the pigment color.

- *RGB*—This model represents color as you would see it on a video screen. In video, red, green, and blue light are mixed to create the colors in the spectrum.

- *CMYK*—This is the color model used by commercial printers. All continuous tone color in printing is composed of combinations of the four process colors. CMYK stands for cyan, magenta, yellow, and black. Use the CMYK model document for process color printing.

- *PANTONE*®—PANTONE colors are premixed spot colors. PANTONE refers to the PANTONE Matching System (PMS), the ink system most widely used by commercial printers. Each color in the system is assigned a number; you specify the color you want the printer to use in your document by specifying its PMS number. Clicking PANTONE in QuarkXPress will display the palette of PMS colors instead of the color wheel. The PANTONE model should be used to specify spot colors for commercial printing, but be careful—always pick the actual colors from a PMS swatchbook because the colors on your screen are not an accurate representation of the real color.

- *TOYO and DIC*—These are Japanese color systems that have come into wider international use. They are color matching systems specifically for spot colors and have one useful advantage over those mentioned above: each color indicates how closely it can be matched with CMYK process colors. Since a spot color system has a much wider range of color than can be produced with just the four process colors, not all spot colors can be accurately reproduced in process printing. Some are a little off and others you would hardly recognize. Each color swatch in these two systems that falls outside the CMYK gamut has one or two asterisks next to the name. One asterisk indicates that it cannot be closely matched in process printing. Two asterisks mean forget it, it won't even be close.

- *TRUMATCH*™ *and FOCOLTONE*®—Version 3.1 of QuarkXPress adds these two new color models. TRUMATCH is a color system designed to produce accurate process color when output on PostScript imagesetters. FOCOLTONE is a similar system, but is geared more toward commercial process color printing. It is designed to reduce the number of trapping and registration problems. Since the colors you see on the screen may not be accurate, both systems should be used with their respective color charts (available from the manufacturers).

- *PANTONE Process*—This is a CMYK process color system developed by PANTONE and includes a wide range of process color combinations.

- *PANTONE ProSim*—This color system is designed to simulate PANTONE spot colors in CMYK.

- *PANTONE Uncoated*—Since ink colors can change slightly when printed on uncoated papers, PANTONE developed this version of their spot color system to give you a better idea of how the colors will look on a non-glossy paper.

If you create a new color and want to print it as a process color you must name it something other than Red, Green, or Blue. QuarkXPress automatically defaults these names to the RGB model and will print them as spot colors.

NOTE

Depending upon the color model you choose, you can select or create colors in the Edit Color dialog box in a variety of ways. (See Figure 7.4.) When using the HSB or RGB models, you can enter a numerical value in the color definition fields or you can use the scroll bars to customize a color. The horizontal scroll bars let you adjust the intensity of the color mix. The vertical scroll bar adjusts the brightness—slide it up to increase brightness and down to decrease brightness. Near the center of the dialog box is a box labeled New on its top half, and Old on its bottom half. When you make color adjustments, the new color will be displayed in the New section of the box. When you're editing an existing color, the original color will be displayed in the bottom of the box so you can see how the color has changed.

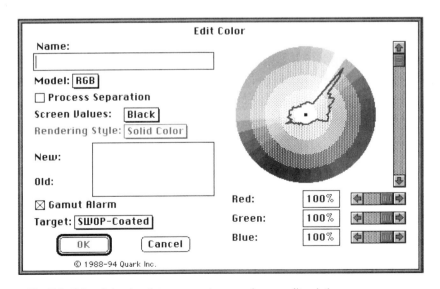

FIGURE 7.4 The Edit Color dialog box lets you create new colors or edit existing ones.

In addition to using the numerical fields and the scroll bars, you can pick a color from the color wheel. Move the pointer over the wheel; it will change to a crosshair pointer. Then click on the desired color. The color appears in the New/Old box, and its values automatically appear in the numerical fields. You can't use the color wheel, however, for CMYK or PANTONE colors.

The check box in the Process Separation area lets you specify whether your color is a spot color or process color. Turning Process Separation on specifies the color as process, and it will be separated into CMYK. Turning Process Separation off makes it a spot color and it will print a single plate for that color when it's output.

Once you've created your color, you'll need to give it a name. You can name it whatever you want; once you click OK that name will appear next to the color in your document's color palette.

Editing an existing color is done in much the same way as creating a new one. In the Color dialog box, click Edit and a new dialog box appears, you then select the name of a color from your document's color palette. Once you open the color, the Edit Color dialog box appears again, but this time the name of the color appears in the Name field. You can then alter the values of the color, comparing the new with the old in the New/Old box. Once you're satisfied with the change, click OK and the new color is available from your color palette.

There are two ways to select PANTONE colors. Bring up the Edit Color dialog box, select PANTONE from the Model pop-up menu and browse through the PANTONE Color Selector using the scroll bar. Once you've found the color you want, select it and its name appears in the name field and the color is shown in the New/Old box. If you already know the number of the PMS color you want, type it into the PANTONE Number field and QuarkXPress automatically scrolls to the color.

You can also use the Colors dialog box to append (add) a color from another document's color palette. For example, suppose you've created a custom color called Peach Parfait in another document. You then decide the design you're currently working on could use exactly that color. Rather than having to recreate the color, you can "borrow" the color palette from the other document. To do this, click Append in the Colors dialog box. This will give you a new dialog box. Find and select the document from which you want to append the color. Click Open, and your current document's palette will include Peach Parfait as well as all the other colors from the appended color palette.

TRAPPING COLOR

When placing two or more colors against each other, you need to overlap the colors slightly to compensate for misregistration on press. This is called *trapping*, and it applies to both spot and process colors. Without an adequate trap, you may see a thin white line between the colors when the piece is printed. (See Figure 7.5.) Discovering this after the piece has been printed can be very annoying (and very costly if your client is displeased). Fortunately, you can adjust trapping values in QuarkXPress.

QuarkXPress offers great control over color trapping. This is very important since trapping values vary depending upon the printing process, the paper, and the kind of printing press your document will run on. Printing processes like silkscreen, for instance, are notorious for being inaccurate and require very large traps, while offset printing on a glossy coated stock requires a much smaller trap.

FIGURE 7.5 The example on the left shows a correct trap, with enough overlap to compensate for plate misregistration. The one on the right shows what can happen if there is no trap or if the trap is too narrow.

In QuarkXPress you can specify trapping values either to the colors themselves or to individual objects within your document. To alter the trapping values of colors, use the Colors dialog box in the Edit menu. In the Colors dialog box, select the color to be altered from the list on the left. Click the Edit Trap button and a new dialog box, called Trap Specifications, appears.

In the Trap Specifications dialog box there are two columns. The column on the left, labeled Background Color, lists all the colors in your color palette. On the right, the column labeled Default lists the trapping values for each color. A numerical value indicates that the color's automatic trapping value has been overridden by a custom value. If a color's value says Automatic, QuarkXPress's automatic trapping values are in place.

The value of some colors might say *Overprint*. Because most printing inks are transparent, any color that exists underneath a color to be printed will show through. Normally, in order to avoid contaminating the color to be printed, the area under that color is "knocked out." This means that all underlying color is eliminated so that the white of the paper is all that's behind the color. *Knockouts* are what makes trapping necessary. Occasionally, however, you may want to create a special effect by overlapping colors, and to do that you must specify that the color is to overprint.

Once you select a color from the list, the Automatic, Overprint, and Trap buttons become active. To apply the default trapping values to the selected color, click the Auto button. To specify that the color is to overprint the color under it, click Overprint. To apply custom trapping values, type a value between -36 and 36, in increments as small as .001 pt, into the Trap field. A negative value will reduce the knockout area of the background color (called a *"choke"*); a positive value will enlarge the object color so that there is a larger overlap over the knockout (called a *"spread"*). Click the button labeled Trap, and the new value should appear in the list next to the color.

Sometimes the background color in a document is indeterminate—not a single color, but a variety of colors, such as when you are printing color type over a color photo. If the Automatic trapping values are applied to a color object to be printed on an indeterminate color, the object's background will be knocked out without trapping unless a value is specified in the Trapping Preferences dialog box. This also applies to backgrounds made up of a variety of individually-colored items.

If you're using QuarkXPress 3.1 or later, you can take advantage of some new and more precise trapping features. First, you can specify the way QuarkXPress applies trapping values by using the controls in the Trapping Preferences dialog box. Go to the Edit menu and select Preferences. From the Preferences menu, choose Trapping. This displays the Trapping Preferences dialog box. In the dialog box is the *Auto Method* pop-up menu. This menu gives you two choices: *Absolute* and

Proportional. These are two formulas for creating traps automatically. If you choose Absolute, QuarkXPress will automatically apply the trapping value specified in the Auto Amount field to either the background color as a choke or to the object color as a spread, depending on which value is darker. If you choose Proportional, QuarkXPress will use a fraction of the Auto Amount based on the difference in value between the object and background color (Auto Amount x object darkness–background darkness). Entering a value in the Auto Amount field specifies the default trapping value.

You can specify a default for trapping against an indeterminate background by entering a value in the Indeterminate field. In the Overprint Limit field you can specify a percentage at or above which an object color will automatically overprint its background color.

Version 3.1 includes another handy feature called the Trap Information palette. Go to the View menu and select Show Trap Information. (See Figure 7.6.)

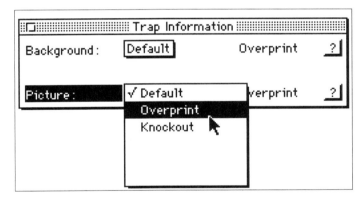

FIGURE 7.6 Use the Trap Information palette to specify trapping values.

In the Trap Information palette you'll see two pop-up menus, a field, and a button. The labels will change depending upon what kind of item is active, but you have six options available in this palette: Default, Overprint, Knockout, Auto Amount (+), Auto Amount (–), and Custom. Use the pop-up menus to choose your trapping options. Select Default if you want to use the preset value in QuarkXPress; that value will be displayed in the field in the upper-right corner of the palette (click on the button with the question mark while holding down the mouse button to display information about trapping values). Choose Overprint if you want to eliminate the knockout under the object. If you want the background color to knock out under the object without trapping, select Knockout. To trap using the Auto Amount values preset in the Application Preferences dialog box, choose Auto Amount (+), which will create a spread; or Auto Amount (–), which will create a choke. Finally, to create a custom trapping value, choose Custom and enter any value between -36 and 36 in the field. Trapping values can only be applied to elements created within QuarkXPress such as rules or boxes. These values have no affect on imported graphic images.

APPLYING COLOR TO GRAPHIC ELEMENTS

In QuarkXPress you can apply color to elements such as type, rules, and boxes. Once you've created a color palette for your document, applying the colors is very simple. To apply color to type or rules, select the element to be modified and choose Color from the Style menu. A sub-menu displaying your color palette appears. Choose a color by highlighting it. To adjust the precise shade or saturation of the color, choose Shade from the Style menu. When the sub-menu appears, select a percentage from the list, or choose Other to enter a custom value.

SHORTCUT

Here's a shortcut for applying color uniformly to a number of elements at the same time. Select all the elements to which you want to apply color and group them by selecting Group from the Item menu. Once the elements are grouped, select Modify from the Item menu, and the Group Specifications dialog box appears. Select a color from the menu, and it will be applied to all the elements within the group uniformly. You can also specify color as a style sheet attribute.

When applying color to rules, you also have the option of using the Modify command in the Item menu. The dialog box contains the other line specifications as well as color controls. This is a convenient way to change several values of a rule at the same time—for instance, both color and width—since all values can be accessed through this particular dialog box.

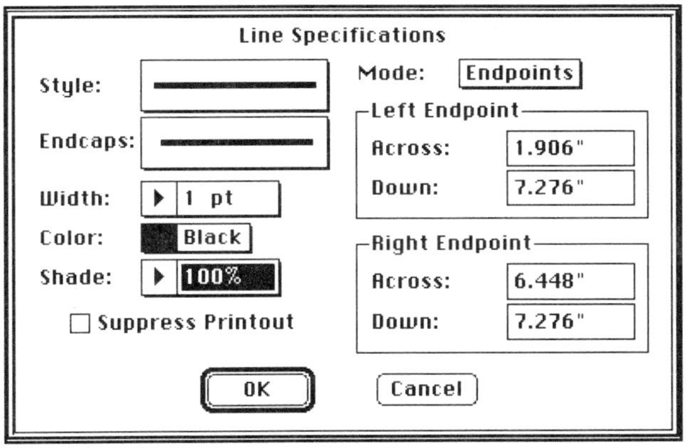

FIGURE 7.7 Use the Line Specifications dialog box to specify color as well as other line attributes.

You can use the Modify command to apply color to box backgrounds. To do this, activate the box to which you want to apply color and select Modify from the Item menu. When the dialog box appears, choose a color from the Background Color pop-up menu. This is an easy way to create a tint block as a background if you want to emphasize a section of text. The dialog box also lets you specify the shade. Consider using a light tint—usually between 5 and 20%, depending on the strength of the color—if you want the text to read well. You can make the background of a box clear by choosing None in the Background Color menu. If you make the box's background clear, any elements behind the box will show through. This is useful if you want to print type over a picture.

To apply color to a box frame, activate the box and choose Frame from the Item menu. When the Frame Specifications dialog box appears, choose a color from the Color pop-up menu.

APPLYING COLOR TO PICTURES

In QuarkXPress, you can apply color to pictures imported into your document if they are black-and-white bitmap images, TIFF or RIFF line art, or TIFF or RIFF grayscale pictures. You can apply color uniformly to line art images or to the shadows and middle tones of grayscale images. You can also apply color to the background of a picture box. This creates an interesting effect, with color showing through the black and gray tones of the picture.

189

To apply color to an imported picture, select the picture, and with the Content Tool selected, choose Color from the Style menu. (See Figure 7.8.) Choose a color from the palette. Use the Shade command to control the color saturation. (The Shade command is available only when the picture box contains a bitmap or TIFF image.)

Applying color to the background of a picture box is just like adding a background color to a text box. Select the picture box, then choose Modify from the Edit menu. When the Picture Box Specifications dialog box appears, select a color from the Color pop-up menu. Click OK, and the color will appear in the picture box.

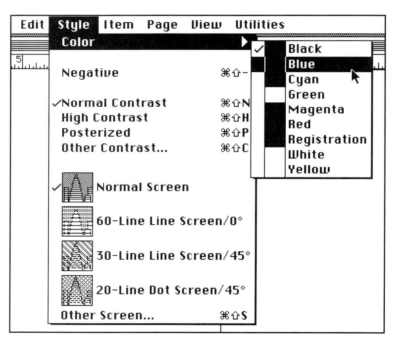

FIGURE 7.8 Apply color to pictures by selecting Color in the Style menu.

THE COLORS PALETTE

There's an easier way to apply color than using the menus. QuarkXPress features color controls in a palette that you can keep open on your desktop. Go to the View menu and select Show Colors. (See Figure 7.9.)

Along the top of the Colors palette is a series of icons. At the far left is a symbol that looks like a frame. This, not surprisingly, is the Frame icon. To the right of the Frame icon is one you'll recognize—either the Text Box or Picture Box icon, depending on which type of box is active. To the right of that is the Background icon, and finally, the Shade pop-up menu. Underneath all that is a scroll list displaying your document's color palette.

To specify a color for a box frame, select the box in your document, then click on the Frame icon in the Colors palette. Then choose a color from the scroll list and select a shade from the pop-up menu. What could be easier? Well, believe it or not, it can be easier. With the Item tool selected in the Tool palette and the Frame icon selected in the Colors palette, click on the color swatch in the Colors palette and, holding down the mouse button, drag the color swatch to the selected box frame and release the button. The color will be applied automatically.

FIGURE 7.9

The Colors palette provides a quick and easy way to apply color to your document.

Similarly, to apply color to the contents of a picture box or a text box, click on the Background icon. Then click on the appropriate box and select a color and a shade or drag the color swatch over the box and select a shade. When you selected the background icon, the Colors palette gained some new controls. There's a pop-up menu that allows you to choose between a solid color and a linear blend. A *solid color* is a background color that is uniform in color and shade. A *linear blend* is a color gradation from light to dark and/or from one color into another.

To create a linear blend, activate a text box or picture box and select Linear Blend from the pop-up menu in the Colors palette. Selecting Linear Blend activates controls that let you specify not only the two colors used in the blend, but also the angle of the blend. You'll notice two radio buttons, labeled #1 and #2. Clicking the

#1 button lets you choose the first color for your blend from the color palette, and clicking the #2 button lets you choose the second color. Remember that you have the option of selecting None instead of a second color. Do this if you want the first color to simply fade into the background. (Note: In order to display both colors in your blend, the Item tool must be selected and the box activated.)

With the Cool Blends XTension installed in your QuarkXPress folder you can also create Mid-Linear, Rectangular, Diamond, Circular, and Full Circular blends.

In addition to selecting colors, you need to select the angle of the blend. Do this by typing a value between -360° and 360° in the angle field.

NOTE

When importing an EPS graphic that contains spot colors into your layout, the new spot colors will be added automatically to the colors palette. Take care that the imported colors do not have the same name as those already in the colors list for that document unless you actually want them to be printed in the same color. For example, if you want a special shade of magenta to be printed as a special spot color, don't call it Magenta or QuarkXPress will automatically print it in process Magenta.

GETTING THE MOST COLOR ON A LIMITED PRINTING BUDGET

Ifyou're planning to have your document printed professionally, keep in mind that color can be expensive. Each color you add can significantly increase production costs. It's always a good idea to consult with your printer if your design uses a lot of color, as printers can be very helpful in showing you ways to keep costs down.

In general, four-color process printing is considerably more expensive than black-and-white or two-color (two-color printing usually refers to black plus one spot color). If your budget allows for only one spot color in addition to black, consider using a variety of shades of the color to create a multicolor effect. Depending on the color you choose, a light tint can take on the character of a completely differ-ent color. You can also use shades of black to create grays.

SUMMARY

In this chapter we discussed how to use color effectively as well as how to actually apply color within a QuarkXPress document. Based on the material in this chapter, answer the following questions.

1. List four guidelines for using color effectively.

2. What is the difference between spot color and process color?

3. What are the four process colors?

4. What are the color models available in the Edit Colors dialog box?

5. What is *trapping*?

6. What's the difference between a *choke* and a *spread*?

7. What's a *knockout*?

8. Describe how you would apply color to text in a QuarkXPress document.

9. What is a *linear blend*?

CHAPTER EIGHT

Working with Printers

A book about graphic design wouldn't be complete without a chapter on printing. After all, a designer's job is to create documents specifically to be printed. Think of printing as the last step in the design process. Your job isn't finished until you have the final printed piece in your hand. Therefore, it's absolutely fundamental that you understand how the printing process works and what printing techniques are available to you. This chapter will answer these questions.

- Why do you need to learn about printing?

- When you talk to your printer it is sometimes difficult to understand what he or she is saying. What does all this talk about *signatures*, *bluelines*, and *hickeys* mean?

- What is *offset printing* and how does it work?

- How do you prepare a document for printing?

- What's a *halftone*?

- What do you need to know about working with a service bureau?

- How do you pick the best paper for your publication?

- Is there some way you can see what the printed piece will look like before it's actually printed?

- Your printer has suggested that you check the job on press. What kind of things should you look for?

- How do you determine the binding technique that's right for your publication?

THE PRINTER'S LANGUAGE

Most printers in this country are bilingual. They speak English, but they occasionally lapse into a mysterious language known only to other printers. What's more, if they sense you don't speak their language they may try to pull the proverbial wool over your eyes. A printer may tell you: Sure, the press sheet doesn't look that good, but there are problems with misregistration due to paper stretch. That he's been chasing slitter dust hickeys and there are ghosts on the sheet and moirés in the duotones. There's nothing he can do. He'll talk like this until your eyes glaze over and you find yourself saying, "Well…if that's really the best you can do…" as you sign your approval on the press sheet. Granted, only the most unscrupulous pressman behaves this way, but believe me, it does happen.

However, if you can respond with a repartee in his own language, perhaps even making suggestions as to how to fix the problems, you'll be surprised how his attitude changes. This chapter provides a crash course in the language of the pressman. Here are some of the most common words.

Accordion fold—A series of folds alternating in different directions like a pleat.

Assembly—Final positioning of all the elements in a publication in preparation for plating.

Backbone—The binding edge or spine of a book, booklet, or brochure.

Basis weight—The weight or substance of a ream of paper in its base size.

Binding—The method of securing the pages at the fold or spine of a publication.

Blanket—In offset printing, the rubber sheet to which an image is transferred before being applied to the paper.

Blanket cylinder—On an offset press, the cylinder on which the blanket is carried.

Bleed—Printed matter that runs off the edge of a finished printed piece.

Blind emboss—A technique in which an image is embossed without ink or foil.

Blueline—An inexpensive proof made by exposing Dylux paper to ultraviolet light.

Case binding—The binding method used for hardback books featuring a squared-off spine.

Cast coating—A coating on a sheet of paper, characterized by a hard, extremely high-gloss finish.

Chalking—A drying problem characterized by a chalky substance on the surface of the printed paper.

Coarse screen—A halftone screen used on newsprint and other porous papers. A coarse screen is generally considered to be anything up to 85 lines per inch.

Coated paper/coated stock—Paper that has been treated with a clay coating to make a smooth hard surface. Most glossy papers fall into this category.

Color bar—A color strip made up of small blocks of ink color in varying densities. The color bar is printed along one edge of the printed sheet and is used to monitor color consistency across the sheet.

Color correction—The alteration of color in a color separation.

Color separations—The process of separating a color picture into the four process colors.

Color swatch—A sample of ink color given to the printer to match.

Contact screen—The screen used to create a halftone.

Cromalin—A dry proofing system.

Cyan—A special blue used in process printing. One of the four process colors.

Damper—Rollers on an offset press that bring water to the printing plate.

Densitometer—An optical instrument used to read the densities of film or inks on the press sheet.

Density—The relative lightness or heaviness of film emulsion or ink color on paper.

Die cutting—A process by which a shape is cut out of paper using a metal die.

Dot etching—A process by which tones are corrected on a negative by etching the emulsion with acid.

Dot gain—The tendency for halftone dots to increase in size through the reproduction process.

Double truck—Two facing pages; a page spread.

Draw down—A strip of ink spread across the surface of a paper intended to test the ink color before it goes into the press.

Drop-out blue/non-photo blue—A shade of light blue that is invisible to litho film.

Dummy—A sample of a job made up of actual materials, intended to show the correct size, paper, and binding method.

Duotone—Two halftones of the same image shot at different densities and printed over each other to produce a wider tonal range. Often one of the halftones is printed in black and the other in color to produce a color effect.

Emulsion—A light-sensitive coating applied to lithographic film and plates.

Final film—The film used for making printing plates. It includes all the elements, such as type, halftones, and line art, that will appear on the final printed sheet.

Finishing—Any operation performed after printing, such as binding, embossing, or foil stamping.

Foil stamping—A method in which an image is transferred to paper by heating foil and applying it under pressure against the sheet with a metal die.

Four-color process—A color printing process in which color is formed by superimposing various densities of the four process colors (cyan, magenta, yellow, and black) on top of one another.

Gate fold—A method in which pages are folded into the center from both sides to form a double gate.

Ghosting—A streaking that occurs on the press sheet as a result of non-uniform application of ink.

Gripper edge—A non-printing area along one edge of the paper, reserved for the gripping mechanism that pulls the sheet through the press.

Halftone—A process in which a continuous tone is simulated by separating a photograph into a pattern of small dots that vary in density depending on the tone (the lighter the tone, the smaller the dot).

Imposition—The arrangement of the pages of a book or brochure on the press sheet so that when the press sheet is folded all the pages will be in proper order.

Impression—The act of transferring an image onto paper.

Letterpress printing—One of the original methods of printing. Ink is applied to a raised metal surface and then transferred to paper by contact and pressure.

Line art—Artwork that is entirely black on white, with no middle or gray tones.

Make ready—Preparation of the printing press before the print run starts. It includes such procedures as inking, hanging plates, and loading paper.

Matchprint—A dry proofing method that simulates what the page will look like when printed..

Moiré—An undesirable pattern in a halftone caused by improperly set screen angles.

Negative—A photographic film or paper used in the reproduction process in which all values are reversed.

Offset—The most common method of printing, in which an image is offset onto a rubber blanket before being transferred to paper.

Overs—A quantity of printed pieces over and above the specified quantity.

Perfect binding—A binding process in which the signatures are gathered and the back trimmed and glued before a cover is applied.

Perfecting—A process in which both sides of the sheet of paper are printed at the same time.

Picking—Damage caused to the surface of the printed sheet during printing due to a defective paper surface or ink that is too sticky.

Plate—A metal plate upon which the printing image is applied, then mounted on a cylinder on the press. It is used to transfer ink to the blanket in an offset press.

Press proof—A proof made by actually printing a test sheet with the proper inks and paper.

Ream—A unit of paper, usually 500 sheets.

Register—Proper alignment of printed color images.

Register marks—Marks, usually lines or crosses, placed in exactly the same position on each plate. When these marks are perfectly aligned on the printed sheet, the forms are in perfect register.

Reverse—To make a positive image white so that it will be legible against a dark area.

Saddle stitching—A common binding process for booklets and brochures, where the pages are bound together with thin wire-like staples.

Scanner—An electronic device that produces halftones and color separations by scanning artwork with a laser or other bright light, reading the tonal densities, and translating the information to digital form.

Sheet-fed—A press that prints individually cut sheets of paper one sheet at a time.

Signature—A group of folded pages within a publication. Multi-page documents are printed on large sheets that are folded into signatures, usually 8, 16, or 32 pages in length. These signatures are gathered together and assembled in the binding process.

Step and repeat—A menu command in QuarkXPress that places an image at precise predetermined intervals. This method is also used in printing to accurately place multiple identical documents on the same sheet of paper.

Stripping—The process of assembling final film for plating.

Web offset—High-speed printing used for long runs such as newspapers and magazines. As opposed to sheed fed, web presses feed the paper through the press in a continuous ribbon from large rolls rather than individual sheets.

Now that you're familiar with basic printing terminology, let's move on to some actual printing techniques. There are numerous methods of printing available, and the method you choose will be dictated by the type of publication you're working on, your printing budget, and the quantity you need. Let's consider some of the options.

ELECTRONIC PRINTING

Working on the computer makes it possible to send your publication directly to an electronic printer such as a laser printer. The laser printer is widely used to print limited quantities of low-end publications like internal communications, newsletters, and flyers. If you've worked with a laser printer, you're probably already aware of what it can and can't do. Its principle advantage is immediacy. Instead of sending your job off to a commercial printer and waiting a week or two to see the result, you can have a printed product in a matter of minutes. At 300 dpi, however, the quality of a laser print is poor, and it's limited to black and white. Some laser printers can produce output af 600 dpi or even 1200 dpi. Desktop color printers are also available, but they're expensive and the quality still falls far short of commercial printing. With both types of printers, you're also limited in your choice of paper.

However, electronic printing is great for proofing your work and presenting visual concepts to clients. Considering that the old method was to create a model by hand with color markers, laser printing is a real time saver and produces much more complete results.

QUICK PRINTING

There is an entire industry made up of printers that specialize in small, one- or two-color publications. Because these companies need less equipment and have lower overhead than the big printers, they are generally more economical for small jobs. In fact, if you need 1,000 copies or less of a standard-size two-color newsletter, a small printer is definitely the way to go. As a bonus, their turnaround is usually quick. However, there are a few things watch out for:

1. *Inconsistent quality*—Quick printers are notorious for wide variations in quality. Often the people running the press have little actual printing experience. These businesses also tend to have a high turnover, so the person who may have done a great job running your last project may no longer be there or may not be assigned to your current job.

Also, small firms sometimes use inferior materials in order to keep costs down. For example, it's not uncommon for them to use paper plates, which are not as precise and are less stable than metal plates. Before you hire any printer, ask to see samples of their work.

2. *Inconsistent pricing*—Don't assume that all printers are comparable in their pricing. Pricing can vary greatly, so shop around. Fortunately, quick printers often publish price lists. If you encounter one that doesn't, get a firm quote before you give them the job.

3. *Limited paper selection*—Because they're small, quick printers don't carry a large paper inventory. If you want quick turnaround, you'll have to settle for paper the printer has on hand. Generally, these papers are inexpensive and they look it. Most printers can order special paper, but expect the cost to go up, sometimes dramatically.

4. *Limited capabilities*—Keep your job simple. Don't give a quick printer anything unusual or complicated. Stick to small formats and standard sizes and inks. Don't expect them to do such things as foil stamping or wire binding.

COMMERCIAL PRINTERS

If your job requires real craftsmanship or must be reproduced in large quantities, find a commercial printer with large presses and a reputation for doing quality work. Since there is often a great deal of money at stake, it's worth taking the time to find out who does the best work and has the best reputation for service. Here are some guidelines to selecting a commercial printer:

1. *Find the right printer for the job*—Not all printers are alike. Unlike small printers, who tend to take on a wide variety of jobs, larger printers often specialize; for example, some may primarily do packaging, others annual reports. Although any printer will probably be happy to bid on your project, try to take advantage of a printer's particular strengths. Avoid giving a printer a project that may not be ideally suited for them. Over time, try to build a stable of printers that you can depend on. Maintain records of who does what, and keep equipment lists on file. Before you add any new printers to the file, meet with a sales representative, look at samples of their work, and try to tour the plant. This may seem like a lot of trouble, but printing is a crucial step in the process. A printer can torpedo all your hard work if they don't know what they're doing.

2. *Always shop around*—Just as printers' equipment and capabilities can vary, so can their pricing. Fitting the job to the printer usually results in a better price. Also, although they may talk about computerized estimating, printers' prices tend to go up when they're busy. (I know of one printer that specializes in annual reports. During annual report season their pricing is exorbitant, but when business slows after the annual report rush, they practically give their services away just to keep the presses busy.) Always get competitive bids, but make sure it's a fair competition. Select three printers with similar capabilities and let them know they're bidding against one another. It keeps them honest and can help you get the best possible deal.

3. *Take a good look at their capabilities*—Some printers offer a lot of services within their plant, while others job out a lot of the work. For example, many printers have a press room and only minimal prepress facilities. Their color separations and film preparation are bought outside, and the finishing work is sent out to a trade bindery. This is a common way for printers to work, but for some jobs you may prefer to have everything done under one roof. For example, if you're on a tight deadline, you could easily lose a day out of your schedule if the film needs to be sent back out to be reworked.

*Designing a publication without a thorough understanding of
printing makes as much sense as an architect designing buildings
without understanding how they're constructed.*

ESTABLISH A WORKING RELATIONSHIP WITH YOUR PRINTERS

Working with printers should be a creative collaboration. It can be extremely helpful to consult with a printer when your design is still in its infancy. If you want to
achieve a certain kind of look in your design, the printer can offer suggestions
about how to achieve it. Especially if you're considering something experimental,
it's far better to consult the printer early in the process. The last thing you want is
to sell an idea to a client and find out on press that it doesn't work. This can be
very embarrassing, not to mention expensive. Developing close working relationships with printers can be tremendously educational. Most designers learn about
print production not from design school, but from working closely with printers
over a number of years. So think of it as an ongoing apprenticeship, and don't
make the mistake of assuming that a printer has nothing to teach you.

DESIGN FOR PRINTING

It may seem obvious that a designer should design with printing in mind, but
most printers will be more than happy to bend your ear about all the times they've
had to deal with designs that were impossible to print. And here's another good
reason to consult with a printer early in the process: Even if your design is print-
able, can it be produced within budget? A lot of things can influence the cost,
including the number of colors, the size, the paper, the quantity, the complexity,
the number and size of pictures, and the type of binding. This is why it's so important to understand what will happen to your job once you turn it over to the printer.
Designing a publication without a thorough understanding of printing makes as
much sense as an architect designing buildings without understanding how they're
constructed.

Working with printers should be a creative collaboration. It can be extremely helpful to consult with a printer when your design is still in its infancy. If you want to achieve a certain kind of look in your design, the printer can often offer suggestions about how to achieve it.

Light Source   Film Negative   Plate

FIGURE 8.1 The first step in the offset printing process is to expose a specially prepared metal plate to light through a negative.

HOW THE PRINTING PROCESS WORKS

By far the most common printing process is offset printing. It's called offset because instead of being transferred directly from the form to the paper, as was done in the old letterpress method, the image is offset to a rubber blanket and then transferred to the paper. Offset printing is based on the principle that oil and water don't mix. Here's basically how it works.

1. The offset press is made up of a system of rollers and cylinders. Attached to one of these cylinders is a metal plate that has been treated with an oil-based emulsion.

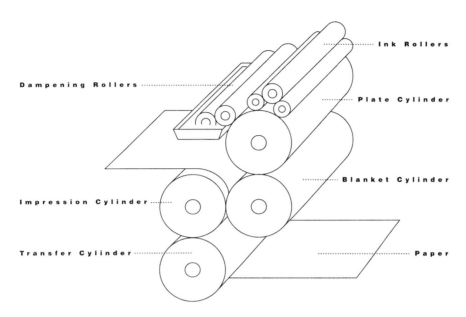

FIGURE 8.2 The offset printing press.

During the pre-press process, a film negative of the printing image is registered to the plate and exposed to light. The light shines through the negative, hardening the emulsion and creating a positive image on the plate. (See Figure 8.1.) The plate is then developed, and the emulsion is stripped away from the surface of the plate except where the printing image has been exposed.

2. Once the plate has been prepared, it is attached to the plate cylinder on the press. A rubber blanket is attached to another cylinder on the press.

3. As the press runs, the plate is dampened. Since the image on the plate is made of an oil-based emulsion, it resists the water.

4. The ink is then applied to the plate using a series of rubber rollers. Since the non-printing areas of the plate are damp, the oil-based ink doesn't adhere to them. It does, however, adhere to the oil-based emulsion, so the printing image is coated with a thin film of ink.

5. As the plate and the blanket cylinders turn against each other, the inked image is transferred, or offset, to the rubber blanket. The blanket cylinder turns against another cylinder carrying the paper, and the image is transferred from the blanket to the paper. (See Figure 8.2.)

This same process is employed for each color used. Each system of cylinders and rollers is called a unit. A two-unit press is capable of printing two colors in-line. A four-unit press can print all four process colors in one pass.

HOW THE ELECTRONIC PREPRESS PROCESS WORKS

Now you have an understanding of the basics of the offset printing process. Where you'll find the computer most useful, however, is in the preparation of the document for printing which includes everything from design to final film negatives that are ready to be plated. This process is often called prepress. It works like this:

1. *Design*—Well, this one should be obvious. It's what we've been talking about all through this book. Design is the process of determining the elements on the page and how they should be arranged. Sometimes the design is developed through a series of preliminary sketches or thumbnails. Once the design is set it is refined in QuarkXPress.

2. *Scanning*—Once you've developed a page layout, the pictures need to be converted to a form that the computer can recognize and use. If you're using illustrations that have been created in the computer in a program like Adobe Illustrator or Aldus FreeHand, they are already in a computer format since they were probably saved in an EPS format. But if you have a photographic print or an illustration rendered using traditional methods, you'll need to have it scanned. A scanner moves a light over the surface of the image, "reads" the colors and/or value densities, and translates that information into an electronic language. Most scanning software lets you save your image in any of the common file formats. Once scanned and saved as, say a TIFF file, the image can be imported into your QuarkXPress layout using the Get Picture command.

3. *Refining the Layout*—Now that you have your rough sketches, your text, and your scanned images, you're ready to create the document in QuarkXPress. This is where you refine your design and make sure everything is just the way you want it. I tend to generate lots of laser proofs at this stage, checking details, and making small adjustments until the layout is perfect.

4. *Processing*—When you save your document on a disk and send it to a service bureau or film house to be processed, it goes through a number of steps. First, a technician will open your document and check everything over carefully. He checks all of the print settings to make sure the file will process correctly. Once he

or she is satisfied, the file will be downloaded to a raster image processor, commonly referred to as a RIP. This is where the magic happens. Your document goes in one end as a QuarkXPress file and comes out the other end as separated film. The process employed by a RIP is similar to a scanner but in reverse. Unlike a scanner which translates visual information into electronic language, the RIP translates the electronic language back into pictures. All the little bits and bytes in the electronic file are converted to tiny dots or squares called pixels which form the image. It doesn't matter if the page is made up of type, pictures, or both. Everything is made from pixels. This process of converting the digital information into pixels is called rasterizing. Connected to the RIP is another machine called an imagesetter. The imagesetter is the device that actually exposes the image onto the film and develops it. Once the film is processed, a proof is made which gives you a pretty accurate representation of what the printed page will look like. This is an extremely important step because you don't want to find out on press that there was a problem in the processing. The proof is also the last chance you'll have to check for typos and other mistakes that may have been overlooked on the laser prints.

5. *Printing*—Once the film and proofs have been created, the job will go to the printer to be plated and printed in the traditional fashion.

SHEET-FED VS. WEB

Offset presses fall into two broad categories: sheet-fed and web. Sheet-fed presses print on pre-cut sheets of paper, sending them through the press one sheet at a time. Web presses, on the other hand, are designed to print on a continuous ribbon of paper feeding off large rolls.

Sheet-fed presses are more common and offer advantages in quality. There is less paper stretch, so color registration is more precise and it's easier to maintain consistent densities throughout the run. Also, sheet-fed presses offer a much greater variety of paper to choose from.

Web presses offer a distinct advantage in speed, printing as many as 50,000 impressions per hour, compared to 4,000 to 12,000 sheets per hour for sheet-fed presses. Web presses are the method of choice for very large-quantity jobs, such as catalogs, magazines, books, and newspapers.

PREPARING ARTWORK FOR PRINTING

You can use QuarkXPress to take your design from concept through final film. Here are some of the advantages of this approach.

- Working with the computer lets you see things such as color breaks, type, and photographs in position.

- Making changes is comparatively quick and easy. Once you're familiar with the software, you can quickly move things around, change trapping values, alter colors, or reset text.

- You have control of the entire process, right up to making the plates and putting the document on press.

- In some cases you can realize a significant savings in your prepress costs (but remember to figure in the time it takes you to do the extra work).

- Much of the work that has traditionally been done by hand is done automatically in QuarkXPress. For instance, instead of drawing crop marks on the mechanical art with a technical pen, you can simply command QuarkXPress to put them in for you.

The disadvantages of using QuarkXPress for preparing artwork for printing have primarily to do with personal choice and the level of commitment that you want to make to the technology. Here are some things to consider before you dive head-first into digital prepress.

- While going direct to film from QuarkXPress can be a real time and money saver, if things go wrong, going back and reworking something can be very expensive. Naturally, the more complex the job, the more likely there are to be problems. Start with very simple one and two-color projects without complicated color traps, and work up from there.

- Do you want to spend time doing your own prepress work when someone else can do it for you? Perhaps you'd rather spend your time doing other things, such as designing. Even if you decide that you don't want to do your own prepress work you need to be aware that this is the wave of the future and a well-rounded designer should understand the mechanics of the electronic prepress process.

- You can't expect to produce work that rivals the best-quality film produced by craftspeople who have been printing for years. Are you willing to invest a significant amount of time learning about this new technology for results that may not be as good as those you may have had in the past?

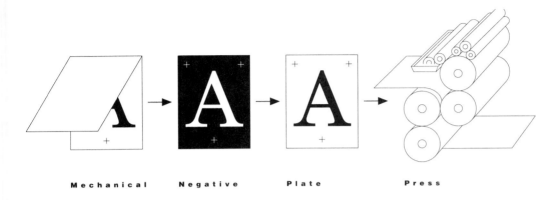

Mechanical   Negative   Plate   Press

FIGURE 8.3 The printing process.

The extent to which you take advantage of QuarkXPress's capabilities is up to you. You may choose to do all of your work electronically or just portions of it.

In order to understand the electronic prepress process, it's important to understand how artwork has traditionally been prepared for printing, since many of the same principles apply. (See Figure 8.3.) Here's a brief overview of the traditional prepress process.

1. The design—The designer determines the document format, arranges all of the page elements, selects the number of colors, the type of paper, and the specific inks, and decides how the photos and illustrations should be treated and how the document should be folded and bound.

2. Production—At this stage the type is set, the photos are shot, illustrations are rendered, and ink and paper swatches are selected.

3. The mechanical—Mechanical art is prepared by pasting all of the page elements in their exact positions on a board, with the edges of the page clearly defined by crop or trim marks. Rough prints of photos and illustrations are sized, cropped, and placed in position. A tissue paper overlay is marked with instructions as to which elements are in color, which elements reverse, and how elements should trap against one another. This crucial step in the process serves as a blueprint for the printer, who will create the final film. All elements must be black on a white background.

4. Film preparation—The mechanical art is placed in a copy camera or on a scanner and photographed. The result is a high-contrast negative. Often the photos

within a page are photographed separately and spliced into position on the final negatives. Photos need to be treated differently because in order to simulate continuous tone with high-contrast film, they must be exposed through a special screen and converted to a pattern of dots called a halftone. The dots are often too small to be easily seen by the naked eye and appear as continuous tones of gray or color. A pattern of dots that are large and close together appear as a dark tone, while small dots spaced far apart appear as a light tone. (See Figure 8.4.) In the final step in film preparation, the final film negative is used as a mask to expose the printing plate.

FIGURE 8.4 Photographs are reproduced by converting them to halftones (patterns of dots that vary in density to simulate a range of tonal values).

5. Printing—The plate with the printing image is attached to the press and the job is run.

QuarkXPress lets you skip the mechanical stage and go straight to film. However, there may be situations where you'll want to use the software to lay out your pages, set the type, and place the graphic elements, but then assemble a traditional mechanical. You can easily have a service bureau run out a high-resolution paper print on a imagesetter, which can be glued to a board and marked up in the traditional manner. (An imagesetter print should not be confused with a laser print. A laser print is a low-resolution proof print on inexpensive paper, while an imagesetter print is a reproduction-quality print produced by a photographic process on a coated paper. It has a resolution up to eight times finer than a 300 dpi laser print.)

Preparing a document for high-resolution imagesetting is easy. Usually you'll send it to a service bureau, which will ask you to specify the name of the document, the software program, the names of the fonts used, the type of output (paper or film), the page dimension, the number of pages to be printed, the desired resolution, the screen size for the halftones, and whether or not you want to include crop marks. Once you've provided this information, all you really need to do is give them your file on a disk. They'll take care of the rest.

PREPARING THE MECHANICAL

There are two primary objectives to preparing mechanical art: accuracy and neatness. The mechanical must be accurate because the printer will work very hard to reproduce the artwork exactly to your specifications. If there are errors on your mechanical, they'll be on your printed piece as well. Neatness is important because the mechanical will be photographed to create the film. Any fingerprints, specks of dirt, or smudges of taco sauce on your board will show up on the film.

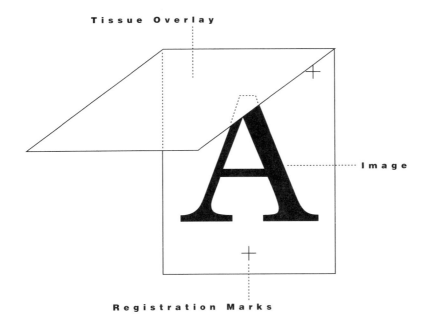

FIGURE 8.5 The mechanical

Since most of the work has already been done in the computer, assembling the mechanical is simple:

1. Paste the pages, with crop marks in place, onto clean white art boards. If your publication has multiple pages, lay them down on the boards as spreads. (See Figure 8.5.)

2. Cover the art with an overlay sheet, a piece of semi-translucent layout tissue paper, and tape the paper along the top edge of the board. You should be able to see the artwork through the tissue paper.

3. Neatly write your instructions on the overlay sheet. Specify colors for all elements and for the background. If your photos are placed only for reference to size and crop, label them for position only (FPO). Mark all elements that should trap to one another. The printer will assume that everything on the mechanical art should print unless you specify otherwise. If there is something in your artwork that shouldn't print (such as a box to show the position of a picture) be sure to note it on the tissue overlay. Remember, this is often the only communication link to the printer, so print carefully and legibly, and make sure all details are noted.

PRINTING DIRECTLY TO FILM

Once your document is set up in QuarkXPress, running the pages out to film is easy. This can save you the trouble of preparing mechanical art, but you must be absolutely sure that the settings in your document are accurate. This especially applies to trapping values. Double-check them! Also, remember that the colors that appear on your monitor may bear little resemblance to the final printed color. Always compare colors to a PANTONE swatch book or a process color chart that has been generated electronically.

Unfortunately, you often don't discover these kinds of problems until your film is run out and a proof is made. Your service bureau can prevent such problems for you if you provide them with the information they need. Be sure to specify that you want film and whether it should be a film negative or a film positive, and whether you want it right-reading with the emulsion side up or down. For offset publication work, the standard is negatives, right-reading, emulsion down. Include the resolution and line screen for halftones, and always specify crop marks.

If you're fortunate enough to have your own imagesetter, you can, of course, bypass the service bureau and run the film yourself, but you'll have to make all of these specifications within QuarkXPress. To prepare the document for printing, go

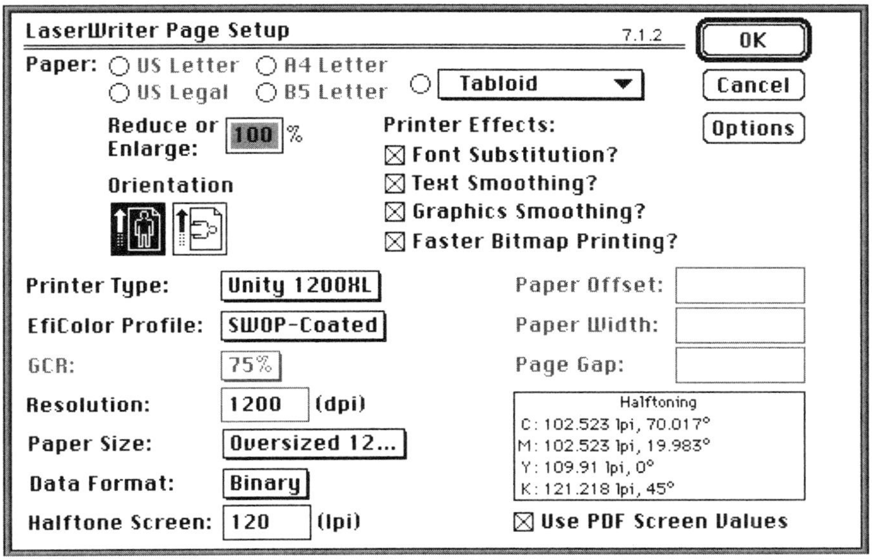

```
┌─────────────────────────────────────────────────────────────────────┐
│ LaserWriter Page Setup                              7.1.2   ╭───────╮ │
│                                                             │  OK   │ │
│ Paper: ○ US Letter  ○ A4 Letter                             ╰───────╯ │
│        ○ US Legal   ○ B5 Letter  ○ │ Tabloid      ▼ │      ┌───────┐ │
│                                                            │Cancel │ │
│       Reduce or  ┌───┐ %     Printer Effects:              └───────┘ │
│       Enlarge:   │100│       ☒ Font Substitution?          ┌───────┐ │
│                  └───┘       ☒ Text Smoothing?             │Options│ │
│       Orientation           ☒ Graphics Smoothing?          └───────┘ │
│       ┌──┐ ┌──┐             ☒ Faster Bitmap Printing?                │
│       └──┘ └──┘                                                      │
│                                                                      │
│ Printer Type:    │ Unity 1200XL │    Paper Offset: ┌─────────┐       │
│                                                    └─────────┘       │
│ EfiColor Profile:│ SWOP-Coated  │    Paper Width:  ┌─────────┐       │
│                                                    └─────────┘       │
│ GCR:             │ 75% │              Page Gap:     ┌─────────┐       │
│                                                    └─────────┘       │
│ Resolution:      │ 1200 │ (dpi)      ┌──────────────────────────┐    │
│                                      │        Halftoning         │    │
│ Paper Size:      │ Oversized 12... │ │ C: 102.523 lpi, 70.017°   │    │
│                                      │ M: 102.523 lpi, 19.983°   │    │
│ Data Format:     │ Binary │          │ Y: 109.91 lpi, 0°         │    │
│                                      │ K: 121.218 lpi, 45°       │    │
│ Halftone Screen: │ 120 │ (lpi)       └──────────────────────────┘    │
│                                      ☒ Use PDF Screen Values         │
└─────────────────────────────────────────────────────────────────────┘
```

FIGURE 8.6 The Page Setup dialog box

to the Chooser in the Apple Menu and select the imagesetter. Then choose Page Setup from the File Menu. (See Figure 8.6.)

When the Page Setup dialog box appears, select the printer from the Printer Type pop-up menu. If you don't see your particular printer in the menu it means that you don't have a PDF (printer description file) or PPD (postscript printer description) installed for your printer. Having a PDF installed for your printer will optimize the printing process. PDFs contain information specific to that particular device such as a screen value set which contains specifics about screen angles, frequency, etc. Check with the printer's manufacturer. They can usually supply you with the appropriate PDF. PPDs are OK too but don't contain quite as much information. Under Paper Type, click the button labeled Film. Specify the desired halftone screen, resolution, and the appropriate material width in the fields in the lower-right corner. Choose Print from the File Menu and fill in the pertinent information in the Print dialog box, including number of copies, desired page range, and whether the document is color or black and white. (See Figure 8.7.) Be sure to indicate if you want to run the pages as spreads, and always check Registration Marks. Check the Color Separations box if your document includes color images that will need to be separated into process colors. When you check Color Separations, the Plate pop-up menu will become active. If you want all the

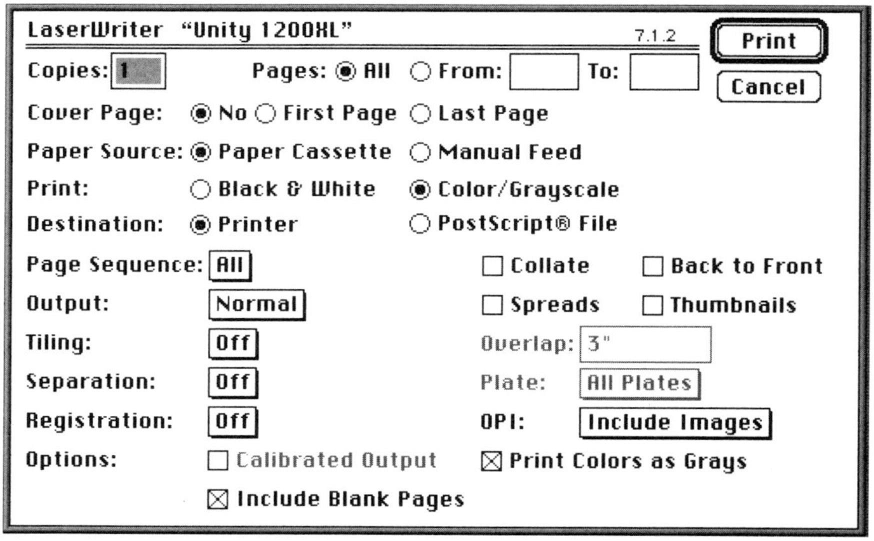

```
┌─────────────────────────────────────────────────────────────────────┐
│ LaserWriter  "Unity 1200XL"                        7.1.2   ╭────────╮ │
│                                                            │ Print  │ │
│ Copies:[1]       Pages: ⊙ All  ○ From:[    ] To:[    ]      ╰────────╯ │
│                                                            ╭────────╮ │
│ Cover Page:    ⊙ No ○ First Page ○ Last Page               │ Cancel │ │
│                                                            ╰────────╯ │
│ Paper Source:⊙ Paper Cassette  ○ Manual Feed                          │
│                                                                       │
│ Print:         ○ Black & White    ⊙ Color/Grayscale                   │
│ Destination:  ⊙ Printer           ○ PostScript® File                  │
│                                                                       │
│ Page Sequence:[All]              □ Collate     □ Back to Front        │
│ Output:        [Normal]          □ Spreads     □ Thumbnails           │
│ Tiling:        [Off]             Overlap:[3"]                         │
│ Separation:    [Off]             Plate:  [All Plates]                 │
│ Registration:  [Off]             OPI:    [Include Images]             │
│ Options:       □ Calibrated Output    ⊠ Print Colors as Grays         │
│                ⊠ Include Blank Pages                                  │
└─────────────────────────────────────────────────────────────────────┘
```

FIGURE 8.7 The Print dialog box.

separation plates needed to reproduce the colors on each page, choose All Plates. Finally, click OK to send the file to the printer.

WORKING WITH A SERVICE BUREAU

A good service bureau should live up to its name. Their business is to make this whole process easier for you, so don't hesitate to consult with one. Like your printer, a service bureau can be a valuable vendor, so it makes sense to find one with a wide range of capabilities and technical expertise and establish a working relationship with them. (I work with several that have proven to be invaluable. The staff are technical wizards who know computers inside and out. If I'm having problems with my system, or if I want information about something technical like how a certain program handles screen angles, they're only a phone call away.)

A word of caution, however: As more and more people embrace computer technology, service bureaus are springing up on every street corner. Anyone with the money to buy an imagesetter can technically call themselves a service bureau, but not all of these places offer the same level of expertise. Look for one that has a staff with solid technical background and a variety of equipment such as scanners, color printers, and color proofing systems, as well as imagesetters.

You can save yourself a lot of grief—not to mention money—if you're prepared when you send your file to a service bureau. Here's a checklist to run down before you hand over your disk:

1. List all the file names and the page numbers you want printed.

2. Note how many copies of each page you need.

3. Specify the page size.

4. Provide the name and version number of the software program you used to create your files.

5. List all of the typefaces used in each document. (If the service bureau doesn't have all of the fonts, you'll need to supply them.)

6. Specify the material you want—paper or film? If film, negative or positive? Emulsion up or down?

7. Note the desired halftone screen, if applicable.

8. Do you want medium resolution (typically 1270 dpi which works fine for most jobs) or high resolution (typically 2540 dpi)?

9. Do you want to include crop marks and registration marks?

10. Specify the percentage of enlargement or reduction, if applicable.

11. Do you require a proof? If so, what kind?

12. Be sure to include any linked graphic files. For instance, if you've placed TIFF or EPS images in your document, you'll need to send along the original files.

13. Send along a laser proof for reference.

USING THE COLLECT FOR OUTPUT UTILITY

Gathering all of the files and information associated with your file for the service bureau can be a tedious task and there's always the chance that you'll forget something that can hold up production. With this in mind, QuarkXPress versions 3.2 and later have a built-in utility that automatically gathers all of the files along with a copy of the QuarkXPress document and places them in a single folder. It also generates a report that provides the service bureau with a lot of valuable information about your job. The report will contain the following:

- The name of the document
- The date
- The total number of pages
- The page dimensions
- The file size
- The version of QuarkXPress in which the document was created
- Any XTensions required
- A list of active XTensions
- A list of fonts used
- A list of graphics used with information about each (file format, size, etc.)
- H&J specifications
- A list of colors used
- Color plates required for each page
- Trapping information

The only thing Collect for Output doesn't do, unfortunately, is gather copies of the fonts. If you have altered your fonts in any way, for example, if you've modified the kerning values within the font itself, you absolutely must provide your versions of the fonts to the service bureau. If you don't, your entire document could reflow resulting in some very unpleasant typographic and pagination variations.

When you're ready to gather your files for the service bureau, simply choose Collect for Output from the File menu. The Collect for Output dialog box will appear asking you to give your report a name and lets you select a location for the files.

QUALITY CONTROL

Whether you give your printer mechanicals or final film, you should see a proof before the document goes to press. A proof is a graphic representation of what the printed page will look like. Proofs are made from final stripped film, so what you see is what you'll get. It's crucial that you look proofs over meticulously becauseg.it's much cheaper to make a change at this stage than when it's on press.

There are a number of different kinds of proofs. The least expensive (and the least reliable) is called a *blueline*. Bluelines, in which the image appears in blue on a white background, are used primarily for one and sometimes two-color jobs and are really useful only for checking type and placement of elements.

A better proof is a *color key*. A color key proof shows each color on acetate sheets, which are layered in register on top of one another to show all of the elements in color. Color keys are not the most accurate proofing system for four-color process work, however, because the acetate has a gray cast that becomes very pronounced when four sheets are layered on top of one another. The gray cast influences the color, rendering it inaccurate.

The best color proofs are dry proofing systems such as Matchprint or Cromalin. In these systems the image is created on a single sheet of paper using dry pigments. They have no layers to look through, and often they can be applied to the actual paper you've specified. These proofs are accurate but very expensive.

Once you've approved the proofs and your document is ready to go to press, it's a good idea to make arrangements with your printer to do a press check. This is a crucial step, especially for large or complex jobs, as the press check is your final quality control checkpoint. If you happened to miss anything on the proofs, this is your last chance to catch it. Also, there are a number of things that can happen while the job is on press. Once you sign off on a press sheet, the printer is responsible for matching the rest of the run to that approved sample.

What kinds of things should you look for at a press check? Here's a short list:

1. Take one last look at the copy. Check for misspelled words or missing type.

2. Check for broken type. Sometimes when the film is being made, small pieces of dust attach to the negative, and these can take a nick out of a letter.

3. Compare the press sheet with the proof. If it doesn't match, the pressman can often make adjustments to make it more accurate.

4. Make sure the color is evenly distributed across the entire sheet. Look for streaks, or ghosts, where the ink is being starved. These are especially noticeable in large areas of solid color.

5. Check for small white spots, called hickeys, that are caused by dust particles on the blanket.

6. If you've specified PANTONE colors, check the colors on the press sheet against the swatchbook.

7. If you're running four-color images, check the color balance in the photographs. Are the skin tones too red? Often subtle adjustments to one or more of the process colors can correct the problem.

Specifying Paper

There are hundreds of different kinds of paper available. How do you choose the best kind of paper for your job? A fundamental knowledge of paper can help you decide. Paper falls into several broad categories.

1. *Coated papers*—These papers are coated with a thin layer of clay or similar material to provide a hard, smooth, and sometimes glossy surface. Coated papers are the best choice for high-quality reproduction. Unlike porous papers, coated papers are less likely to absorb ink, making a more precise image. They are also more reflective, which tends to make colors appear brighter and tonal ranges deeper and richer.

2. *Book papers*—This kind of paper is typically used for books. Book papers are porous and have a rough or textured surface.

3. *Text papers*—Text papers are uncoated papers that come in a wide variety of colors and textures. They are widely used for such documents as announcements, letterheads, and flyers, and are often available with matching envelopes.

4. *Cover papers*—These papers cover a wide range of categories. Their distinctive characteristic is their weight, which is heavier than most papers. They are designed to be a durable outer leaf for brochures and booklets.

5. *Bond papers*—Bond papers are used primarily for stationery. They are light in weight and often come with matching envelopes. They come in a wide variety of colors and have surfaces specifically designed to accept typewriter and writing inks. Many bond papers are partially made of cotton fibers. As a rule, the more cotton fiber, the more expensive the paper.

6. *Bristol boards*—These papers are noted for their stiffness and durability. They are relatively inexpensive and are commonly used for packaging.

7. *Label papers*—Label papers are very lightweight, and generally only one surface is prepared for printing. Often the back side is left uncoated or is applied with an adhesive. As their name implies, they are used for packaging labels.

Within all of these categories are numerous subcategories. Paper companies manufacture swatchbooks with samples of their papers in all available colors, textures, and weights. These swatchbooks can be obtained through your printer.

Specifying the thickness or substance of a paper, referred to as its basis weight, can be tricky. Over the years, the paper industry has developed a formula for determining an approximation of a paper's basis weight (the formula provides only an approximation because it doesn't take into account the density or bulk of the paper).

The formula works like this: A ream of paper (500 sheets) in its basis size is weighed, and that weight is considered the basis weight. While the number of sheets weighed is consistent between types of paper, the basis size is not. The basis size for bond paper, for instance, is 17" x 22", while the basis size for book is 25" x 38". In paper swatchbooks, basis weight is expressed in pounds, such as 65lb cover or Sub. 65 cover. When specifying paper, you need to include the name of the paper, the color, finish, and basis weight. Paper swatchbooks make it easy, since they include clearly labeled samples of colors, finishes, and weights.

Choosing the right paper is an important part of the design process. Each kind of paper has a different character. The finish and texture, color, and weight of the paper should be consistent with the tone of the publication printed on it. For example, a brochure printed on white glossy paper would have an entirely different character if it were printed on colored text paper with a textured surface. Before you make your final paper selection, have your printer give you a preview by making dummies out of several samples of stock in the correct size and with the correct number of pages.

BINDING OPTIONS

There are a number of binding styles to choose from, and the one you choose should depend on the number of pages in your publication, how the publication will be used, and the durability that is required. The basic commercial binding styles include.

1. *Case binding*—This is a common and durable binding, in which the pages are sewn together at the spine, and a hard cover, or case, is attached. This is the typical binding for hardcover books. It requires enough pages to form a squared spine.

2. *Perfect binding*—This is the familiar paperback binding. In this method, the

pages are gathered together, the spine is trimmed, and the squared spine is roughed up and glued. A paper cover is then glued to the spine.

3. *Spiral wire*—In this binding, a series of holes are drilled through the pages along the spine edge. A wire spiral is then wound through the holes. This is a good binding choice if your publication must lay flat when opened. For this reason it's often used for cookbooks and reference manuals.

4. *Comb binding*—This method is similar to wire binding, but instead of wire being threaded through the holes, a wire or plastic comb is inserted into the holes and bent closed.

5. *Saddle stitch*—This is the most common binding method for brochures. In this method, the pages are held together by wire staples along the fold. This is a good option for publications that have too few pages to be viable candidates for other binding methods.

SUMMARY

This chapter provides an overview of the printing process from start to finish. While it only touches on the basics, it provides essential knowledge for anyone designing publications for print. Take a few minutes to review the material in this chapter by answering these questions.

1. What are some of the things to consider when choosing a printer for your publication?

2. Why is it important for a designer to understand the printing process?

3. What's the difference between *sheet-fed* and *web* printing?

4. What are some of the advantages of electronic prepress?

5. What is a *mechanical*?

6. What information does a service bureau need to process your job?

7. What kinds of things should you look for at a press check?

8. What is a *blueline*?

9. What are the fundamental paper categories?

10. What are the basic binding styles?

Creating a Small Space Ad

In this exercise you will design a small black-and-white advertisement using QuarkXPress functions to set up the page structure, import and format text, and import and crop an illustration.

Ads must attract attention and communicate a message in a matter of seconds. Since they tend to have so few elements, their components must be carefully balanced and placed in a way that can be read easily and quickly. It's also important to consider where the ad will be reproduced. For instance, a small-space ad such as the one we will create here often shares a page with other ads, which compete for attention. This makes it even more important that the ad's message be clear and easy to grasp.

The paper on which the ad will ultimately be printed is another important consideration. For example, glossy coated paper holds a great amount of detail, while newsprint is very unforgiving. When you're preparing an ad for reproduction on a soft porous paper like newsprint, keep the graphic elements simple and avoid a lot of detail. You will prepare the ad in this exercise to be reproduced in a newspaper.

STEP 1

First let's set up the page. Open QuarkXPress by double-clicking on the icon, then go to the File menu and select New (Command-N). The first dialog box to appear will ask you to type in the page dimensions. Let's set up this ad to be 6" wide by 8" tall. Next, type in .25" for the top, bottom, left, and right margins, and enter 1 in the Columns box. Click on the Automatic Text Box button, then click OK. You should be looking at the page with the margins defined by the edges of a text box (see Figure 1.1E).

FIGURE 1.1E

After the page is formatted in Step 1 it will look like this.

There are three methods of placing text into a document: You can cut and paste it from another QuarkXPress document, you can import it from another document such as one created on a word processing program, or you can create and edit it directly on the page in QuarkXPress. In this exercise you will use the latter two options. Let's begin by typing in a headline.

STEP 2

Create a new text box by selecting the Text Box Tool (the tool with the letter A in it). The cursor will change to a cross. Click in the upper-left corner of the page, and holding the mouse button down, drag it across the page. Stretch the text box from margin to margin and make it 1.5" deep. You should see a cursor blinking in the upper-left corner of the box. Now type in the words The Brush Off. This is the ad's headline.

It's always important to consider how a reader will absorb the information in an ad. Generally the headline and the illustration work together to communicate the ad's essential idea. In this exercise, they need to work in concert to make a visual point, so you'll want to give the headline a lot of emphasis.

When selecting a typeface for your ad, consider how quickly it will need to be read. Legibility is very important. When you thumb through a magazine or newspaper, how much time do you spend reading advertising? Ads that are hard to read won't be read; in fact most ads are passed over or are given only a cursory glance because they are poorly conceived or designed. The best ads seize your attention and make you want to read them.

STEP 3

Let's set this headline in Helvetica Bold. Select the headline by holding down the mouse button and dragging the cursor across it. It should be displayed inside a bar. Pull down the Style menu and open the Fonts menu. Find and select Helvetica.

You've changed the style of the headline, but it's still too small. Use the Measurements palette to change the size of the type. If it's not already on your desktop, activate the palette by selecting Show Measurements from the View menu (see Figure 1.2E). The measurements inside the Measurement palette show up only when a text box is activated. With the headline still highlighted, drag across the number in the upper-right corner of the Measurements palette that indicates point size. This will select it. Then type 80 and hit the Return key. The type size will change on your page. (You may have noticed that the headline no longer fits in the box. Don't panic! We'll fix that later.)

| X: 0.25" W: 5.5" △ 0° ⚲ auto ▤ ▤ Ⓓ Helvetica ▶ 80 pt |
| Y: 0.25" H: 1.5" Cols: 1 ◇◇ 0 ▤ ▤ P B I Ⓞ Ⓢ Ⓤ U W K K ▲ ▼ |

FIGURE 1.2E The Measurements palette.

STEP 4

In the Measurements palette, notice the five little rectangles with horizontal lines in them. These buttons will change the text alignment. Click the box in the upper-middle to center the headline. While you're there, click on the little box with the bold letter B. This will make the type bold.

STEP 5

Now let's get the headline to fit in the text box. We'll do that by making the letter-forms more vertical and spacing them more tightly. Making sure the type is still selected, pull down the Style menu and select Horizontal Scaling. This function lets you to compress or expand the letters. Type 80 into the box and click OK.

Return to the Measurements palette. In the middle of the box you should see the value 0 next to two back-to-back horizontal arrows. This is the tracking tool. (Remember, tracking refers to adjustment of spacing between the letters.) There are two ways to adjust the tracking with the tracking tool: You can drag across the number and type a new value over it, or you can click on the left arrow to remove space or on the right arrow to add space. Close up the headline by clicking once on the left arrow. The value should read -10.

Another way to put text into a document is to import it from another software program. This is an extremely useful function because copy is often contained in a word processing program such as Microsoft Word. Importing text directly from the other program ensures accuracy and saves you the trouble of retyping it.

N O T E   *Horizontal scaling can radically change both the character and the legibility of the letterforms because it actually distorts them. To avoid loss of legibility, you might consider limiting horizontal scaling to a range of 80 and 120 percent, although the program allows for a much wider range.*

STEP 6

Select the original text box (the text box that was created automatically when you set up the page) by clicking on it. When the text box is activated, you will see tiny boxes, or handles, attached to the box's corners and centerpoints. Clicking and dragging these handles lets you change the size of the box. Grab the handle at the center top and drag it down so the top of the text box is 2" from the top of the page.

Next, insert the exercise disk that accompanies this book in your drive. If it's not already selected, click on the Content Tool in the toolbox (that's the tool containing the little hand, second from the top). With the text box activated, pull down the File menu and select Get Text (Command-E). Navigate through the dialog box until you find the file called Ad Copy on your exercise disk. Select it and click Open. The text should automatically flow into your text box.

STEP 7

The new text now needs to be formatted. With the text box still active, pull down the Edit menu and click Select All (Command-A). This will highlight all the text. Using the Measurement palette, change the type style to Times and the size to 13 pt.

Notice that none of the words in the document are hyphenated. QuarkXPress can automatically break words in the proper places and add hyphens. The program also allows you to customize exactly how, or if, words break at the end of a line. To use the automatic hyphenation feature, make sure the text box is active, then pull down the Edit menu and choose H&Js. When the dialog box appears, click Edit. In the new dialog box that appears, click Auto Hyphenation and OK. Click Save, and the text will be hyphenated.

STEP 8

Importing pictures into a QuarkXPress document is just like importing text, except that you use a picture box instead of a text box. QuarkXPress lets you import Paint, TIFF, RIFF, PICT, and EPS files that have been scanned or created in other programs. These files can be either color or black-and-white. In this exercise you will import two black-and-white EPS files.

There are four different kinds of picture box tools in the tool box: the Rectangular Picture Box Tool, the Rounded-corner Rectangle Picture Box Tool, the Oval Picture Box Tool, and the Polygon Picture Box Tool. Picture boxes contain crossing diagonal lines that look like the letter X. As you can see, each box has a different shape. Click on the tool with the box that looks like a rectangle. Starting on the lower-right corner of the page, hold the mouse button down and drag the box upward diagonally so that the upper-left corner of the picture box is 1.5" from the left side of the page and 1.75" from the top. Your page should now look like Figure 1.3E.

The Brush Off

We're the Cleanup Crew and we'd like to make your building shine! We're a property maintenance service with nearly 20 years of janitorial experience. But here's the best part: we think we can save you both time and money! Because the Cleanup Crew offers an unusually wide range of services, one call to us can usually take care of all your cleaning problems. Since there's no need

FIGURE 1.3E

After you create a picture box in Step 8, your page should look like this.

With your picture box still active, pull down the File menu. Notice that when a picture box rather than a text box is active, Get Text changes to Get Picture. Select Get Picture (Command-E) and use the dialog box to locate the file on your exercise disk called Ad Art. Click Open. This should place the picture in the picture box.

FIGURE 1.4E

Centering the image in the picture box as described in Step 9.

The Brush Off

We're the Cleanup Crew and we'd like to make your building shine! We're a property maintenance service with nearly 20 years of janitorial experience. But here's the best part: we think we can save you both time and money! Because the Cleanup Crew offers an unusually wide range of services, one call to us can usually take care of all your cleaning problems. Since there's no need

STEP 9

QuarkXPress imports graphics at the same size they were created, so often they need to be resized to fit into a QuarkXPress document. To resize the picture, select Modify from the Item menu. In the upper-right corner of the dialog box you'll see Scale Across and Scale Down, followed by value boxes. Change the value in each to 60%. While you're in the Modify dialog box, change the background color to None. Click OK, and the picture should appear larger in the picture box. Now hold the mouse button down on the picture box. Notice that the pointer changes to a hand. This hand lets you to move the image inside the picture box. Center the image in the box, as shown in Figure 1.4E.

The Brush Off

We're the Cleanup Crew and we'd like to make your building shine! We're a property maintenance service with nearly 20 years of janitorial experience. But here's the best part: we think we can save you both time and money! Because the Cleanup Crew offers an unusually wide range of ser-vices, one call to us can usually take care of all your cleaning problems. Since there's no need

CLEANUP CREW

FIGURE 1.5E

Once you've placed the logo, your page should look like this.

228

Now create a new picture box in the lower-right corner of the page. This is where you will place the logo. Make the box .75" wide by 1" tall, leaving a .25" margin at the right side and the bottom. Using the Get Picture procedure you used to import Ad Art (Command-E), import the file on your exercise disk called Logo. Resize it to 18% and center it in the picture box (Command-shift-M). Your page should now look like the one shown in Figure 1.5E.

Here's a quick and easy way to center a picture in a picture box: hold down the Command and Shift keys and type M.

SHORTCUT

STEP 10

You may have noticed that the text of this ad doesn't completely fit on the page. You'll fix that by creating a runaround. A runaround is a typographic term for text that follows the contour of a picture. In this case, the runaround will utilize the space more efficiently, allowing you to get more text in a smaller space.

To create the runaround, activate the large picture box by clicking on it. Pull down the Item menu and select Runaround (Command-T). In the dialog box under Mode, select Auto Image. This command will wrap the text automatically around the image. However, if you don't tell QuarkXPress to leave a margin it will butt the text right up against the image. To create the margin, type a value of 12 in the Text Outset box, then click OK. Finally, with the Picture Box still active, select Bring To Front from the Item menu. Click outside the page to deactivate the window. You should see the text running around the illustration.

To see the final result better, pull down the View menu and select Hide Guides. The ad is finished!

FIGURE 1.6E The finished ad.

Designing a Stationery Set

O ne of a company's most important vehicles of corporate image is its stationery. It is widely circulated and often creates that critical first impression. For these reasons, it should do more than just list the organization's
name and address—it should reflect the company's personality. The size and placement of the elements; the character of the type; the color, texture, and weight of
the paper; and the color of ink should all work together to create a visual harmony
and a sense of the kind of business it represents.

There are practical considerations to designing stationery as well. Remember that
the letterhead is a frame for a letter. Always consider the letterhead a design element and be sure to leave ample room for it. Also keep in mind that the stationery
and envelopes may be used in a laser printer, copier, or fax machine. The type
should have enough contrast to reproduce well under all these circumstances.

In this exercise you will create a letterhead, a business card, and an envelope
using QuarkXPress's functions to set up page formats, import text and graphics,
format text, and (for those using QuarkXPress 3.1 or later) apply color in the form
of a linear blend.

STEP 1

Open QuarkXPress and select New Document from the File Menu (Command-N). In the New dialog box (Figure 2-1E) there is an area labeled Page Size. In its upper-left corner is a button that says US Letter. Click on this button and QuarkXPress will automatically set your page to 8.5" x 11". (While some letterheads are created with odd shapes and sizes, it's far more economical to stick to the standards. For instance, if you decide to make your letterhead larger or smaller than 8.5" x 11", you'll probably need to order custom envelopes, which are much more costly than the off-the-shelf standard variety.)

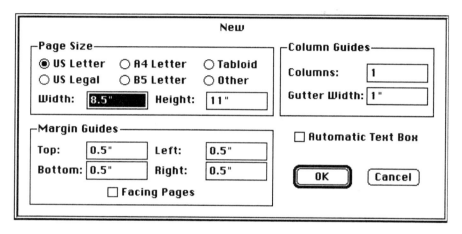

FIGURE 2.1E   The New dialog box.

Going back to the New dialog box, set all your margin guides at .5" and type 1 in the Columns field. Click OK, and the page will appear on your desktop.

STEP 2

In this exercise you will design materials for a fictitious resort called Largo Reef Beach Club. Start by importing its logo from your exercise disk. Using the Picture Box Tool, create a picture box approximately 1" square and place it in the upper-left corner of the page. Align it so it rests against the page's top and left margins. (See Figure 2.2E.)

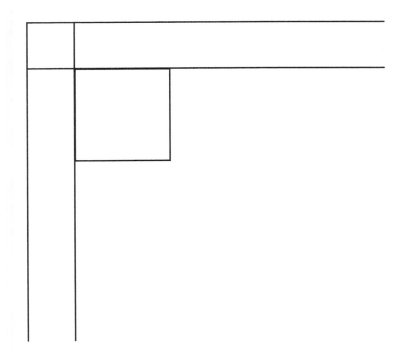

FIGURE 2.2E

Align your picture box with the top and left margins of the page.

Press Command-Shift-F to automatically resize a picture to fit perfectly in a picture box.

SHORTCUT

With the picture box active, select the Content Tool and choose Get Picture from the File menu (Command-E). When the dialog box appears, select the file called Resort Logo from the exercise disk. Once it's selected, click Open and it will be placed in the picture box. The logo is much too large to fit in the picture box, so with the picture box still active, go to the Item menu and choose Modify. When the Picture Box Specifications dialog box appears, type 20 into both the Scale Across and Scale Down fields and click OK. This will reduce the size of the logo proportionally to 20 percent of its original size. With the Content Tool selected, place the cursor over the picture box. The cursor will change to a little hand. Use this hand to position the logo in the box, pushing it into the corner of the box until its edges are as close as you can get them to the top and side edges of the picture box. (Be careful not to push the logo out of the box, or part of it will be cut off.)

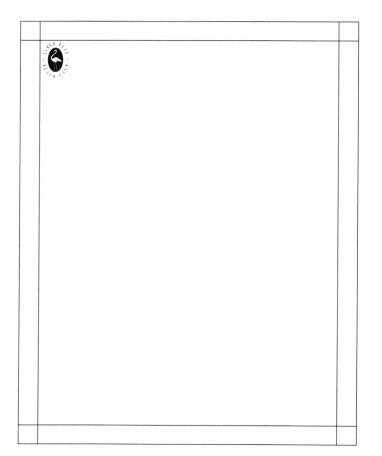

FIGURE 2.3E

The page with the logo imported, sized, and positioned.

STEP 3

Now let's place the resort's address on the page. Using the Text Box Tool, create a text box 1" high and 2" wide and drag it to the lower-left corner of the page, positioning it against the left and bottom margin guides. Although it's often easier to type simple addresses into the text box, in this exercise you'll import the text. Activate the text box, and with the Content Tool selected, choose Get Text from the File menu (Command-E). Using the dialog box, locate the file called Stationery Text on your exercise disk. Click Open to place the text in your text box. (See Figure 2.4E.)

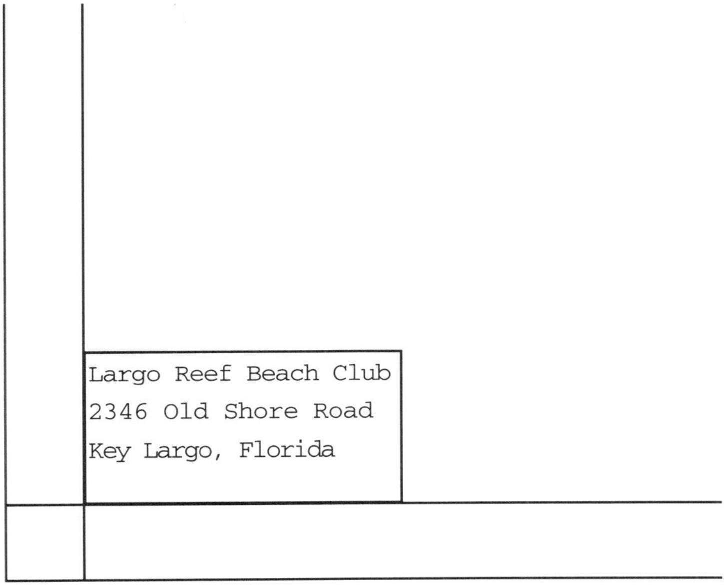

FIGURE 2.4E

The text box with the company address placed.

```
Largo Reef Beach Club
2346 Old Shore Road
Key Largo, Florida
```

STEP 4

The text may not entirely fit in your text box, so don't worry if you don't see the complete address. To reformat the text, hold down the Command key and tap A to select everything in the box. (This selects the entire contents of the box, whether it shows or not.) Change the typeface by choosing Times from the Font menu under Style. With the text still selected, pull down the Style Menu, and in the Size submenu choose Other. This will display a box with a field labeled Font Size. Type 8 in the field and click OK. Now your text should be in 8-pt. Times.

Now let's give the type some character by adding some leading to the lines and by tracking the letters open. If the Measurements Palette is not on your desktop, open it by choosing Show Measurements from the View menu. Making sure your text is selected, use the Measurements palette to open up the leading to 20 points. You can do this easily by clicking on the little arrow that's pointing up until the number next to the arrow reads 20. If the text no longer fits in the text box, use the handles on the box to enlarge it.

Now use the Measurement palette to open the tracking. To do this, you'll use the arrow that points to the right. Click on it until the tracking value reads 20, then click outside the text box to deselect it.

Notice that some of the letter pairs—including La, Ro, and Ke—are too widely spaced. Use the tracking control in your Measurements palette to adjust their kerning: place the Text Insertion Bar between the letters and either click on the arrows or type in a new tracking value.

Now let's make the name of the resort stand out by setting it in bold text. Drag the cursor across the first line of text to select it and click the Bold button (the one containing the letter B) in the Measurements palette. (See Figure 2.5E.)

FIGURE 2.5E

This is how your text should look once it's formatted in Step 4.

Largo Reef Beach Club

2346 Old Shore Road

Key Largo, Florida 33037

(305) 482- 5740

STEP 5

Now you've created a simple and functional letterhead. The logo and text are placed where they won't interfere with the letter, and the page is balanced and tasteful. But let's add a bit more character to it by introducing a graduated color bar along the right side. (Even if you don't have a color monitor, complete the following steps—you may sometimes need to put color into your documents even if you can't see the color on your screen.)

Start by drawing a text box 1/2" wide and 11" tall. Position it so that it aligns with the top, right, and bottom edges of the page. Now let's add a new color to your document's color palette. Select Colors from the Edit menu. When the dialog box appears, click the New button. This will open the Edit Color dialog box. You're going to use a Pantone color, so select Pantone from the Model pop-up menu. You should see the Pantone color palette on the right. We'll use PMS 170—kind of a flamingo pink that looks tropical and ties conceptually to the flamingo in the logo. Simply type the number in the Pantone No. field in the lower-right corner and click OK. Click on Save in the Colors dialog box the new color will be added to your document's palette. (See Figure 2.6E.)

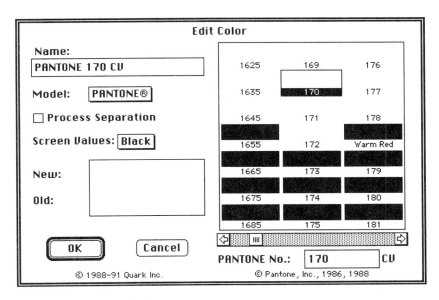

FIGURE 2.6E The Edit Color dialog box.

STEP 6

If you're using QuarkXPress 3.1 or later, you can use the Colors palette to create a linear blend. Open the Colors palette on your desktop by choosing Show Colors from the View menu. Activate the box and choose Linear Blend from the pop-up menu in the Colors palette. Two radio buttons should appear in your palette. Click on button #1 and select Pantone 170 from the scroll list. Now choose 10% from the pop-up menu in the upper-right corner of the palette. This will establish the color and shade for one end of the blend. Now click button #2 and again choose Pantone 170 from the scroll list, but this time set the shade to 100%. Type 90 in the angle field, hit Return and the blend should fill the box, going from dark at the top to light at the bottom. (See Figure 2.7E.)

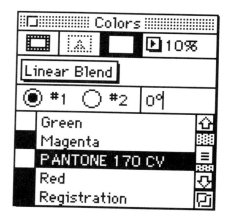

FIGURE 2.7E

The Colors Palette.

STEP 7

Since we want the color bar to bleed, or extend to the edges of the page, the print-er requires that the image actually extend beyond the edges by 1/8th" to allow for any inaccuracies in trimming. This is easily done. Simply use the handles on the top, bottom, and sides of the box to pull the edges out to the proper distance. (See Figure 2.8E.)

Use the techniques in this exercise to create a business card and envelope, follow-ing the models in Figures 2-9E and 2-10E. When sizing these elements, keep in mind that the standard size for a business card is 1 1/2 x 3" and a business envelope is 4 1/8 x 9 1/2".

FIGURE 2.8E The finished letterhead.

Largo Reef Beach Club

2346 Old Shore Road

Key Largo,

Florida 33037

(305) 482- 5740

FIGURE 2.9E

Business card.

FIGURE 2.10E Business envelope.

Designing a Flyer

If you're working as a designer, at some point a client will probably ask you to put together a flyer or brochure. While most flyers are small, often small enough to fit in a business envelope or a display rack, a brochure can take many forms. Some companies produce elaborate publications describing the company, its philosophy, history, products, and services. But small companies rarely have the resources to do something on this scale, and for them, a flyer or brochure can provide an economical means of self promotion.

For this exercise we will produce a small 4-page flyer for a fictitious business. In the process we will utilize QuarkXPress to set up the page format, import text and graphics, apply color and shades, track text, and create an initial cap.

STEP 1

Open QuarkXPress and select New Document from the File menu (Command-N). In the New dialog box, type 3.5 in the Width field and 7 in the Height field. Go to the Margin Guides section and click the box labeled Facing Pages. This will set the pages up as spreads and display them facing one another. Next, type .4 in the Top, Inside, and Outside fields, .6 in the Bottom field, and check Automatic Text Box. (Remember, as discussed in Chapter 4, leaving a bit of extra space in the bottom margin will give the page a more pleasing visual balance.) Finally, type 1 in the Columns field and click OK.

Step 2

The basic page structure should now be displayed on the screen (Figure 3.1E). If the Document Layout palette is not already on your desktop, open it now by choosing Show Document Layout from the View menu. In the palette you will see a single page labeled 1A. Since this is a four-page flyer, you'll need to add three more pages, setting them up so you can view them as spreads. Add a new page by clicking on the Master Page icon at the top of the palette and dragging the page into position in the palette, just to the right of Page 1A. The new page will automatically be labeled 2A. Now create and position Page 3A under 1A, and Page 4A to the right of 3A (see Figure 3.2E).

Now you're ready to begin placing elements on the pages. Double-click on Page 1A in the Document Layout Palette to display Page 1 on your screen, and choose Fit in Window from the View menu. Fit in Window automatically sizes the page to the dimensions of your screen. You should see a spread, with Pages 1 and 2 joined together.

Step 3

Your first task will be to create a logo for the fictitious company. Create a text box 1/4" high by 2" long near the center of page 1. (Don't worry about getting it in the exact center of the page right now. We'll position it more precisely later.) Once the text box is created, choose the Content tool and you'll see the flashing Text Insertion Bar at the left edge of the box. Type the word ARBOREUS, in all caps. Select the word by dragging the cursor over it or by choosing Select All from the Edit menu. When the word is highlighted, go to Alignment in the Style menu and choose Centered from the pop-up menu or click the Centered icon in the Measurements palette. Going back to the Style Menu, select Times from the Font menu and set the point size to 14 pt., either by selecting it from the Style menu or by typing a new value into the Size field in the Measurements palette.

Now let's track the letters to fill the space within the text box and then shift the word down so that it's centered vertically. Using the Measurements palette, type 135 in the Tracking field. Then go to the Style menu and locate Baseline Shift. Baseline Shift is a command that lets you adjust the baseline of a line of text up or down. When you select Baseline Shift, a small dialog box will appear. Type –3 in the field and click OK. The type should now be centered in the text box.

FIGURE 3.1 E

After page format values have been set in Step 1, your page will look like this.

With the text box still active, choose Modify from the Item menu (-M). When the Text Box Specifications dialog box appears, find the area labeled Background. Set the color to Black and the shade to 100%, and click OK. Now the text box should become a solid black bar; if your text is still selected, it will appear as an empty bar. The type has disappeared because you've specified black type on a black background. To change the type to white, highlight the text, choose Color from the

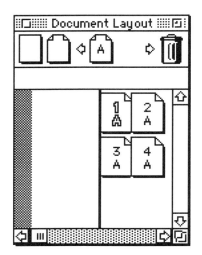

FIGURE 3.2E

After adding pages 2, 3, and 4, your Document Layout Palette will look like this.

Style menu, and select White from the color palette. Then click outside the text box and look at the result (see Figure 3.3E).

STEP 4

Now that you've finished the logo, you'll want to position it in the visual center of both Pages 1 and 2. To help position it accurately, use a guide. Click on the ruler at the top of the page and drag down. (If the rulers aren't displayed on your desktop, select Show Rulers from the View menu.) Place the guide 3 1/4" from the top of the page. You'll need to position separate guides at the same spot on both pages. (Remember that the visual center of a page is slightly higher than the mathematical center; that's why the guides are slightly higher than the exact middle of the page.) Depending on how your preferences are set, you may find that the guides have disappeared behind the text boxes. You can remedy that by activating the text box, choosing Modify from the Item menu (Command-M), and changing the background color to None in the Text Box Specifications dialog box.

With the Item Tool selected, click on the logo and drag it to the guide. Align the top edge to the guide and center it horizontally so that there is 3/4" of space on each side (Figure 3.4E). You can align the object using the top ruler.

FIGURE 3.3E The finished logo

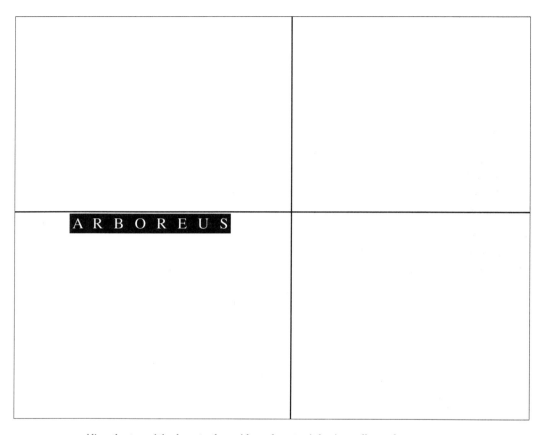

FIGURE 3.4E Align the top of the logo to the guide and center it horizontally on the page.

STEP 5

Now you need to position the logo on the back page. Make a copy of the logo by selecting it with the Item Tool and choosing Copy from the Edit Menu. Double click on Page 2 and choose Paste from the Edit menu. You now have a second logo. Using the procedure outlined above, center the logo on the page.

Make another copy of the logo and center it on the inside spread, straddling the fold between Pages 3 and 4.

STEP 6

The next step is to import the text. Before you do that, though, you need to link the text boxes on Pages 3 and 4. Select the Linking Tool from the Tool palette and click on the text box on Page 3. The text box will change to a moving dashed line. Now click on the text box on Page 4. An arrow will appear, pointing from the lower-right corner of the Page 3 text box to the upper-left corner of the Page 4 text box. This shows you how the text will flow.

Insert the exercise disk into your drive. Click on the Page 3 text box to activate it, and with the Content Tool, choose Get Text from the File menu. Locate Arboreus Text on the exercise disk, select it, and click Open. Since the text boxes are linked, the text will flow from the left page to the right page. There are several blocks of text that will need to be moved to other places in the document, but before you move them you need to create places to put them.

Double-click on Page 1 in the Document Layout palette. At the top of Page 1, draw a text box 1½" square. Align the top of the box with the top margin and center the box horizontally so there is an inch to the right and the left. Using the Copy and Paste commands, copy the box and paste it onto Page 2. Align the box in the same relative position as the box on Page 1.

Use the Document Layout palette to move back to Page 3. At the top of the text block are three lines that read "Landscape Designers and Horticulturists." Using the Cut and Paste commands, move this text to the text box on Page 2. Similarly, move the address and phone number to the text block on Page 1. Change the text in both text blocks to 9-pt. Times Italic and center it. Finally, use the Measurements palette to increase the leading to 30 pt. To do this, you can either click on the little arrow that points up until the value reads 30, or you can simply select the current value 30 and type over it. Pages 1 and 2 should now look like Figure 3.5E.

STEP 7

Go back to Pages 3 and 4. There may be a couple of blank lines left over at the beginning of the text block. To get rid of these, drag the cursor down the left side to select them and press the Delete key on your keyboard.

Now let's run the text around the logo in the center of the spread. Select the logo with the Item Tool and choose Runaround from the Item menu. Change all the values in the Runaround Specifications dialog box to 15 and click OK. Select all of the text. Use the Measurements palette to change the font to TimesItalic and the size and leading to 14/18. (This is how a typographer would specify 14-pt. type on 18 pt. leading.) Since you're using a fairly large point size relative to the line width, make sure that Auto Hyphenation is on. If the words in your document are not hyphenated, choose H&Js from the Edit Menu. When the H&Js Specification dialog box appears, check the box next to Auto Hyphenation and click OK. (You can also take this opportunity to change any of the hyphenation values.) Now your text should almost fill both columns (see Figure 3.6E).

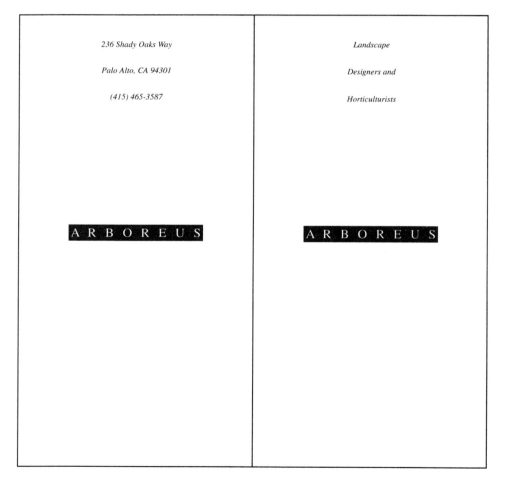

236 Shady Oaks Way

Palo Alto, CA 94301

(415) 465-3587

Landscape

Designers and

Horticulturists

A R B O R E U S

A R B O R E U S

FIGURE 3.5E Pages 1 and 2 should look like this after you've completed Step 6.

Remove the background color from each of your text boxes by first selecting the boxes (with the Item Tool you can hold down the Shift key and click on each box to select them all at the same time) and then choosing Modify from the Item menu (Command-M). Specify None in the Background pop-up menu in the Text Box Specifications dialog.

Walking through the garden gate, you have the sense of entering another world. It's a peaceful place, silent but for the musical chirp of birds and the creak of a hammock swaying with the light breeze. The beauty is almost palpable. The lawn is a carpet of deep green splashed with amber light and bordered by a symphony of floral color. Roses, Impatiens, Tulips, and Pansies nestle among the ferns and jasmine. There's something special here... a harmony, a completeness... whatever it is, you know you'll be in no hurry to leave.

Perhaps you've been to a place like this. We're in the business of creating them. We know it's a big challenge but, frankly, we think there's something pretty special about creating environ-

ARBOREUS

ments of living beauty, whether it's a park, a commercial landscape, or a back yard. We have a combined experience of some 50 years working with plants and designing outdoor environments. Our clientele includes large commercial developers, civic organizations, and architects as well as a host of private homeowners.

If you have an interest in creating a special outdoor environment, why not let us help? Just give us a call at (415) 465-3587 and we'll arrange for a free, no-strings-attached consultation. Who knows? Maybe the next time you walk through that garden gate it will be your own.

FIGURE 3.6E Proper formatting of the text on Pages 3 and 4.

STEP 8

Let's set an initial cap to create a strong focal point where the text begins. Select the first paragraph and choose Formats from the Style menu (Command-shift-F). When the Paragraph Formats dialog box appears, click the box labeled Drop Caps. You'll see the dialog box expand to include two new fields: Character Count and Line Count. Type 1 in the Character Count field and 3 in the Line Count field. This specifies a one-letter drop cap that is three lines deep. Now click OK. Finally, select the initial cap and change it from Italic to Plain (see Figure 3.7E).

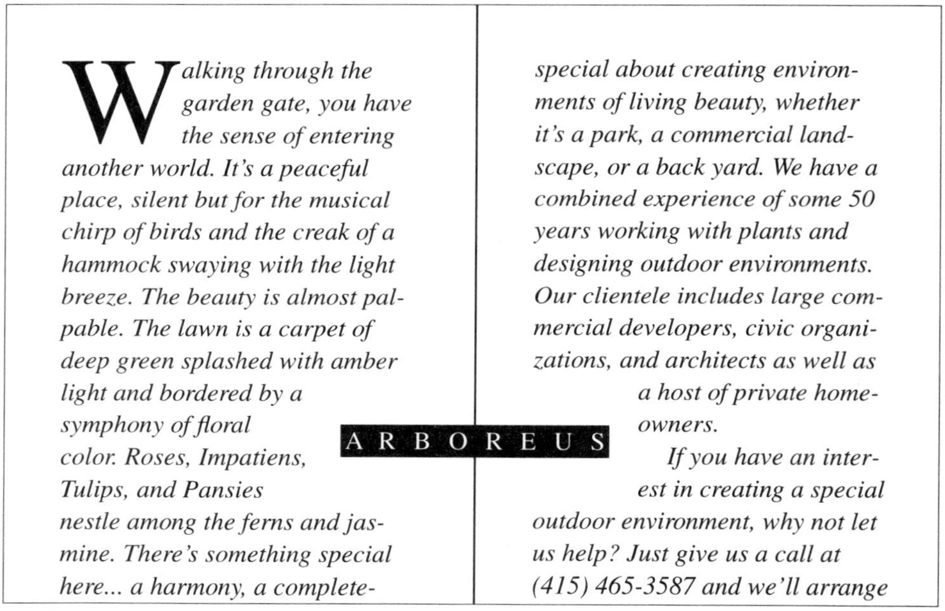

Walking through the garden gate, you have the sense of entering another world. It's a peaceful place, silent but for the musical chirp of birds and the creak of a hammock swaying with the light breeze. The beauty is almost palpable. The lawn is a carpet of deep green splashed with amber light and bordered by a symphony of floral color. Roses, Impatiens, Tulips, and Pansies nestle among the ferns and jasmine. There's something special here... a harmony, a complete-

ARBOREUS

special about creating environments of living beauty, whether it's a park, a commercial landscape, or a back yard. We have a combined experience of some 50 years working with plants and designing outdoor environments. Our clientele includes large commercial developers, civic organizations, and architects as well as a host of private homeowners.

If you have an interest in creating a special outdoor environment, why not let us help? Just give us a call at (415) 465-3587 and we'll arrange

FIGURE 3.7E The initial cap

STEP 9

The flyer is looking pretty good typographically, but it needs some visuals to add interest. The next step is to import some high-contrast graphic images of leaves and print them in color in the document's background. Before you do that, however, you need to add some new colors to the document's color palette.

Choose Colors from the Edit menu, and when the dialog box appears, click New. In the Edit Color dialog box, select PANTONE from the Model pop-up menu. Type 3268 into the PANTONE No. field and click OK. Use the same procedure to add PMS 173 to the document color palette. Click on Save.

Go to Pages 1 and 2 and draw a picture box. The graphic images will take up the entire background of each spread. Remember that when images bleed, the picture box must extend beyond the trim edge, so the picture box should cover both pages and extend 1/8" beyond the edges (see Figure 3.8E). If you can't see the logo and text through the picture box, select None as a background color in the Picture Box Specifications dialog box. (Command-M).

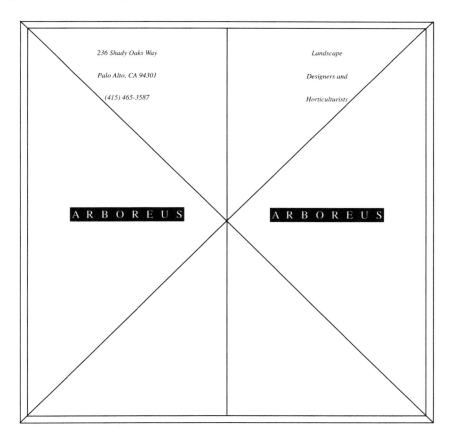

236 Shady Oaks Way

Palo Alto, CA 94301

(415) 465-3587

Landscape

Designers and

Horticulturists

ARBOREUS

ARBOREUS

FIGURE 3.8E A picture box with a bleed

STEP 10

With the Content Tool selected, choose Get Picture from the File menu. Locate a file called Leaf on your exercise disk, select it, and click Open. Use the Picture Box Specifications dialog box to resize the image to 200% and position it in the box as shown in Figure 3.9E.

Now use the same procedure to place the image titled Branch on Pages 3 and 4. Enlarge it to 300% and position it as shown in Figure 3.10E.

236 Shady Oaks Way

Palo Alto, CA 94301

(415) 465-3587

Landscape

Designers and

Horticulturists

A R B O R E U S

A R B O R E U S

FIGURE 3.9E The leaf image positioned on Pages 1 and 2

STEP 11

Right now, the pages look confusing, but you will remedy this by applying color and shading to the pictures to minimize the contrast between type and image. (While the following procedure looks better on a color monitor, apply it even if you're working with a monochrome monitor. You'll still be able to see the effect of the shading.)

Click on the picture box on Pages 1 and 2 to activate it. With the Content Tool selected, choose Color from the Style menu and PANTONE 3268 from the pop-up menu. From the Shade menu, select 30%. Choose Send to Back from the Item menu. Now change the color of the picture on Pages 3 and 4 to PMS 173 and the shade to 30%. The flyer is finished! (See Figure 3.11E.)

FIGURE 3.10E The branch image positioned on Pages 3 and 4

FIGURE 3.11E

The finished flyer

Designing a Newsletter

M any professional organizations produce newsletters to keep their audiences informed about such things as company events, new employees, new products or services, and noteworthy achievements. Newsletters are often widely circulated both inside and outside an organization. But often, surprisingly little attention is given to the visual presentation and quality of these publications. A common attitude seems to be "after all, it's just a newsletter." But a newsletter can be just as effective at building corporate image as it is at communicating information. It might not need to be as polished as the company's annual report, but it should be well designed and functional.

In this exercise you will design a format for a newsletter and use QuarkXPress to set up a master page, format text, import a photographic image and apply color to it, set up style sheets, and anchor rules to text. While this exercise focuses on the opening page of the newsletter, the style guides will make it easy to expand to other pages.

STEP 1

Open QuarkXPress and select New from the File menu. When the New dialog box appears, click the radio button labeled Tabloid. This will automatically set the page size to a tabloid format (11" x 17"). This is a popular format for newsletters; its larger size has more impact but it can still be folded to the standard 8½" x 11" inches for placement in a standard envelope or press kit folder.

Set the top, left, and right margin guides to .5" and the bottom guide to .75". Now set the column guides to 4, with a .5" gutter. Click OK, and the basic master page is set.

STEP 2

To create the logo for the newsletter, draw a text box 3" deep and 8" wide in the center of the page. Select the Content Tool and type the word VISION in the text box. Select the word and choose Times from the Font menu. In the Style menu, select Horizontal Scaling. When the dialog box appears, type 80 in the field. If the Measurements palette isn't already on your desktop, open it now by choosing Show Measurements from the View menu. With the text still selected, use the Measurements palette to change the point size to 225 pt and the tracking value to –15. Click anywhere on the page to affect the changes. The type should fill the box and should be set pretty tightly. (You wouldn't want to set body text this tight, but in this size and for this application it's fine.)

Notice that all the letter pairs are kerned tightly and fairly evenly except for the V and I. Place the Text Insertion bar between these letters and use the tracking controls to change the kerning value to –20.

STEP 3

The design calls for the logo to be placed on its side in the upper-right corner of the page. Use the Item Tool to activate the text box and choose Modify from the Item Menu. Find the field labeled Box Angle and replace the value currently in the field with 270. While you're at it, go the Background pop-up menu and change the background to None. When you're done, click OK. The text box should be on its side, with the word VISION reading from top to bottom. Using the Item Tool, align the box to the top and right margins. (See Figure 4.1E.)

STEP 4

Draw a new text box just underneath the logo. It should be 1" deep and the same width as the column. Position it so that its sides align with the column guides and the top of the box hangs at the 8½" mark on the vertical ruler. (If the rulers aren't showing on your screen, choose Show Rulers from the View menu.) Switching to the Content Tool, type these words into the text box: The Official Newsletter of OptiMax Corporation. Select the text and set it in 14-pt Times with 15-pt. leading. Remember, you can use the arrow controls in the Measurements palette to adjust the leading.

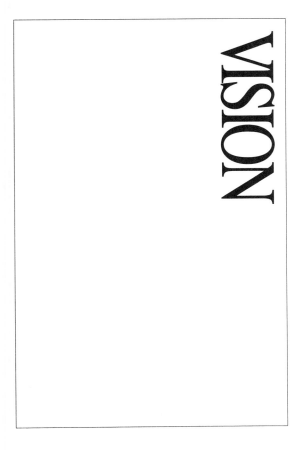

FIGURE 4.1E

The final logo in position after Step 3.

STEP 5

The covers of newsletters often feature a section that highlights items of interest inside. This is called billboarding. Let's use the rest of the right-hand side of the page for billboarding. Use the Text Box Tool to create a new text box within the column. It should start 12½ inches from the top of the page and align with the column guides to the left, right,and bottom. Now insert the exercise disk into your drive. With the Content Tool selected, choose Get Text from the File menu. From the dialog box, select a file called Billboard Text on the exercise disk and click Open.

STEP 6

Now let's format the billboard text. Drag your cursor across the word INSIDE to select it, and use the Fonts menu to change the font to Helvetica. Go to the Measurements palette, change the font attribute to Bold and the tracking value to 330. The word should now appear spaced out across the width of the text box. Select the block of bulleted text underneath and change this text to 16-pt. Times Italic. Set the leading to 19 pt.

Notice that the second line of each item wraps under the round bullet. You can use tabs to align the text and "hang" the bullets out to the left. This not only looks neater, it also calls more attention to the bullets. Select the paragraph and choose Tabs from the Style menu. You'll see a small ruler appear above the selected paragraph. Making sure that the Alignment pop-up menu reads Left, click on the ruler at the 1/8th" mark and then click OK. The tab stop is now set. Place the cursor between the bullet and the beginning of the first line. Use the Tab key to move to the preset tab stop. Set a hanging indent character by typing Command-\ and the rest of the lines should automatically align themselves. Follow this procedure for the other bulleted items.

STEP 7

Select the Text Box Tool again and draw three text boxes. (Since these boxes should be identical in size, you can draw one box and copy and paste it twice.) To help position the text boxes, pull down a guide from the horizontal ruler at the top of the page and align it with the 8" mark on the side ruler. Now position another guide at the 81/2" mark. Place the first text box in the far left column, aligning it with the lower guide on top and with the column guides on the bottom and sides. Place two more text boxes in the same relative positions in the second and third columns. Now draw a horizontal text box the width of the three left columns, aligning it with the guides on the 8" and 81/2" marks. Sometimes when text boxes overlap it causes the text to disappear. If this happens, go to the Item menu and select Runaround (Command-T). Now the page should look like Figure 4.3E.

STEP 8

Using the Linking Tool, link the three vertical text boxes together, beginning with the box on the left and working toward the right.

FIGURE 4.2E

The newsletter's cover after completion of Step 6.

STEP 9

Activate the vertical text box on the far left, and with the Content Tool, select Get Text from the File menu. Find the file called Esprit Text on your exercise disk and click Open.

STEP 10

Select the text with the Content Tool and set it in 14-pt. Times on 19-pt. leading. If Auto Hyphenation is not turned on, turn it on now by clicking on the box in the H&Js Specifications dialog box in the Edit menu.

FIGURE 4.3E

The position of the text boxes after completing Step 7.

VISION

The Official Newsletter of
Optimax Corporation

I N S I D E

• *OptiMax Signs*
  Japanese Distributor

• *Your Vision After 40*

• *OptiMax Introduces*
  Non-glare Lenses

• *How to Lengthen the*
  Life of Your Contacts

STEP 11

Select the article's title, and cut and paste it to the horizontal text box above. Once it's in its own text box, select it and set it in 19-pt. Helvetica. Make it bold by clicking on the B in the Measurements palette. Now locate the subhead "How the Technology Works" and set it in 13-pt. Helvetica Bold.

STEP 12

Often you'll want to apply a given set of attributes to all the headlines or subheads in a newsletter. You can simplify that task in QuarkXPress by setting up style sheets. To set up a style sheet for this exercise, select the headline with the Content Tool and choose Style Sheets from the Edit menu. When the Style Sheets dialog box appears, click New. You'll see a new dialog box called Edit Style Sheet. Notice that the attributes listed in the box are those of the selected headline. Now you need to save those attributes in the computer's memory so that you can apply them automatically to any other headlines in the document. All you need to do now is give the style sheet a name. Type HEADLINE in the name field and click OK. Notice that the name of the new style sheet appears in the scroll box in the Style Sheets dialog box. Click the Save button, and the style is committed to memory. To activate the style, select the type you want to style and choose Style Sheets from the Style menu, then simply select a style from the pop-up menu.

Now repeat this procedure to create a style sheet for subheads based on the attributes of the subhead in the text.

STEP 13

Now that all of the newsletter's text is in place, let's add a couple of rules, or lines, to add visual interest to the page and to better organize the information. The first rule will be a vertical rule separating the main body of text and the billboarding. Select the Line Tool and draw a line down the center of the gutter between the columns, beginning at the 12½" mark and bleeding off the bottom of the page (remember to extend it 1/8th" beyond the edge of the page). Notice that the Measurements palette now displays line specifications. To change the style of the line, select from the pop-up menu closest to the center of the palette. For this line, choose the style that looks like a row of dots. Now change the width of the line by typing .5 in the Width field. (See Figure 4.4E.)

Now let's hang a rule above the subhead. If there's not already an extra line of space above the subhead, add one now. You'll need to anchor this rule to the paragraph so that it will move with the text if the text moves. Select the subhead and choose Rules from the Style menu. When the Paragraph Rules dialog box appears, check the box labeled Rule Above. This specifies that we want to place the rule above the text. The dialog box will expand to include some new fields. In the Length pop-up menu, choose Indents. Type 100% in the Offset field, .5 in the Width field, set the color to black, the shade to 100% and choose the standard unbroken rule, then click OK.

STEP 14

To complete the page, you need to add a photograph. Create a picture box with the Rectangular Picture Box Tool and position it in the upper-left corner of the page, aligning it with the top and side margins. Use the handles to align the right side with the right-hand edge of the third column from the left. (If your logo disappears, choose Runaround from the Item menu and select None in the pop-up menu.) Align the bottom of the picture box with the 7½" mark on the side ruler. (See Figure 4.5E.)

FIGURE 4.4E

The newsletter's page with rules in place.

STEP 15

Activate the picture box, and with the Content Tool, select Get Picture from the File menu. Find the file on your exercise disk entitled Vision Photo and click Open. Type 190 in the Width (X%) and Height (Y%) fields of the Measurements palette to resize the picture to 190%. Finally, use the Content Tool to reposition the image as shown in Figure 4.6E.

FIGURE 4.5E

The page with the picture box in place.

263

STEP 16

Sometimes putting color in the background can add character to a black-and-white photograph. When you add background color, be careful not to use a color that's too bright or too dark—the color should be used only to tint the picture.

Let's add some background color to the photo in the newsletter. Activate the picture box and choose Modify from the Item menu. Use the pop-up menus in the Background area to change the background to cyan and the shade to 20%.

FIGURE 4.6E

The photo positioned within the picture box.

Since you're applying color, why not change the logo color as well? Select the logo, choose Color from the Style menu, and choose cyan. Finally, add some color to that vertical rule at the bottom of the page as well. Activate it, choose Color from the Style menu, and select cyan.

Although the newsletter is technically done, few designs are ever really finished. There's always something you can do to make it better. Take a close look at it and fix anything that needs fixing. Experiment with kerning, rearrange the elements, change the colors—be creative!

QuarkXTensions

QuarkXTensions™ are add-on software modules designed to enhance the capabilities of QuarkXPress and facilitate the processing of QuarkXPress documents through service bureaus. Some XTensions are included with your application software, while others can be obtained through independent software developers and as shareware.

Following is a list of some the extensions I have found to be useful in my work. Because new products are continually being developed, this cannot be a complete list of the available products. There are literally hundreds of extensions available.

Magpie—Once your QuarkXPress publication is ready to go the service bureau or printer, this XTension makes a copy of your document, gathers all of the linked files, and places them in a new folder. Sounds a lot like the Collect for Output feature in QuarkXPress doesn't it? But there's one important difference. Magpie also gathers all of the fonts used in the document. This is very important, especially if you've altered the fonts in any way.

Kitchensink—This XTension is designed to give you one-click access to basic Quark functions. It includes a variety of handy palettes that speed up such things as scrolling, nudging, zooming, text scaling, and much more.

Layer Manager II—As QuarkXPress documents become more and more complex it can become difficult to move between elements that are stacked on top of each other. This XTension makes navigating between layers much easier.

Dashes— You may have noticed that QuarkXPress sometimes has funny ideas about how words should be hyphenated. This XTension gives you better hyphenation by providing a more sophisticated internal hyphenation code.

Relink—Once numerous text boxes are linked throughout a document, to reorder them often requires unlinking them then manually chaining them together again. This utility automates this complicated process.

Time Logger—If you're a professional designer or desktop publisher and charge for your time working on Quark documents, you may find this XTension useful. It keeps a running tally of all the hours spent on each Quark document giving you an accurate time record for billing purposes.

The Kerning Palette—Most computer fonts fall short of the quality of professional typesetting because they come from the manufacturer with too few kerning pairs. The Kerning Palette provides a handy palette within QuarkXPress that allows you to customize your fonts easily as you work. When you encounter a poorly kerned pair of letters you can fix it immediately and permanently without leaving the application. You can also make the change to the font itself so the improved fonts can be used in other applications as well.

Image XTensions—This is actually a series of XTensions that are designed to add image editing features to QuarkXPress. Change pictures from CMYK to RGB or Grayscale, retouch, color correct, create masks, or add special effects without leaving your Quark document.

XTension Manager—As you add more and more XTensions you may find this one useful. It allows you to easily turn XTensions on and off as you need them. Since XTensions can use up a lot of memory, you may want to turn on only those needed for a particular document. You can also use XTension Manager to group your XTensions into sets.

XTensions can be obtained through online services such as CompuServe or America Online or ordered through a company called XChange; for a catalog, call (800) 788-7557.

Standard Page Sizes

Paper mills manufacture paper in standard sizes. When specifying the dimensions of a publication it's important to determine the best cut out of the sheet so there is little paper waste. With this in mind, page sizes have been standardized by the printing industry. This not only saves trees, it saves money. Use this chart to select the page sizes for your publications. Let's say you want to produce an 8-page, 8 1/2" x 11" brochure. Go down the chart until you come to the section for and 8 1/2" x 11" page size. Now choose the line that specifies 8 pages. Using this chart you can determine that the printer will buy paper in the standard mill size of 35" x 45", then cut it down to a press sheet size of 22 1/2" x 35". (This is the size paper that will go through the press.) Each mill sheet will yield 4 brochures.

Page Size	No. of Pages	Paper Size	No. Out of Sheet	Press Sheet Size
3 x 6	4	25 x 38	24	6 1/4 x 12 1/2
	8	25 x 38	12	12 1/2 x 12 1/2
	12	25 x 38	8	12 1/2 x 18 3/4
	16	25 x 38	6	12 1/2 x 25
	24	25 x 38	4	18 3/4 x 25

Page Size	No. of Pages	Paper Size	No. Out of Sheet	Press Sheet Size
3 1/2 x 6 1/4	4	28 x 44	4	7 1/4 x 13
	8	28 x 44	12	13 x 14 1/2
	12	28 x 44	8	13 x 21 3/4
	16	28 x 44	6	14 1/2 x 26
3 3/4 x 6 7/8	4	32 x 44	24	7 3/4 x 14 1/4
	8	32 x 44	12	14 1/4 x 15 1/2
	12	32 x 44	8	15 1/2 x 21 3/8
	16	32 x 44	6	14 1/4 x 31
	24	32 x 44	4	21 3/8 x 31
4 x 5 1/2	4	25 x 38	16	8 1/4 x 11 1/2
	8	25 x 38	8	11 1/2 x 16 1/2
	12	38 x 50	12	16 1/2 x 17 1/4
	16	25 x 38	4	16 1/2 x 23
	24	38 x 50	6	16 1/2 x 34 1/2
	32	25 x 38	2	23 x 23
4 x 6	4	25 x 381	8	8 1/4 x 11 1/2
	8	38 x 501	8	12 1/2 x 16 1/2
	12	38 x 50	12	16 1/2 x 17 1/4
	16	25 x 38	4	16 1/2 x 23
	24	38 x 50	6	16 1/2 x 34 1/2
	32	25 x 38	2	25 x 33
4 x 9	4	25 x 38	12	8 1/4 x 12 1/2
	8	38 x 50	12	16 1/2 x 18 1/2
	12	25 x 38	4	18 1/2 x 24 3/4
	16	38 x 50	6	16 1/2 x 37
	24	25 x 38	2	24 3/4 x 37
	32	35 x 45	2	33 x 37

Page Size	No. of Pages	Paper Size	No. Out of Sheet	Press Sheet Size
4 3/4 x 6 1/4	4	28 x 421	6	9 3/4 x 13
	8	28 x 42	8	13 x 19 1/2
	12	32 x 44	6	13 x 29 1/4
	16	28 x 42	4	19 1/2 x 26
	32	28 x 42	2	26 x 39
5 x 7	4	32 x 441	8	10 1/4 x 14 1/2
	8	32 x 44	8	14 1/2 x 20 1/2
	12	32 x 44	6	14 1/2 x 30 3/4
	16	32 x 44	4	20 1/2 x 29
	24	28 x 42	2	21 3/4 x 41
	32	32 x 44	2	29 x 41
5 x 8	4	35 x 451	6	10 1/4 x 16 1/2
	8	35 x 45	8	16 1/2 x 20 1/2
	12	28 x 42	4	20 1/2 x 24 3/4
	16	35 x 45	4	22 1/4 x 35
	24	28 x 42	2	24 3/4 x 41
	32	35 x 45	2	35 x 45
5 1/2 x 7 1/2	4	35 x 451	6	11 1/4 x 15 1/2
	8	35 x 45	8	15 1/2 x 22 1/2
	12	38 x 50	6	15 1/2 x 33 3/4
	16	35 x 45	4	22 1/2 x 35
	32	35 x 45	2	35 x 45
5 1/2 x 8 1/2	4	35 x 451	6	11 1/4 x 17 1/2
	8	35 x 45	8	17 1/2 x 22 1/2
	16	35 x 45	4	22 1/2 x 35
	32	35 x 45	2	35 x 45

Page Size	No. of Pages	Paper Size	No. Out of Sheet	Press Sheet Size
6 x 9	4	25 x 38	8	12 1/2 x 19
	8	25 x 38	4	19 x 25
	16	25 x 38	2	25 x 38
	32	38 x 50	2	25 x 38
7 x 10	4	32 x 44	8	16 x 22
	8	32 x 44	4	22 x 32
	16	32 x 44	2	32 x 44
7 1/2 x 10	4	32 x 44	8	16 x 22
	8	32 x 44	4	22 x 32
	16	32 x 44	2	32 x 44
8 x 10	4	35 x 45	8	17 1/2 x 22 1/2
	8	35 x 45	4	22 1/2 x 35
	16	35 x 45	2	35 x 45
8 1/2 x 11	4	35 x 45	8	17 1/2 x 22 1/2
	8	35 x 45	4	22 1/2 x 35
	12	35 x 45	2	35 x 35
	16	35 x 45	2	35 x 45
9 x 12	4	25 x 38	4	19 x 25
	8	25 x 38	2	25 x 38
	16	38 x 50	2	38 x 50

Standard Envelope Styles and Sizes

Commercial & Official	
No.	Size
5	3 1/16 x 5 1/2
6	3 3/8 x 6
6 1/4	3 1/2 x 6
6 1/2	3 9/16 x 6 1/4
6 3/4	3 5/8 x 6 1/2
7	3 3/4 x 6 3/4
7 1/2	3 3/4 x 7 5/8
7 3/4 (Monarch)	3 7/8 x 7 1/2
Data Card	3 1/2 x 7 5/8
8 5/8 (Check)	3 5/8 x 8 5/8
9	3 7/8 x 8 7/8
10	4 1/8 x 9 1/2
10 1/2	4 1/2 x 9 1/2
11	4 1/2 x 10 3/8
12	4 3/4 x 11
14	5 x 11 1/2

Booklet	
No.	Size
2 1/2	4 1/2 x 5 7/8
3	4 3/4 x 6 1/2
4 1/4	5 x 7 1/2
4 1/2	5 1/2 x 7 1/2
5	5 1/2 x 8 1/2
6	5 3/4 x 8 7/8
6 1/2	6 x 9
6 3/4	6 1/2 x 9 1/2
7	6 1/4 x 9 5/8
7 1/4	7 x 10
7 1/2	7 1/2 x 10 1/2
8	8 x 11 1/8
9	8 3/4 x 11 1/2
9 1/2	9 x 12
10	9 1/2 x 12 5/8
13	10 x 13

Ticket

No.	Size
3	1 5⁄16 x 4 7⁄16

Window

No.	Size
6 1⁄4	3 1⁄2 x 6
6 3⁄4	3 5⁄8 x 6 1⁄2
7	3 3⁄4 x 6 3⁄4
7 3⁄4	3 7⁄8 x 7 1⁄2
8 5⁄8	3 5⁄8 x 8 5⁄8
9	3 7⁄8 x 8 7⁄8
10	4 1⁄8 x 9 1⁄2
11	4 1⁄2 x 10 3⁄8
12	4 3⁄4 x 11
14	5 x 11 1⁄2

Remittance

No.	Size
6 1⁄4	3 1⁄2 x 6 (3 3⁄8" Flap)
6 1⁄2	3 1⁄2 x 6 1⁄4 (3 3⁄8" Flap)
6 3⁄4	3 5⁄8 x 6 1⁄2 (3 1⁄2" Flap)
9	3 7⁄8 x 8 7⁄8

Policy

No.	Size
9	4 x 9
10	4 1⁄8 x 9 1⁄2
11	4 1⁄2 x 10 3⁄8
12	4 3⁄4 x 10 7⁄8
14	5 x 11 1⁄2

Catalog

No.	Size
1	6 x 9
1 3⁄4	6 1⁄2 x 9 1⁄2
2	6 1⁄2 x 10
3	7 x 10
6	7 1⁄2 x 10 1⁄2
7	8 x 11
8	8 1⁄4 x 11 1⁄4
9 1⁄2	8 1⁄2 x 10 1⁄2
9 3⁄4	8 3⁄4 x 11 1⁄4
10 1⁄2	9 x 12
12 1⁄2	9 1⁄2 x 12 1⁄2
13 1⁄2	10 x 13
14 1⁄4	11 1⁄4 x 14 1⁄4
14 1⁄2	11 1⁄2 x 14 1⁄2

Baronial

No.	Size
2	3 3⁄16 x 4 1⁄4
4	3 5⁄8 x 4 5⁄8
5	4 1⁄8 x 5 1⁄8
5 1⁄4	4 1⁄4 x 5 1⁄4
5 1⁄2	4 3⁄8 x 5 5⁄8
5 3⁄4	4 1⁄2 x 5 3⁄4
6	5 x 6

Metal Clasp

No.	Size
0	2 1/2 x 4 1/4
5	3 1/8 x 5 1/2
10	3 3/8 x 6
1	4 1/2 x 10 3/8
14	5 x 11 1/2
15	4 x 6 3/8
25	4 5/8 x 6 3/4
35	5 x 7 1/2
50	5 1/2 x 8 1/4
55	6 x 9
63	6 1/2 x 9 1/2
68	7 x10
75	7 1/2 x 10
80	8 x 11
83	8 1/2 x 11 1/2
87	8 3/4 x 11 1/4
90	9 x 12
93	9 1/2 x 12 1/2
94	9 1/4 x 14 1/2
95	10 x 12
97	10 x 13
98	10 x 15
105	11 1/2 x 14 1/2
110	12 x 15 1/2

Announcement Text

No.	Size
A-2	4 3/8 x 5 5/8
A-6	4 3/4 x 6 1/2
A-7	5 1/4 x 7 1/4
A-8	5 1/2 x 8 1/8
A-10	6 1/4 x 9 5/8
Slim	3 7/8 x 8 7/8

Wallet Flap

No.	Size
10	4 1/8 x 9 1/2
11	4 1/2 x 10 3/8
12	4 3/4 x 11
14	5 x 11 1/2
16	6 x 12

Coin

No.	Size
1	2 1/4 x 3 1/2
3	2 1/2 x 4 1/4
4	3 x 4 1/2
4 1/2	3 x 4 7/8
5	2 7/8 x 5 1/4
5 1/2	3 1/8 x 5 1/2
6	3 1/8 x 6
7	3 1/2 x 6 1/2

Power User Techniques

QuarkXPress is a powerful productivity tool that can dramatically speed up your work. If you're new to Quark, you'll be amazed at how much more efficient it will make you. If you've been using it for a while, however, you may get to the point where you find that the familiar techniques and procedures are no longer fast enough. Desktop publishers are always looking for new techniques that will speed up their work. This chapter will give you some tips that can make you a real Quark power user.

SPEED SCROLLING

If you're computer isn't very speedy or if you're working with documents that have a lot of graphics, you may find it frustrating scrolling around the page and waiting for the screen to redraw every time you make a move. Checking Speed Scroll in the Application Preferences dialog box speeds up this process by "greeking" pictures, text, and blends while scrolling. When you're finished scrolling, the elements are redrawn normally. In the same dialog box you can adjust the speed at which the application scrolls the page.

WINDOW TILING

If you're the kind of person that likes to do numerous tasks at the same time, you might find this a handy feature. If you have multiple documents open at the same time, choosing Tile Documents in the Windows menu will stack the document windows on your screen so you can see them all at once. This is often more convenient than overlapping the documents one on top of another. If you have more than one monitor, checking Tile to Multiple Monitors in the Applications Preferences dialog box will tile the documents across all of your screens.

USING TEMPLATES

When you save a document in QuarkXPress, you have the option of saving it as a document or a template. What's the difference? Saving your document as a template creates a standard document that is difficult to save over by accident. A file saved as a document is active. When you make changes to it, then save it, the original version of the document is written over. If you start with a template and add to or edit the file, when you try to save it you are only allowed to save it as a new document, leaving the template untouched. This is a great productivity tool if you're working on documents that are based on a standard format. For example, let's imagine that you're responsible for producing a monthly newsletter. The page grid, masthead, and other elements are the same in each issue. If you set up the basic elements in a document and save it as a template, you can use that same template each month as the basis for the new issue instead of starting from scratch. This can be a real time saver. What's more, with QuarkXPress 3.2 or later, you can share templates with other users over a network, allowing numerous people to work on the same publication at the same time. But what if you need to change the template? Simply open the template, modify it, then save it as a new document with exactly the same name.

APPLE EVENTS SCRIPTING

Here's the ultimate efficiency tool. Apple Events Scripts are little macros that "memorize" a series of commands and perform them automatically in a single step. For example, let's say your publication design requires a large initial cap at the beginning of each article. It's not a difficult task to create an initial cap in QuarkXPress, but it takes a number of steps. Multiply that number of steps by the number of articles in your document and it can add up to a lot of keystrokes or clicking. Creating a script for this procedure reduces it to a single step.

Apple Events Scripting isn't something built into QuarkXPress but is a function of the Macintosh System 7 software. Any Macintosh application can be automated with Apple Events and you can only use it for QuarkXPress it if you're running System 7 or later and have QuarkXPress 3.2 or later with UserLand Frontier.

Scripts are actually simple programs that are written in a special programming language such as Frontier's UserTalk. If you're a "techie" you can easily write your own customized scripts using either UserLand Frontier or Apple's AppleScript. (Refer to your Macintosh documentation or the folder labeled For Advanced Scripting in your QuarkXPress folder.) If you have no interest in trying your hand at programming but still want to use scripts you can find a plethora of preprogrammed scripts on online services such as America Online or CompuServe. If you want to take a script for a test drive you can try some of the sample scripts on the Apple Events Scripting Disk that came with your QuarkXPress application.

KEYBOARD SHORTCUTS

What initially attracted me to the Macintosh was the "point and click" nature of its operating system. I thought it would be great if I could avoid using the keyboard and memorizing a lot of commands. While I still like to keep any memorizing to a minimum, I've learned from experience that using key commands instead of the mouse can really save time. Even remembering the key commands for the basic functions like Save, Cut, or Paste can make you more efficient. With that in mind, here are some of the keyboard shortcuts I've found most useful:

New Document	*Command-N*
New Library	*Command-Option-N*
Open	*Command-O*
Close	*Command-W*
Save	*Command-S*
Save As	*Command-Option-S*
Get Text/Get Picture	*Command-E*
Document Setup	*Command-Option-Shift-P*
Page Setup	*Command-Option-P*
Print	*Command-P*
Quit	*Command-Q*

Undo	*Command-Z*
Cut	*Command-X*
Copy	*Command-C*
Paste	*Command-V*
Select All	*Command-A*
Find/Change	*Command-F*
H&Js	*Command-Option-H*
Plain Text	*Command-Shift-P*
Bold Text	*Command-Shift-B*
Italic Text	*Command-Shift-I*
Underlined Text	*Command-Shift-U*
Small Caps	*Command-Shift-H*
Superscript	*Command-Shift-+*
Subscript	*Command-Shift-hyphen*
Flush Left Text	*Command-Shift-L*
Centered Text	*Command-Shift-C*
Flush Right Text	*Command-Shift-R*
Justified Text	*Command-Shift-J*
Delete	*Command-K*
Group	*Command-G*
Ungroup	*Command-U*
Fit in Window	*Command-0*
Actual Size	*Command-1*
Show/Hide Rulers	*Command-R*
Show/Hide Invisibles	*Command-I*
Show Measurements	*Command-Option-M*

Scroll to Beginning of Document	*Control-A*
Scroll to End of Document	*Control-D*
Scroll to Previous Page	*Control-Shift-K*
Scroll to Next Page	*Control-Shift-L*

This is a good list to start with but if you want to learn more keyboard shortcuts refer to the list in the back of your QuarkXPress documentation. The key commands listed above will work on any standard keyboard. If you have the extended Macintosh keyboard you can simplify the process even further by using function keys. Here is a list of the standard pre-programmed function keys:

F-1	Undo
F-2	Cut
F-3	Copy
F-4	Paste
F-5	Bring to Front
F-5 + Shift	Send to Back
F-5 + Option	Bring Forward
F-5 + Option + Shift	Send Backward
F-6	Lock/Unlock
F-7	Guides On/Off
F-7 + Shift	Snap to Guides On/Off
F-7 + Option	Baseline Grid On/Off
F-8	Show/Hide Tools
F-8 + Option	Next Tool
F-8 + Option + Shift	Previous Tool
F-9	Show/Hide Measurements

F-9 + Shift	Edit Font
F-9 + Option	Next Font
F-9 + Option + Shift	Previous Font
F-10	Show/Hide Document Layout
F-11	Show/Hide Style Sheets
F-11 + Shift	Edit Styles
F-11 + Option + Shift	Edit H&Js
F-12	Show/Hide Colors
F-12 + Shift	Edit Colors
F-12 + Option	Show/Hide Trap Info
F-12 + Option + Shift	Trap Preferences
F-13	Font Usage
F-13 + Option	Picture Usage

Index

PMS (PANTONE Matching System), 182

point size, changing, 120

points, 79

Polygon Picture Box, 58, 59

Polygon Picture Box Tool, 34, 160-161

posterization, 171-173

post-modern design, 50

power user techniques, 277-282

    Apple Events Scripting, 278-279

    keyboard shortcuts, 279-282

    speed scrolling, 277

    templates, using, 278

    window tiling, 277-278

PPDs (printer printer descriptions), 213

prepress process, 4-5, 206-207

press proof, 199

printer description files (PDFs), 213

printer fonts, 85

printer printer descriptions (PPDs), 213

printing, 195-220

    binding options, 219-220

    Collect for Output utility, using, 215-216

    color documents, 177-180

    with commercial printers, 202-203

    design for, 203-204

    direct to film, printing, 212-214

    electronic prepress process for, 206-207

    mechanical art, preparing, 211-212

    offset, 204-206

    paper for, 218-219

    preparing artwork for, 208-211

    presses, sheet-fed vs. web, 207

    pros and cons of electronic, 200-201

    and quality control, 216-218

    with quick-print firms, 201

    service bureaus, working with, 214-215

    terminology, 196-200

    working with printers, 203, 204

process color, 180-181

professional photographers and illustrators, working with, 152, 154-155

    creativity issues, 155

    personality issues, 154-155

    pricing, 155

    quality of work, judging, 154

    style, evaluating, 152, 154

proofs, 216-217

publishing, computers and, 1-2

Q

QuarkXTensions, 267-268

quick printers, working with, 200

quotation marks, 126

R

ragged edge, 109

ragged right, 102

raster image processor (RIP), 207

readability of type, 87-88

ream, 199, 219

Rectangular Picture Box Tool, 34, 159

register, 199

mixing, 111
modifying forms of, 112-113
and rag, 109, 110
readability of, 87-88
sans serif, 76, 81
scaling, 127-128
serif, 76, 81
size and weight of, 97-98
terminology, 75-80
and tracking, 95-96
uppercase, 89
using Style Sheets with, 139-141
weight of, 76
and widows and orphans, 113-114
and WYSIWYG, 85-86
typography, typesetting vs., 74-75

U

units, 206
Unlinking Tool, 35
uppercase letters, 76-77, 89
user interface, 30-32

V

value, 15, 17
visual center, 48
visual literacy, 16
visual paths, 44-47
visual texture, 12, 14

W

web offset, 200
web presses, 207
weight (of typefaces), 76, 97-98
white (negative) space, 12, 14-15
widows, 80, 113-114
window tiling, 277-278
Windows metafile format, 157
word processor, QuarkXPress as, 114-115
WYSIWYG, 85-86

X

x-height, 77
XPress Tags, 117-118
XTension Manager, 268
XTensions, 267-268

Z

Zoom Tool, 34, 55